STRICTLY THE WORST

CARRIE ELKS

CHAPTER
ONE

TESSA

"I'm taking you off the project," my boss tells me. He's standing in the corner of his over-expansive office, holding a putter as he squints at the golf ball in front of him. He lightly swings it, gently murmuring to himself as though he's having his own personal pep talk.

"I'm sorry?" I frown because my ears are ringing and it's been almost impossible to hear anything for the past three days. I spent the weekend becoming close friends with a circular saw and even though I wore ear protection all I can hear is constant buzzing. It's like a family of crickets has moved into my brain and thrown a party.

I wait for him to repeat his words. After he does, I'll tell him what I thought he said and we'll both laugh.

"You're off the Exuma project." He's still glaring at the golf ball like it's his nemesis. "A hundred and thirty-two," he mutters. "I scored better than that when I was a beginner." He finally looks up, his gaze meeting mine. "Did you know

Salinger can score seventy without batting an eyelid? That's professional level. Damn it, I'm never gonna beat him."

My heart is slamming against my chest, not least because Roman Hampshire seems more interested in his golf score than the fact I've been working on the Exuma project for the past six months.

I swallow hard, trying not to hyperventilate. Because this project is the big one. It's my first multimillion dollar budget, and my one chance to prove that I can create a PR plan for a huge client. And yes, there's the sizable bonus that I'll get at the end to consider, too.

I need that money. I've already spent it in my mind on a kitchen that actually has cupboards and a nice sink with faucets that don't leak, along with a counter top that isn't made of crates stacked on top of each other.

"We're supposed to be doing the pitch in two weeks," I say, as Roman taps the ball and it veers around the hole of his makeshift green in the corner. "I've been working on it for months. I'm all ready for it."

He shrugs, as though it doesn't matter that I've spent every waking hour I'm not demolishing my home making mock ups of brochures and social media campaigns. I can't remember the last time I actually watched the television or read a book. I work and I renovate and I take care of my daughter.

"Is the client unhappy with my work?" I ask. Because the last time I spoke with the marketing team they loved the direction we were taking. He's not the decision maker – that's James Gold, the owner of Gold resorts. But the marketing director is a pretty big cheese.

"James is fine," Roman says. "He just wants to take things in a different direction."

"What kind of direction?" I'm already thinking of the printing budget I've spent and the draft contracts I've agreed to with influencers.

This is not good. Not good at all.

"He wants the pitch to be presented on Exuma itself."

I blink. The presentation is supposed to take place at Gold Resorts' head office on Fifth Avenue. I've already scoped out the room – thanks to a connection I have over there. In my head I've planned where everybody will sit. I enjoy planning. It's my superpower. And though I know a lot about the Exumas – an archipelago of little islands in the Bahamas – what I don't know is the audiovisual equipment they'll have at the hotel.

I think I'm going to hyperventilate.

"Why would James want us to present the pitch on the island?" I ask.

"Because he thinks we need to experience the resort itself." James shrugs. "I can't say I disagree. You should have thought about that months ago."

"You said you wanted me to keep within budget," I say. "How could we do that *and* fly to Exuma?"

I'm shaking. I need to sit down. I can't remember if I ate lunch today. I don't think I did. I was too busy on a conference call during lunch. My assistant brought me a coffee at about two, and insisted I drank it. But apart from that...

There's a knock at the door and Roman grabs his ball and club and puts them into the golf bag that's leaning against the wall. "Don't tell him I was practicing, okay? I don't want him to know he's gotten me riled up."

"Who don't you want me to tell?" I ask, completely confused.

A moment later my question is answered when Roman yells out for whoever is knocking to come in and the door opens wide. I turn around, my gaze taking in the sharply cut suit, the thick shoulders, and broad chest, tapering down to a slim waist.

"Salinger," Roman calls out, beaming like Linc Salinger is his best friend and not another employee. "Come on in. I was just updating Tessa on our chat with James Gold on the course earlier."

"You were playing golf with James Gold?" I ask. "Why didn't you ask me to come along?"

"Do you play golf?" Roman asks. I'm aware of Salinger's gaze on my face. He's been working for Roman for the last year. His official title is Head of Client relations, but he's basically Roman's right-hand man. On paper, we're equals – we both report to Roman.

But as far as everybody else here at Hampshire PR is concerned, Salinger and Roman are the head honchos around here.

"No," I say tightly. "I don't play golf." I never had the chance to learn. I remember wanting to every Saturday morning when my ex-husband would head for the golf club, leaving me to nurse a baby with one arm and replying to emails with the other.

"That's a shame," Roman says.

Linc still hasn't said anything. I turn to look at him and his dark blue gaze hits mine. "Carmichael," he says softly, not moving his gaze at all. I swallow hard, because as much as I hate it, this man is stupidly attractive.

"Salinger."

He's not in the New York office very much, because his job requires him to fly to whatever client is threatening to leave at any given time. I've seen him in action. The man could smooth talk anybody. He has this way about him that makes everybody love him.

Everybody but me. Because, no, my insides aren't tingling like they've just touched a frayed piece of electrical wire. Not at all. I'm not interested in this man with the sharp jaw and god-like charm.

And yes, part of that is professional jealousy. I've been working for Hampshire PR for the last nine years. Managed to claw my way up to Head of Social Media Marketing. And then Salinger sails in a year ago pretty much above my head and Roman thinks the sun shines out of his rather fine behind.

"Salinger agreed that he can give the pitch," Roman tells me, smiling as though he's doing me a favor. "You just need to meet with him to give him all the details. The videos and whatnot."

And whatnot. I blew out a mouthful of air. There's no point in explaining that whatnot involves many hours of my life. Or that I've fallen in love with this project.

"This isn't fair," I say, aware I sound like a kid who's just been told to go to bed. "This is my project."

Roman lifts a brow and I know I've spoken out of line.

But they can't give Exuma to *him*. That's just wrong.

"James specifically asked for Linc to take over," Roman says. "He knows you're not able to travel at short notice because…" he waves his hand, as though my reasons are unimportant.

As though Zoe is unimportant.

Linc still says nothing. I turn to look at him and he presses his lips together, his vivid blue eyes still trained on my face. I know he doesn't like me much either. I also know that's because he knows I don't like him.

So why is the air sizzling between us like somebody's just popped it into a Soda Stream?

It's uncomfortable, because there's not many people I dislike.

My ex-husband. Obviously.

His girlfriend. Who is also his boss' daughter.

And Ryan Sharp from first grade who stole my favorite *Peanuts* pencil topper and threw it down the boy's toilet.

That's it. I like everybody else. Except him…

Linc Salinger is part of a very favored few. And from the way he's looking at me, he knows it.

"Okay," I say, because I need to get out of here. My throat

is doing that weird ticklish thing it always does before I start to cry. And I'm not going to let Salinger know he's upset me. "Is there anything else?"

Roman shrugs. "No, that's it."

I nod wordlessly and turn around, wrenching his door open and stepping outside.

"Sixty-eight," Roman says. "How the heck do you score that?"

"Practice," Salinger replies. "And a little bit of genius."

———

"He can't do that," my assistant, Gina, whispers, horrified. She's force feeding me a Snickers bar – king sized – and a mug of coffee. As soon as I walked into the large office full of desks she took one look at my pale face and forced me to sit down while she took care of me. So I'm in her chair while she's perched on her desk in front of me, pointing half a candy bar at my mouth.

"Eat," she says.

I shake my head. "I can't eat any more."

"Just one more bite," she urges, like she's talking to a child. "It will do you good."

I appreciate her, I really do. But all I really want is to be alone. And maybe scream at the world, because it really isn't fair.

She gives me the most sympathetic of smiles. "Maybe Roman will change his mind."

"He won't," I say. "He's already given it to Salinger."

"Stupid dumbass nepo babies," Gina mutters. And this is why I love her, because I know she doesn't mean it. She likes Linc. Like most of the female employees at Hampshire PR, when he first arrived she had a crush on him.

Now it's more of an admiration. And I know for a fact that she stalks him on Instagram. Because she insists on showing me all the beautiful women he dates in what seems like every city in the world.

That's the beauty of his job. He flies wherever the business needs him. He can be in Paris one day, London the next, and then suddenly he's on an airplane to Dubai. He rarely spends any time in New York, much to Gina's – and everybody else's – disappointment.

"I thought you liked him," I say. Because she definitely runs to the bathroom to touch her lipstick up whenever he walks into the office.

"I don't," she tells me. "I just want to tear his clothes off and climb him like a tree."

I'm not going to imagine him with his clothes off. I'm just not.

"So what do we do now?" she asks me. "Do you still get the account if they decide to give it to us?"

"I don't know," I say honestly. And that's the most upsetting part of all. The Exuma project was supposed to be my opportunity to show Gold Leisure what I can do. With an aim to win all their PR and social media business across the US as well as Exuma.

It would guarantee me a job for life in Roman's eyes. But now I don't know if I'll have one next week.

I take a deep breath. "We're going to have to package everything we've worked on into a neat bow so we can pass it over to Salinger."

Gina snaps her head to look at me. "Seriously?"

"Seriously." I nod. Because yes, we've done all the work, but Salinger will take the glory.

"Maybe we should sabotage it," she says, a wicked glint in her eye. "We could put subliminal messages in the videos."

"What kind of subliminal messages?" I'm only humoring her, but right now I need something to make me smile. And if anybody can make me smile it's Gina.

She's been my assistant for the last four years and nobody could ask for anybody better. She knows everything about me. She was there when I found out about my ex – Jared's affair, and she was there when I filed for divorce.

When I need somebody to vent to, or a shoulder to cry on she's always there. Gina is part of my very small circle of trust.

"I don't know what messages, but I'll think of something," she promises.

I can't tell if she's kidding or not. Mary Beth, one of Salinger's two assistants, walks past us and shoots us a look.

And I open my mouth to remind Gina that we're better than that, and that we're all supposed to be on the same team, but then my phone rings.

Zoe's name lights up on the screen.

There aren't many people that I rush to answer. I much prefer to write a message than talk on the phone. Unlike Linc Salinger, I'm not always great with a speedy answer. I need to think about things before I respond and messages help with that.

But this is my daughter. And at thirteen years old she calls a lot.

"I'll just get this," I tell Gina, leaving her to her evil plans for retaliation as I walk into my office. It's small but perfectly formed. Gina's desk is right outside – she pretty much acts as my gatekeeper. And my feeder, if the stash of candy bars in her drawer is anything to go by.

"Hey honey," I say after closing the door and swiping the screen to accept Zoe's call. "Is everything okay?" I glance at my watch. It's almost five o'clock. This week she's at her dad's. We share custody. It's supposed to be fifty-fifty, but it never is.

"Dad's late," she tells me. "And I can't get ahold of him. He's not answering my calls."

I let out a long breath. I shouldn't be surprised. This isn't the first time he's left her stranded, and it probably won't be the last.

But today is Zoe's orthodontist check up. The office is about a five-minute walk from her school, so she'd agreed with Jared to meet him there.

"Did you call his office?" I ask, trying not to sound annoyed.

"Yeah, they said he's in surgery."

"Now?" My voice lifts. Jared is a cosmetic surgeon. He can choose his hours. And he knows about this appointment because I reminded him four times.

"Yeah. So I called Melissa and she spoke to the orthodontist and he did the check up anyway. But she can't come and get me. She's at a salon on the other side of town."

Melissa is Jared's twenty-four year old girlfriend.

It's kind of laughable that she's more responsible than Jared is when it comes to our daughter. And I'm almost certain that the orthodontist has broken some kind of code by seeing Zoe without a parent being present. But I'll work through that one later.

"Why didn't you call me earlier?" I ask her. Even though I probably would have been in Roman's office at the precise moment she called, I still would have answered. And I would have rushed to the orthodontist to be with her.

"Dad told me not to call you every time he's late," she says, her voice small, because she thinks it will piss me off.

"You can always call me," I tell her. "Always. No matter what. Okay?"

"Okay," she says, still sounding uncertain.

"I'm leaving now," I tell her. "Hang tight and I'll be there in twenty minutes."

"They're closing up."

"Let me talk to them," I say. "Don't leave the office without me, okay?" I'm already picking up my jacket and purse, and pulling open my office door.

"Hello?" a voice says down the phone. "This is Doctor Archer's office."

"Hello, this is Tessa Carmichael. Zoe's mom. I'm afraid there's been a mix up. I'm heading over to pick her up now, but it's going to take twenty minutes. Can you make sure she's safe until I'm there to meet her?"

A huff comes down the line. "It's very inconvenient."

"Gotta go," I mouth to Gina. She frowns and I gesture at the phone. "Zoe."

She nods and I run down the corridor.

"I understand it's inconvenient," I say. "But it's all I've got. Please just make sure my daughter isn't left alone in the middle of the street."

"Okay then. But you need to organize your children better," the person says, and I immediately want to scream. But I need their help so I'll save it for later.

Zoe comes back on the line and I promise her I'll see her soon, right as I turn around the corner and stop short.

But not short enough. Because I barrel into the one man I'd like to avoid for the rest of my life.

CHAPTER
TWO

LINC

"Can I have a word please, Carmichael?" I ask her. And I'm trying to keep my voice even because I can't quite believe what I just heard. That her team is planning to sabotage the presentation. I need to nip this in the bud before it gets out of hand.

She looks up at me through those thick eyelashes of hers. If she wasn't so annoying she'd be deadly attractive, with her soft skin and her pink rosebud lips. My gaze dips to take in the way the top button of her blouse has come undone. I don't think she knows it has, but my eyes do. I can just about see the top of her cleavage and my body reacts even though I don't want it to.

"Sorry, I don't have time," she says, shrugging as though this isn't the most important thing right now. "I have to pick up my daughter."

"Well, can you make time, please?" I say, my voice tight. And yeah, I'm more than a little pissed. I'm doing her a damn favor. I didn't ask for this project, I didn't want it. Either I fly to Exuma on her behalf or she loses the whole damn thing.

She stops walking and stares at me, those pretty eyes flashing. "Seriously, I'm in a rush. I'm sorry. Can we do this tomorrow?"

"Not really. I have exactly two weeks to prepare for a presentation that most people would take months over."

"I *have* taken months over it," she says, her voice thick. She's started walking again and I follow her because she's really annoying me. "And when I hand it to you it'll be perfect."

"That's funny, because I heard you might sabotage it."

She turns to look at me, her eyes flashing. "What? Where did you hear that?" She shifts her feet.

"A little bird told me." I catch her eye.

"Of course she did." Tessa rolls hers.

"What's that supposed to mean?" I ask.

She looks at her watch. "Nothing. I have to go."

I let out a long breath, because I have no idea how to deal with her. From the moment I started working at Hampshire PR, she's disliked me. I'm grateful that I don't spend much time in the office where I have to deal with it. Roman brought me in to deal with our overseas clients, which requires a lot of travel. Roman used to do it, but after his second heart attack his doctor advised him to slow down.

So now he plays golf in the mornings – badly – and works in the afternoons. And I fly to Paris or Exuma or wherever he needs me to in order to smooth out problems with his best paying clients.

I like this job. I like the travel. I feel better when I'm not stuck in one city for too long. Carmichael is the one sexy fly in the ointment.

For a minute neither of us say anything. We both stare at each other, and I feel that pull again. Why am I attracted to her when she's being a bitch?

Because you want to tame her. You want to win whatever game this is she's playing.

She pushes the door to the parking lot open and grabs her keys from her bag. "I'll talk to you about it tomorrow," she says. "Call my assistant and set up a time."

"I have meetings all day tomorrow. Jesus, will you slow down?"

I lightly touch her shoulder and she swings around to look at me, a neutral expression on her face. But I'm almost certain that underneath her calm exterior she's fuming.

I don't like the way we always clash, I really don't. Keeping everybody happy is my superpower.

In every aspect of my life, I'm the peace maker.

I keep clients happy by day, and friends and family happy by night.

But I can't make this woman smile no matter what I do.

My fingers are still touching her shoulder, and beneath her blouse I can feel the heat radiating from her. Like she's so full of energy it doesn't know where to go.

She's so damn closed up not even a nuclear missile could penetrate her.

And now I'm thinking about penetration. With her. *Great.* I push that thought right out of my mind.

But it keeps trying to climb back up with an image of her face all soft and full of pleasure.

"I'll get Gina to liaise with you," she mutters. "You'll be fully briefed. You don't need to worry about that."

Here's the thing about Carmichael. She's the best that Hampshire PR has. She knows it. I know it. Everybody in the damn building knows it.

But her people skills leave something to be desired, which is why she'll never climb up the greasy pole. It annoys me, because if she tried, she could do so much better. With her looks and the way she holds herself she could be dynamite if she wanted to be.

She clicks her keys and her car beeps. "I have to go."

"I really didn't know Roman hadn't told you about the project," I say as she reaches for the car door.

She takes a long breath, her chest lifting. Then she touches her dark hair, as though she's worried a strand is out of place.

"It doesn't matter," she says, in a voice that tells me it does matter, a lot. "It's done. I'm sure you'll do great."

"If you can travel to Exuma, I'll back out," I say magnanimously. Okay, not so magnanimous. I don't want to be the asshole that stole her project. Truth be told, I want nothing to do with it.

"I can't do that." Her lips press together.

I wrack my brain about what to say. Right now all I can see is a red flashing light, warning me of danger.

"Why not?" I frown at her. If it was me, I'd jump at this opportunity.

"Because I can't exactly leave my child to fend for herself."

"Can't your husband look after your kid for a week?"

She looks at me coolly. "My *ex*-husband is probably busy." She slides into the car seat. I try not to notice as her skirt rides up, revealing perfectly toned thighs.

I'd forgotten that she was divorced. And now my mouth feels dry because I'm the asshole that stole a project from a single mom.

"Maybe we can work together," I suggest, my hand on the car roof. I'm leaning down and talking to her through her open car door. "I'll do the client facing stuff. You can be the backseat driver."

Her brows knit. "What?"

"We can split the bonus," I offer.

Her rosebud lips form a little 'o' as she exhales heavily. "I'm not a charity case. It's fine. Roman's made his decision. I'll work on something else." She waves her hand, as though to dismiss me.

My phone buzzes. I look down at the screen and sigh, because it's rare that I go an hour without a call from a client. The one that demands most of my attention – Celine – is the CEO of a makeup company in London. She's as needy as my inner child. But I have to take this call, because that's my job. If she calls Roman, he'll be pissed that I didn't pick up first.

Plus, I know we're hemorrhaging clients, thanks to them all believing that they no longer need a PR firm when AI should take up the reins very nicely, thank you very much.

"Sorry. I have to take this."

"Sure."

She slams her car door shut, and as I accept the call and put the phone to my ear, I can't help but wonder what it would be like to make her smile. To make her laugh. She's been married, she has a kid. Her ex-husband must have made her smile at least once.

"Celine," I say, my eyes still on Carmichael as she starts her engine and the car pulls away. "How are you today?"

————

TESSA

I end up taking Zoe out for dinner – because there's still no sign of Jared or Melissa and I don't want to drop her off at their apartment until at least one of them is there. Not because I don't trust her alone, but because I don't trust them to actually come home. And if she's home alone all night I'll have to drive back over and pick her up. So, we're at a diner near their apartment.

Zoe has a manga on the table in front of her, using one hand to turn the pages while she eats her burger with the other. She's obsessed with anime, has been for the last two years. She laughs at something on the page and I smile.

Damn, I love this girl.

Her phone rings. She licks some ketchup from her hand before answering. "Hey Dad," she says. "Where are you?" Her eyes catch mine and she rolls them.

I try not to listen in to their conversation. I'm not even mad that he was late picking her up anymore. I got to spend more time with her which is fine by me.

"Actually, I just ate a burger," she says.

And then his voice becomes louder that I can hear it from across the booth.

"I was hungry. And I didn't know when you were coming home," Zoe replies. She looks at me and I shoot her a smile but say nothing. She's a strong kid and can handle her dad for the most part. I only step in if I'm needed. "Okay," she says to him. "Bye."

"Why can't I come home with you?" she asks when she hangs up the call. "I want to help choose the colors."

The paint samples for the living room walls have arrived. I need to choose the color before we refinish the floor, which will happen after the electrics are rewired. Trying to juggle everything at the house is a full-time job.

"Because it's your dad's week," I remind her.

"He's never home. I have to sit with Melissa and we have nothing to talk about." Zoe frowns at me. "Did you know she's only eleven years older than me?"

"Yes," I say patiently.

"She's almost twenty years younger than Dad," Zoe continues. "Isn't that weird? That she's much closer to my age than his?"

"Very weird," I agree, motioning to the waitress to get the check.

Ten minutes later we're at Jared's apartment. It's a four-bed condo with a view over the river. Zoe hits the buzzer at the entrance and the door opens and we head toward the elevator, pressing the eleventh floor.

Jared is waiting for us as soon as we get there. He pulls the door open and motions Zoe inside. Then he looks at me.

"Go on then," he says. "Tell me what a terrible father I am."

I let out a low breath. So today he's playing the martyr.

"Anything could have happened," I tell him. "She's a kid alone in the city. If you couldn't make it to her appointment, why didn't you call me?"

"I thought I had it covered," he says, looking petulant. "I don't understand why you keep criticizing me. I'm doing my best here."

Melissa comes to the door, her long blonde hair flowing over her shoulders. She's not wearing any makeup – her face is glowing and I assume she's just had a facial. Either way, she looks absolutely gorgeous.

"Hi Tessa," she says. "Sorry about Zoe."

I give her a tight smile. "Not your fault," I say.

"It's *my* fault," Jared tells her, his voice saying the opposite. "The man who can't do right for doing wrong."

I'm exhausted. I haven't even thought about the Exuma project since leaving the office. I need to go home, drown my sorrows in a home that's full of holes and life-endangering bare wires, then work out what I'm going to do about my career.

"Just call me next time," I say.

He opens his mouth to say something, and I'm pretty sure it's going to be salty bullshit, but then he closes it, saying nothing. Sensing conflict, Melissa wisely lifts her hand in a goodbye and walks back inside the apartment.

"Whatever." Jared shrugs.

"I'm going, Zoe," I call out. "I'll see you on Saturday."

She runs to the door and hugs me. "Thank you," she whispers in my ear.

"Any time." I kiss her soft cheek, and revel in the smell of my only child. It's funny, no matter how old she is, she still smells the same way she did as a baby. "I'll call you tomorrow," I whisper. "I love you."

"Love you too." She walks back into Jared's apartment and I try not to feel sad. Every time she's gone I miss her. It's like my right arm has been cut off.

"Goodnight Jared," I say.

"Yeah." His eyes won't quite catch mine. "See you around."

———

Even though it's half falling apart and half put back together, I absolutely adore the condo Zoe and I chose after the divorce was finalized. It's tiny, set in the lower floor of a larger house with four stories, each with a condo inside it. But it's mine, or at least it's mine and the mortgage company's.

When we heard our offer was accepted, Zoe and I did a happy dance. Her room is the only one that's fully decorated. Not that you can see much of the pale blue walls beneath all her manga and Kpop posters.

Our next big job is tackling the living room. And right now I'm standing in front of the fireplace wall with Angela, my best friend, who arrived at my door carrying a bottle of wine and three giant size bars of chocolate after I told her about the shit show at work.

"This Salinger guy sounds like an asshole," Angela says. "I can't believe he stole your project."

Like Gina, she's always on my side. Angela and I have been friends since we collided into each other – literally – on our first day at college. She was carrying an enormous cup of coffee, I was wearing a white blouse. It could have gone either way, but we both found it hysterically funny.

She's been with me through thick and thin. She was the maid of honor at my wedding, she held me while I sobbed after I found out about my husband's affair with his boss' daughter.

"He's not an asshole," I say begrudgingly. "He's just..." I sigh, trailing off. It's hard to put into words. "I don't know, he just gets all the breaks you know?"

"That's because he's a guy," Angela says, passing me a glass of wine. "They always have it easy."

"His dad and Roman are friends," I say. And I hate this. I feel churlish not liking him. It's really not like me.

"You think that's why Roman gave him the project?"

"I don't know," I say honestly. "But everything just seems so easy for him. He charms everybody."

"Except you," Angela points out. "I think that middle one is best."

"Which middle one?" I look at the chessboard pattern of green squares in front of us.

"That one." She points to a square that is to the left of the middle.

"Isn't it too grassy?" I ask her.

"I don't know. I don't even know what that means. Can something be too grassy?" She looks at me and we both laugh. "Does anybody look at a field and say *'that's beautiful, but it's a little too... grassy for my tastes.'*?"

I love the way she's more sarcastic than anybody I've ever met.

"This is stupid," I say. "I need to just choose a color."

"Yes you do," Angela agrees. "What about the one at the top? It's more mossy."

"How's that different to grass?" I ask her, genuinely confused.

"Moss only grows on north facing areas," she says, as though that explains it. If you hadn't guessed, she studied environmental biology in college. But now she works in an investment bank.

"I'm going to buy the grassy one," I tell her, making the

decision because I want a room Zoe and I can relax in after work. Once it's painted, I'd hoped to fully furnish it, but I may need to divert that budget to the kitchen.

I guess we'll be sitting on boxes for a while longer.

"Maybe you're just triggered," she says. "Because he's friends with the boss."

I take a minute to realize we're back on the subject of Lincoln Salinger again. And for a moment an image of him flashes through my mind. His tall, strong body, clad in a designer charcoal suit. His dark, perfectly styled hair. And that jawline that could launch a thousand crushes.

"Why would I be annoyed because he's friends with Roman?" I ask her.

"It could be a trigger," she says. "Jared is also friends with his boss."

I try not to laugh at the way she spits out my ex-husband's name. It's like she can't bear it to be on her tongue. "It's his boss' daughter who was the problem," I say lightly. Because I'm over it.

"Yeah, well. It's still hurtful, right? These guys who get over friendly with the boss. Then before you know it they're tearing families apart."

I can't help it. I laugh again. And this is why I love Angela so much. She's my biggest fan. My biggest protector.

"It's just a bit of pop psychology." Angela shrugs. "But I still don't get why you don't like him."

"Maybe I'm a little envious of how much everybody likes him," I muse.

"Everybody likes you." Angela looks at me, and from her expression I can tell she's being completely honest.

"No they don't." I shake my head. "I think we both know that."

"They do. You're kind. Caring. A nice person. Why wouldn't they like you?" Angela asks. "And I like you better now that you've decided about the wall." She pauses, tapping something down on her phone.

"What are you doing?" I ask her, hoping she's on that dating site again. Her dates are legendary. In an awful way. The last guy she met ordered the most expensive items on the menu and then escaped out of the bathroom window.

She's tried to get me to sign up, and I keep telling her I'm not ready.

"I'm writing the paint name down. I'm going to order you five gallons of it."

"I'll order them," I say.

"No, you won't. You'll dither and second guess the choice and it'll take you at least two weeks to pick up the phone and do something about it."

"Okay then," I say, grinning, "I'll order it in two weeks."

"You won't be here in two weeks," Angela tells me.

"Of course I will." I shoot her a strange look. "And I'll order the paint."

"No, you won't," she says, turning to face me. And I know that expression on her face. It's the same look she gave me when Jared asked for a second chance. The same one she gave me as she held my hand while I was giving birth because Jared had decided to go away on business at the end of my third trimester.

"You're going to Grand Exuma," she says.

I laugh. "No, I'm not."

"Yes you are. You're going to ask Jared if he can have Zoe for the week." She holds her hand up when she sees my mouth open, ready to protest. "And if he can't do it, I'll come here and stay with her. I can move some work around. Make sure she goes to school. And don't look at me like I'm an idiot."

"I'm not looking at you like that. I was just going to remind you I'm off the project."

"Then get back on it." She rolls her eyes.

"How?" I'm genuinely curious because she seems to have all the answers. Not that I'm going to go.

"By telling Roman that you've changed your mind and you want to go to Exuma." She says it like it's so simple. "You need to go. You've already told me it's a tropical paradise."

It really is. Blue skies, even bluer seas, lush trees that form a canopy to block the hot rays of the golden sun.

"I don't know…"

She pouts at me. "Either you go to Exuma or you sign up for this dating site. It's time for a new beginning."

I look around the living room, taking in the peeling walls – now complete with green squares – and the holes in the floor. Maybe she's right.

A few days in paradise – even for work – could take me away from all this.

"And you'll also be able to get one over on this annoyingly sexy guy," Angela says, a sly look on her face. "Salinger, was it?"

"Yeah." I nod, not bothering to correct her. Because he is annoying. *And* sexy. He exudes appeal if you're into that kind of thing, which I'm so not. Because there's one thing I know, men like Salinger are dangerous. I don't need sexy and annoying, I need nice. There has to be somebody out there like that. "I'm going to do it," I tell her, because I'm not going to let Salinger win. It's time to start making a stand and be the woman I want to role model for Zoe.

"Yes!" She fist bumps the air and then hugs me tight. "That's my girl. Back in action."

CHAPTER
THREE

LINC

I wake up covered in a cold sheen of sweat. My skin is overheated, my muscles tensed, and my breath is coming way too fast. I reach up and swipe the damp hair from my brow, sitting up and looking around.

I'm in bed. That's good at least. Swinging my legs over the side of the mattress, I plant the soles of my feet on the floor and lean forward, closing my eyes as I try to recapture my breath.

That damn nightmare again. It doesn't come often anymore. Not like it did when I was a kid and I was scared to go to sleep at night.

But when it comes, it's a doozy.

I'd think about it, but that would just make me feel worse, so I pad to my bathroom and turn on the shower. It's a double size one. Like the rest of the bathroom, the shower walls are clad with marble tiles, and within moments water droplets are clinging to them as the air steams up and I step into the hot stream raining down from the shower head.

God, I need to get laid or something.

Seriously, it's been way too long. I blame my brothers. We all used to go out together. You'd be surprised how easy it is to find good company when you're one of six good-looking men. Women used to flock to us like we were the Hemsworths.

Now all but one of them has settled down and they're all disgustingly content. Sure, I'm happy for them.

But I miss the old days.

Squeezing out a palmful of the shampoo my stylist insisted I buy at my last haircut, I lather it into my hair, rinse it out, then add the conditioner I also had to buy – mostly because I'm a chump – and then I clean myself, tidy up the loose hairs, because nobody loves a bad manscape, and finally get out of the shower.

Usually I head down to the gym in the complex's basement on Saturday mornings. I try to go most days. My way of decompressing. But today I'm meeting my brothers for brunch because they all happen to be in Manhattan at the same time and we have some things to plan. So I pull on a pair of expensively ripped jeans and a gray t-shirt, then grab my phone and check every cab app I have, choosing Uber this time, because there's actually a car around the corner.

By the time I make it down to the street level, the car is waiting. I lift a hand at him and he nods at me.

"Hey Linc," he says as I climb inside.

"Hey Adi, how are you doing?" I ask him. Sure, we've never met before, but we know each other's names through the beauty of technology. We're practically besties.

"All good," he tells me. "It's a beautiful day, isn't it?" He pulls away from the curb and the car behind us immediately blasts their horn at him. The smile doesn't waver on his face. You have to be a special kind of person to drive for a living on this island. The same kind of person who'd happily fight a lion with their bare hands in eras gone by.

Still, I'm relieved that he doesn't give a damn about the other cars, because I'm late – as always. It's one of my faults, or at least that's what my previous girlfriends have told me. Along with my inability to commit, my selfishness, and the way I always laugh every problem I have off.

Which probably explains why I don't have a girlfriend right now.

I five star Adi, then add a big tip and thank him before climbing out of the car and walking toward the Carter Hotel – my big brother Myles' nest of choice whenever he has to tear himself away from his family in West Virginia and visit the big bad city for business.

Though this time isn't about business. It's about Holden, who has also traveled up from West Virginia. In fact, four of them traveled together – Myles, Liam, Eli, and Holden. They chartered a plane last night, because that's the kind of shit my brother loves.

Okay, I love it too. Why travel first class when you can travel without anybody else to mar the view?

Of course, all five of my brothers are sitting around a large circular table when the Mâitre D' shows me to my seat. They stand as one – like they're at school and I'm the teacher, which is kind of laughable, then one by one they give me a huge hug.

I secretly like it. Mostly because our relationships weren't always like this. There was a time when my four eldest brothers kind of hated Brooks and me. Brooks is the youngest brother. And we all have a very complicated relationship.

Myles, Liam, Eli, and Holden all have the same mom. Brooks and I have a different mom. We share the same dad, but there's a lot of evidence that his relationships with our moms overlapped a little.

And for a while, our four eldest brothers kind of blamed me and Brooks for taking their dad away from them. Or that's what it felt like, anyway.

But then we all grew up, and those kind of stupid resentments got pushed away. Nowadays, we all have a great relationship. Since the four of them moved out of New York, I miss their faces. So when I tell them it's great to see them, my words are genuine.

"How come you live the closest and you're the one who's late?" Myles murmurs, slapping my back a little too heartily.

"Because I still have a life," I tell him. "One that isn't taken up with two point four kids and a dog."

"What was her name?" Brooks asks, grinning.

I shrug. "Can't remember." I'm not going to tell them I slept alone last night.

"Can I bring you a mimosa?" the server asks me as I finally take my seat.

"Yes please. And a coffee. Black."

"Certainly, sir."

There's about ten minutes of small talk before we get down to business. Myles tells us how his kids are – he has two now. Charlie is the oldest, and he's the funniest kid you'll ever meet. Myles and his wife, Ava have recently had a second child, Laura. She doesn't do a lot except scream and shit, but I have high hopes for her.

Liam joins in, along with Eli and Holden because all of them have kids or, in Holden's case, a nephew in law that they're absolutely obsessed with. I smile and nod when they talk about swimming lessons and some TV show with animals that save lives, but really I'm thinking about Tessa Carmichael.

She never talks like this about her daughter. I don't think I've ever heard her mention any after-school activities or kids' tv. Hell, I don't even know how old her kid is.

I wonder why she rarely mentions her. And now I'm remembering how she stood up to me yesterday, her eyes flashing with anger, her body tense as fuck.

My ex-husband…

I wonder what went wrong with them? And I ignore the little voice in the back of my head telling me she's now available.

Not interested, thanks.

"So, what do you think?" Holden asks.

"Swimming lessons are great." I shoot him a smile.

"I was talking about the wedding."

"Okay…" Was he?

That's why we're here after all. Holden and his fiancée, Blair, are getting married. The ceremony will take place at our dad's estate in Virginia. It's the perfect location. Full of rolling hills and lakes. We spent every summer there growing up.

I try to get there when I can, but the truth is I'm constantly traveling. It's gotten worse since I started working for Hampshire PR. They have a lot of overseas clients who need nurturing.

And that's my job. I nurture.

"Well, about the bachelor party, actually." Holden shrugs. He's probably the brother I'm closest to out of the older four. Until last year he lived here in Manhattan. He's a pediatric oncologist, and yeah, he's pretty much superman.

And now he's stupidly in love.

"I'd like you to organize it," he says.

I blink. "Me?"

He nods. "Yeah. Eli's the best man, but you know what he's like. He can't organize his own day, let alone an event."

"I said I'd do it," Eli sighs.

"No," Holden corrects him. "You said you'd get Mackenzie to do it." Mackenzie is Eli's wife. She's a fabulous organizer. But I wouldn't want her arranging my bachelor party. I wouldn't want any of my brothers' partners doing that.

Don't get me wrong, I love them all. But we don't need a bachelor party at a spa.

"Sure, I'll do it." I shrug, trying to look nonchalant, but

actually I'm pretty excited. Not just because I love parties. But because for once my brothers are trusting me to do something. And yeah, I kind of wanted to be Holden's best man, but it was always going to be Eli. We kind of pair off in our family. Myles and Liam, Eli and Holden, Brooks and me.

Which makes me look at my brother – younger than me by just over a year. "Wanna help?" I ask him, because I always include him. Being the youngest sucks.

"Was hoping you'd ask." He grins. "I already have some ideas."

"No strippers," Holden says firmly.

Brooks and I exchange a glance. "Wasn't planning on having any," I murmur.

"It needs to be PG," Myles intones, even though it has nothing to do with him. But that's Myles. Always the leader. "Otherwise Ava will kill me."

I stifle a laugh. "What exactly does PG entail?" I ask him.

"I don't know." He shakes his head, his brows knitting. "Just not… what you're thinking."

"It's fine," Holden says. "Just run things past me before you book anything."

"Sure." I nod. "Anything else? Want me to get us matching velour pant suits with our names on the butt?"

"Don't joke about velour pant suits," Liam says, wincing. "Remember when our moms got matching ones?"

Ugh, yes I do. Our moms are best friends. Which to most people sounds weird. They were love rivals at one point, but you'd never believe it now. They spend a lot of time together, go on vacations together.

Sometimes with my dad and his latest wife.

No wonder we're all messed up.

"Okay then. One bachelor party, coming up," I say. "Same date we agreed on before?"

"Yep." Holden nods. It's just under a month away.

"Cool. I'll start booking things. I'll keep you updated from Exuma."

"You're going to Exuma?" Brooks asks. "Why?"

"A work thing."

Myles laughs. "Only you would go to a tropical island for a work thing."

"Right?" Holden grins. "How'd you get to be the luckiest sonofabitch in New York City?"

"Because I'm good at my job." I arch an eyebrow at him. And he has the good grace to look a little embarrassed. Because that's the other thing about being the second youngest in our family, I rarely get any praise for doing what is actually a hard role.

Sure, it's a dream traveling all over the world. But when I get there I'm often faced with angry clients threatening to leave, occasionally threatening to sue the company. And it's my job – and only mine – to soothe them. To make them feel special. And nine times out of ten I come away not only with a happy client but also with a renewed contract and an increased budget.

Holden couldn't do it. Eli couldn't either. Liam could possibly, but Myles, he'd scare them off before he opened his damn mouth.

And sure, I couldn't do their jobs either. But at least I give them credit for how hard they work.

Which makes me think about Tessa again. The way she looked when I waltzed into her meeting with Roman. Even worse, her expression when he told her I'd be going to Grand Exuma.

I rarely get stuck on things like this. Easy come, easy go.

But damn, there's a feeling of guilt in my stomach I don't like at all. It makes the mimosa taste weird. I much prefer being annoyed with her.

"So, about those strippers," Brooks says, taking a bite of

one of the pastries the server put in the center of the table. "Can we have maybe just a couple?"

———

TESSA

It's late on Monday afternoon and I can't put it off any longer. So I hold my hand up and rap on Roman's door. His executive assistant has left for the day. In fact, most people have. Zoe is at a friend's house for dinner, and I don't have to pick her up until eight, so I took the opportunity to finish up some work while I had the time.

And I can't leave until I've spoken to Roman. Otherwise Angela will kill me. She's been calling all afternoon to ask if I've met with him yet.

Of course I've ignored her calls. But I know her well. She'll come to the house if I don't pick up soon. So I've pulled up my big girl panties and I'm going to get this project back even if it kills me.

"Come in," Roman calls out after I've knocked twice.

When I push the door open, I see him on the treadmill in the corner of his expansive office. He's wearing jogging pants and a t-shirt, with one of those thick headbands with speakers built-in that all the runners seem to be wearing at the moment.

He pulls one ear down. "Tessa. Is everything okay?"

"It's fine. I just wondered if I could have a word."

He looks at the display on his treadmill, then at me again. "Sure. Let's walk and talk."

This would be fine if he had two treadmills. But he only has one so I have to kind of stand next to him, around a foot lower than he is, and pretend to walk while he does the real thing on the rubber belt of his machine.

And yes, this is weird. But this is Roman. And I have bigger fish to fry than worry about looking like an idiot while I walk in place.

"So how can I help you?" he asks me. He's out of breath. And I can smell his sweat. It's not pleasant.

"I wanted to talk to you about the Grand Exuma project." I glance over at his face. Am I supposed to be looking at him? Or are we supposed to both be facing ahead?

I've no idea.

"I know you're disappointed. But there's nothing we can do. We need somebody who can travel there." He tries to shrug but it puts him off his stride. He slips back on the rubber belt and has to grab the rails to steady himself. "Damn, this is a tricky course."

"I can travel there," I tell him. "That's what I wanted to tell you. There's no need to send anybody else. I can still take the lead."

"What about your little girl?"

"Zoe," I remind him. *Again.* I don't bother pointing out that she's not little anymore. "Her father will watch her." I spoke with him on Sunday. He huffed and puffed but finally agreed to swap our dates. Or rather Melissa did, because she was the one who told me they'd do it.

Roman leans forward to hit the off switch, as though I've finally grabbed his attention. When he turns to look at me I can see how red his face is. I let out a sigh of relief because I can finally stop pretending to walk too. It's harder than it looks.

"Have you spoken to Linc about this?" Roman asks me.

"No. I wanted to speak to you first."

"Call Linc. He's probably already made his flight arrangements." Roman presses his lips together. "Actually, I'll call him now."

"Okay. Thank you."

I follow Roman to his desk, where he grabs a towel to

wipe his face. Then he takes a long swallow of mineral water. He hits the intercom button. "Can you get me Linc Salinger?"

"I think your assistant has left for the day," I tell him. He screws up his face.

"Damn." He grabs his phone and it takes him about a minute to actually find Linc's contact details and hit the green phone button. Within a moment, I hear Linc answering.

"Hey. Good to hear from you. Ignore the wind sounds. I'm on a boat."

Of course he is. Probably in a pair of swim shorts and nothing else, his stupidly toned chest looking bronzed in the sun. I try to keep my face neutral.

"No problem," Roman says, as though he constantly has to track his staff down on expensive floating devices. "I was wondering, have you booked your flight to Grand Exuma yet?"

"Your assistant booked it. Why?"

"Turns out Tessa can make it after all." Roman clears his throat and looks at me. Then a big grin pulls at his lips and his eyes widen, like he's just discovered the meaning of life. "Hey," he says, slowly, blinking those same eyes like he can't believe his luck. "I have a great idea. I'm going to send you both. The dream team. Between the two of you, you're sure to get the deal closed."

My jaw drops.

What? He can't be serious. There's no need to have two of us traveling to Grand Exuma. "Roman," I whisper. "I can deal with it alone."

"Sorry, the wind is terrible." Linc is shouting now. "What did you say?"

For a moment, the only thing that's keeping me going is the thought that he'll be as horrified as I am at Roman's suggestion.

The thought of us spending a week together on an island makes every drop of my blood run cold.

"I said you and Tessa are going to Exuma together," Roman shouts back. I'm pretty certain the entire office could hear him, if any of them are still at their desks. "You're my dream team. Gonna bring that baby home."

"Still can't hear you," Linc says. "I'll call you back."

It doesn't matter. Because I heard him. And I'm pretty sure that Roman will make sure that Linc does, too.

And my eyes widen in horror. This is worse than not going to Exuma at all. I don't want to go to the Bahamas with Linc Salinger. Yes, he's pretty. Okay, stupidly handsome with a smile that lights up cities whenever he walks into them. And yeah, every woman in the office would be fighting to take my place if they knew I was about to spend five days in paradise with Hampshire PR's very own panty-melting god.

My skin is tingling right now at the thought of being that close to him for days on end, but I'm putting it down to early-onset heat rash at the thought of a trip to Exuma with him.

How did this happen? How did I think I was winning and yet I'm walking out of Roman's office feeling like Linc's just got one over on me without even trying.

I close my eyes, trying to center myself, but all I can see is his slow sexy smile. I hate every perfect tooth in Linc's imaginary grin.

And now I have to share paradise with that ass.

———

LINC

"This is pointless," I say to Roman when he finally tracks me down the next day. I'm on a video call in Paris and he asks me to stay behind so he can talk to me. There's no pretending it's windy or that I can't hear him.

Hampshire PR has state of the art videoconferencing tools. We use them so much, Roman invests a lot of money in them.

"Why send both of us to Exuma? It's expensive and I have a ton of work to do. Send Carmichael in on her own, she'll be fine."

"I don't want fine, I want us to win that account. I need you both there. This isn't negotiable, Linc."

I loosen my tie, because it's getting hot in the conference room. And yeah, I might have caught the sun a little too much on the boat with our European clients yesterday. "Tessa and I don't always see eye to eye on things," I tell him.

"Then get yourself some glasses or something. I'm sick of you two sniping about each other. You're supposed to be my two best employees so start acting like it." He lifts a brow, letting me know there's no arguing with him. "Think of it as a chance to bond. Get to know each other outside of work. I have plans for both of you, but I need you to play on the same side here." He drops his voice. "Charm her like you do everybody else. I need you to rub off her hard edges. Come on, Linc, this is why I employ you. To bring home the bacon."

"And in this case the bacon is… Carmichael?"

"No, the account. Tessa is the farmer. You're the butcher."

I shake my head because I'm not liking this analogy. First of all, why do I have to be the bad guy butcher? I want to be the farmer.

And second of all, I'm picturing Carmichael in a milk maid's outfit. And fuck, she'd look good in it. She'd look good in anything.

If she wasn't such a she-devil, I'd actually be looking forward to spending time with her. Truth be told, she's the most interesting person at Hampshire PR. And yes, I mean interesting in an attractive, bitchy kind of way. But she's also prickly and has made it clear she hates my guts.

"Okay," Roman takes my non-answer as an answer.

"Great, I've already booked Tessa on your flight. Don't let me down, Linc."

Before I can say anything else the screen flickers to black and I sit back in my chair and groan.

Roman wants me to rub off her hard edges. And now all I can think about is Carmichael all soft and pliant, her eyes dazed with the pleasure I know I could give her.

Fuck. Why are Carmichael and sex sharing the same thought space in my head?

Because you've always wanted what you can't have. Since you were a little boy.

I blink that thought away. Not true at all. Maybe it's just that I only know one way to soften a woman.

And the thought of doing that to Tessa Carmichael is making every part of my body feel as hot.

Fucking Exuma. This might be Roman's worst idea ever.

CHAPTER FOUR

TESSA

Two Weeks Later...

I let out a long breath as we taxi toward the tiny yellow terminal nestled at the end of the runway. The sun is blasting through the porthole windows, warming my face, and I can't help but stare out of the one next to me as we come to a stop. A gentle breeze rustles the leaves of the palm trees on either side of the low, red-roofed building.

It's everything I'd read about, and more.

The seatbelt sign turns off and everybody stands up in the tiny airplane.

"Ready?" a voice asks me.

"Yeah." I nod at Linc. He's wearing a pair of jeans and a black t-shirt that hugs his chest. And I can still smell the aroma of his cologne despite us both having spent hours traveling. Our first flight was from JFK to Nassau, and it was fully booked, which meant I didn't have to sit anywhere near Linc for the first three and a half hours of our journey.

Then we had a two hour layover before this flight, which was only forty minutes in the smallest of planes.

Luckily he fell asleep. And I stared out at the ocean below us.

As soon as we're through immigration and customs we make our way outside to be picked up by the hotel limo. The driver greets us with his hand out, shaking mine first and then Linc's. He tells us his name is William and before we've even made it out of the airport he and Linc are chatting like they're old friends. And I realize I actually like it. Traveling with Lincoln Salinger has been better than I expected.

Because he does it so much, he knows all the tricks and shortcuts. He's a member of the best business lounge in JFK, and he knows the bartender well enough to get the best champagne.

Even in Nassau he bumped into two people he knew working at the check-in desks. And for the first time I relaxed.

Maybe being in the Bahamas for a few days with this man won't be so bad after all. Most people would kill to be here.

These islands really are beautiful. Even after all the research I've done on the area in the past few months, I didn't expect the beaches and trees and sea to be so stunning in person. Maybe Gold was right. Being here is worth a hundred hours of research.

And for the next five days I get to really experience what the Exumas have to give. We're due to give our final presentation to Gold the day before we leave. Which means we have four days to record material, rewrite the presentation, then show him exactly what we can do on the fly.

William pulls out of the service road. They drive on the left here, a hangover from

when the Bahamas were British colonies. It takes some

getting used to, especially as I'm sitting on the right side of the backseat.

The ocean is so blue it looks like somebody has dyed it just for us.

"Nice, huh?" Linc asks me.

"It really is," I agree, putting my straw hat on to protect my face from the sun.

"Why are you wearing that?" Linc asks, nodding at it.

"I haven't put on any sunscreen," I tell him. I don't want to get sunburn."

"It's three strides to the hotel lobby, Carmichael. I think you'll be okay."

I lift a brow at him. "Skin cancer is no laughing matter. You get burned if you like, but I'm taking precautions.

He rolls his eyes as William helps us out of the car and a porter appears to take our luggage.

"Welcome to the Grand Exuma resort," he says. "Please go inside and take a seat. Emma will be with you in just a moment.." He points at a pair of sparkling glass doors with *GR* frosted on the front, and we walk inside, the air-conditioned interior of the reception building cooling my skin.

Within a minute, we're served drinks. Luckily, these are non-alcoholic because I'm already feeling a little wobbly on my feet to tell the truth. I drink the refreshing lemon-based soda drink, closing my eyes because it tastes so good.

And when I open them, Linc has his phone trained on me.

"Are you recording me?" I ask him.

"Thought I'd get a few shots in. For our presentation. We want to capture the entire experience, right? Including check in."

"True." I nod.

"Miss Carmichael, Mr. Salinger," the receptionist says, walking over with a clipboard. "We have you all checked in. We just need your signatures." She passes Linc a pen. "And

Mr. Gold sends his apologies that he's not here to greet you himself. He's flying in on Friday."

"That's fine," I say.

"And he's given us a list of the things he'd like you to include in your presentation. So I've booked you for some of our trips. Now William will take you down to your accommodation." She smiles widely. "With an ocean view, of course."

William has already taken our cases and loaded them up on the white golf cart with Gold Resorts emblazoned on the sides. He leads us out, and Salinger climbs into the front seat next to him, while I slide into the back.

He keeps up a steady chat about the resort. He used to work for another hotel, but since this one opened last year, he's been happier than ever. He tells us he saw the resort being built a couple of years ago and assures us that we're going to love the stilted cottage that we've been upgraded to.

"Cottages," I correct.

He turns to look at me. "No," he says. "Cottage. For the both of you."

I look over at Linc, expecting him to laugh. But he looks as confused as I am. I widen my eyes at him and he shrugs, then turns to look at William.

"There's been some miscommunication," he says. "We need separate beds. We're not a couple."

William stops the cart and turns to look at us both. "The cottage sleeps four. There are separate beds. One in the bedroom and a sofa bed in the living room." He grins. "Unfortunately there's only one bathroom."

Linc turns around and our eyes meet. He lifts a brow and I shrug. There's not much we can do about it now. The receptionist told us they were fully booked, and it's not like we have to share a bed or anything.

Maybe it'll even be useful, having a shared space to work in.

"It's fine," I say, my voice tight.

It's Salinger's turn to shrug, but he looks distinctly uncomfortable. "All good," he tells William, who nods and continues the drive to the cottage.

The warm breeze lifts my hair as I climb out and look around.

Our accommodation is a low wooden cottage on stilts, built right along the beach, nestled among palm trees. It's far enough from the other cottages to make you feel like you're in your own private piece of paradise. My first thought is how much Zoe would love it, and I feel a little pang in my chest because I'm missing her already.

I can't remember the last time I was away from her for this long.

"You okay?" Linc asks and I realize he's already taken a few steps toward the cottage while I've been staring out, my head full of thoughts. I blink them away. If we get this contract my bonus will be enough for me to pay for the rest of the renovations in the apartment and take Zoe away during her school vacation.

"I'm fine. Sorry."

William is already carrying our cases up the stairs. Linc follows him up and I trail behind, with my hat on again, suddenly feeling apprehensive. This man is big and built and the cottage is small.

The thought of sharing it with him – even for a few days – makes me feel strange. Just as I reach the bottom of the steps a tiny bird flies down and lands on the rail in front of me. It has a purple neck and a brown body with a long, thin beak. It turns to look at me as though sizing me up.

"Look at this," I whisper to Salinger. He turns around and a smile plays on his lips as the little bird starts to hop up the rail like it's walking up the stairs.

I hate the way I react to his smile. Like I'm one of his Hampshire PR girls.

"That's a Bahama Woodstar," William tells us. "A male, because he has that coloring."

"He's a little show off," I say as he flutters is little wings. "Why is it always the men that have the brightest coloring?"

"Because we have to find a way to get the girl," Linc says dryly.

I clear my throat, and the noise makes the tiny bird fly off. He disappears into the trees right as William opens the door to the bungalow and steps to the side so we can walk in.

The next five minutes are taken up with a tour of the cottage. He proudly tells us about the history of the resort, how he has lived in Exuma for the last fifty years, having relocated here with his family from Nassau where the tourist industry exploded. There's a control pad by the door for the blinds and lights that he explains to us. Then he takes us into the bathroom and explains how the rainfall shower, complete with light effects, works, then shows us to the bedroom.

It feels very crowded with the three of us in here.

I try not to look at Linc. Instead I shift my feet. It's his turn to clear his throat until I finally let my gaze rise up.

"You have dinner reservations at the beach restaurant at seven-thirty," William tells us, after he's shown us the sofa bed and explained that the maid service can make it up each night. "We will pick you up at seven-fifteen."

"How far is the restaurant?" I ask him.

"About a quarter of a mile that way," he says, pointing out of the window. I can't see the building, but I'm getting the idea.

"Can't we walk there?" I ask. Because I want to get to know the place. It feels wrong to have him driving us everywhere when we're perfectly capable of using our feet.

"It'll still be hot," he tells us.

"I don't mind if you don't," I say to Linc. He shrugs, easy going as always.

"Okay then." William nods. "If you need anything at all, use the phone by the sofa. It will connect you directly to me."

"Thank you." I smile at him because he's so very kind. "We appreciate it."

William touches the tip of his white baseball cap and makes his way out, walking back down to the buggy before driving away.

And for a long moment neither Linc nor I say anything. I'm staring through the open doorway to the beautiful bed, made up with white linens. This cottage is lovely, but it's not big enough for the two of us.

I'm not sure a whole building would be big enough for that.

"I guess I'll be taking the sofa then," Linc says, eyeing the white cotton sectional that looks way too small for his long, muscled body.

"No need," I say. "We can toss for it."

He lifts a brow at me. I take a deep breath. "Either way, can we just… try not to snap at each other while we're here?" I ask him.

"I don't snap," he tells me. "You bite."

I know I do. And I hate that. It's not his fault he looks this good. Or that it's been so long since I had sex that I'm actually finding him attractive in an annoying way. "Peace?" I say, looking at him. "Please?"

He runs his thumb along his jaw. "Okay, on one condition."

"What?"

He takes the sunhat off my head. "You stop wearing this hideous thing everywhere we go."

I snatch it back off him. "No deal. Being friends with you isn't worth getting melanomas."

CHAPTER
FIVE

LINC

I lose the toss. Which is kind of unfortunate because I know for certain I'm not going to get any sleep on that tiny fucking piece of furniture in the corner of the living room. Not that I'm going to let Tessa know that. She's still holding that hat like I'm about to take it off her again.

I don't know why it annoys me so much. Maybe it's because it's kind of adorable and Carmichael is anything but adorable.

Anyway, even if she'd lost, I would have found a way to give her the bed. I'm not that much of an asshole.

As she puts the dime back into her purse, I check my watch, trying to keep the peace she'd asked for even though she rejected my deal. "We have an hour until dinner. Want to walk down the beach?"

"I should call my daughter," she says. "And then get ready."

"Sure." I nod. "I'll go anyway. Take a look around."

"Sounds good."

"I'm just gonna get changed," I tell her. "Can I use the bedroom for a minute?" See, I can do nice.

Her cheeks pink up like I've suggested I'll be doing something much worse than changing clothes in the only bedroom in the cottage. "Oh, um yeah. Sure. I mean you're going to need to use it too, right? And you'll need half the closet space. And some drawers."

"I'll just keep my clothes in my suitcase." I shrug.

"Won't they get wrinkled?" she asks me.

"Probably. But I know how to use an iron." I grab my luggage and walk into the bedroom, putting it on the luggage rack and opening it up, before taking out a pair of shorts and a t-shirt from the clothes I threw in there this morning. I grab a pair of slides for my feet, and within two minutes I'm ready to leave.

"Okay. I'll be back in half an hour or so." I hook my sunglasses into the neckline of my t-shirt.

She nods. "Over dinner we should talk about our plan."

"What plan?"

"We need to review the presentation. Decide how we're going to incorporate the new videos into it." She's looking at the list of excursions the receptionist gave us, already making notes on it.

"Okay," I agree. "Let's talk about it over dinner. Do you need anything else?" God, my mom would be proud of me.

"No. I'm all good."

"Okay then. I'll be back in around half an hour." It won't take longer than ten minutes for me to shower and get changed when I get back from my walk. And I get the distinct impression she needs to be alone right now.

Not that I can blame her. I kind of feel the same way. In fact, I'm kind of kicking myself for not double checking our reservation. I know the staff think they're doing us a favor by giving us one of their nicer cottages, but it's made for couples and families, not co-workers. I should have specified that we needed two separate cottages, not beds.

I guess I'm lucky she's going along with my stupid mistake. Most people wouldn't. And if my spine is tied up in twenty different knots by the morning, that's the price I pay for being an idiot.

I lift my hand in goodbye and head out to the deck, taking in a long breath of air. It really is beautiful here. I've traveled to a lot of places. I spend half my life on an airplane, after all, at Roman's behest. I've even been to the Bahamas a few times before. But this is my first time on Grand Exuma and I'm kind of blown away.

And that's when I decide it's time to start being a professional. I pull my phone out – state of the art with a hell of a great camera included – and start recording some video of the cottage and surrounding area. I even manage to catch a few seconds of the Bahama Woodstar bird that is hanging around our cottage before he flies up into the trees.

As I make my way around the cottage ready to head to the ocean, I suddenly hear Tessa's voice.

"Yes," she says. "One bungalow. As in I have to share with him. And get this… there's only one bed."

I can't hear the other side of the conversation. She must not have the call on speaker phone. But my curiosity is piqued anyway.

Yes, I know that eavesdroppers never hear good of themselves. But they also don't get blindsided. And right now, I want to hear her pure, unadulterated response to having to share a bungalow with me.

"Of course he took the sofa," she's saying. "He's an asshole, but not that much of an asshole."

I blink, because that's almost exactly what I said to myself. Damn, are we that similar?

No. She's nothing like me.

"Oh shut up," she says quickly, giving an awkward laugh. And it's at this point I realize she's not talking to her daughter. I should have guessed that earlier. Why would she be telling a little kid she was sharing a cabin with me? But anyway, it makes me want to hear more. So I stay completely still.

"I'm not going to ask him to share a bed with me," she whispers. "Stop that." And hell, now I'm more than interested.

I'm fucking fascinated. I never for a moment considered that we'd share a bed. Heck, I'd be worried about getting covered in spikes because she can be that prickly. But now I can't stop listening if I tried.

"It's not one of your romance novels, Ange," she says. "And no. Because…"

Because what? I stand as still as a statue, waiting to hear her response. I'd kill to hear the other side of the conversation. A bird flies down and lands at my feet, pecking around the sand.

"You know why," she says softly.

I grimace. *No I don't. Tell me!*

There's a long sigh. "You know how long it's been. Two years."

Since what? Her divorce? Since she's been on vacation?

Since she had sex? Fuck, that's a long time. And now another part of me is interested. Because the idea of being the first man to touch Carmichael in two years makes me feel like a caveman.

I want to unfreeze the ice queen.

"You know he's hot. You just looked him up," Tessa says. And a grin slowly forms on my lips. "If you like that kind of thing," she adds, the grin kind of freezes.

There's a pause. "I'm not going to have sex with Lincoln Salinger," she says firmly.

My mouth drops open. Dear fucking God, is this what

women talk about on the phone? I guess that's my cue to leave. Not just because I shouldn't have been listening in the first place, but because there's a weird taste in my mouth that I can't quite get rid of. I pull my sandals off and tiptoe around the cottage to the stairs, taking them quickly and hurrying down the beach in case she decides to look out of the window.

I'm not going to have sex with Lincoln Salinger.

Huh. Nobody asked her anyway.

And if she wanted to?

I let out a low breath. Because if she did, I'd probably say yes.

I'm an asshole. But I'm also human. And Tessa Carmichael is a beautiful woman. She's also a challenge I'm not sure I can win.

And I always like to win.

———

TESSA

Linc walks back into the cottage right as I'm walking out of the bedroom. After calling Angela and then talking to Zoe who seems as happy as she can be at her dad's house, I showered quickly, not bothering to wash my hair because I did it this morning and there's not enough time to dry it right now. Instead, I've put it up into a kind of topknot, with some strands falling out around my face.

I'm wearing one of the new dresses I bought during an emergency shopping trip with Angela last weekend. It's white and strappy, the bodice tight and the skirt floaty. It makes me feel good.

Linc has the weirdest expression on his face as he looks at me. I have to double check my dress to make sure the hem isn't tucked into my panties, but it's flowing perfectly down to just above my knees.

And he's still staring at me.

"The bathroom's a little steamy," I tell him. "I've had the fan on but it doesn't seem to be doing much."

He nods and it strikes me that I've never seen Linc Salinger so quiet before. He has words for everything. It's unnerving.

"Are you okay?" I ask him, actually starting to get worried. "Did something happen while you were out walking?"

"What do you mean?" His voice sounds strained.

"You just seem…" I trail off because I don't know the right word. "*Off*?"

"I'm not being off," he says quickly.

"Okay then." I shrug. Backing off.

"I'm just wondering if I'll actually be able to make my way to the shower," he mutters. "It looks like the sixth ring of hell in there."

Okay, so the bathroom is kind of full of my stuff. I brought three toiletry bags – one for my hair, one for the shower, and one for my makeup – but there aren't enough surfaces in the tiny room and they've kind of spread out. "You want me to move my things out?" I ask him.

"It's fine. I'll just put my bottle of shampoo somewhere," he tells me.

"I'm certain you didn't just bring a bottle of shampoo." I narrow my eyes at him, because he's the kind of man who brings just as many bottles and sprays as I have. "I bet you have three bags, too."

His eyes catch mine. "Two."

"There you go. And you don't need to wear makeup so that's pretty much the same as me."

"You don't need to wear makeup either," he says gruffly, then passes me as he walks into the bathroom and pushes the door shut. I blink. Did he really just say that? It sounded weirdly like a compliment, but I have no idea what to do with that thought.

The shower is turned on immediately, and it's as loud out here as it was when I was standing under it. I guess the walls in this place weren't built for privacy.

No, they were built for love. I tip my head to the side, wondering if we can somehow use that in the PR pitch.

"Fuck." A loud thump comes from the bathroom, making me jump.

"Are you okay?" I call out.

"You heard that?" he calls back. He sounds kind of annoyed. Did a fish bite him or something?

"Yep."

"Of course you fucking did," he mutters.

I open my mouth to tell him that I heard that too, but nobody likes a smart ass, and I'm pretty sure Linc knows I can hear him. I also hear the thud of his clothes as they fall to the floor, then the change in the sound of the water spray as he climbs underneath it.

Naked. Linc Salinger is naked. And I start to blush because I hadn't thought about how sharing this cottage with him would feel so intimate. And of course it should. This whole resort is made for lovers, including this cottage. It's all Angela's fault for planting that seed in my brain. If she hadn't said I should choose Linc as my first post-divorce sex partner I wouldn't even be thinking like this.

I know he'd be good. I just know it. He has that cockiness to him that only men who know what they're doing in bed have. He exudes sex, and I hate that.

I try to forget what Ange said, because I definitely won't be going near Salinger.

There's a buzz from the sofa and I realize that Linc must have left his phone on the back of it before he walked into the bathroom. Curiosity gets the better of me, and I lean over to see what kind of notification he has on his phone.

Hi, handsome. Long time no see. Want to join me and Catriona on a yacht next week? We'll have it all to ourselves, just the three of us. A fun time guaranteed!

It's from some woman named Liliana. And it makes my stomach feel slightly sick. Not because I'm in any way, shape, or form attracted to this man. I'm not. It's just the thought of him and two women.

It's like somebody has thrown a bucket of ice cold water over me. And I'm thankful, really. I needed something to bring me back to reality.

He's not my type. And I'm never going there. To try to push the image of Linc Salinger and two women out of my mind, I grab my own phone and check my messages, then send a quick email to Gina to make sure I haven't missed too much at the office.

By the time I hit send the bathroom door opens and Linc walks nonchalantly into the living room, his body glistening with water, a white towel wrapped around his hips.

For a moment I openly stare at his chest. At the defined rise and fall of his pectorals, the way his stomach is ridged, and the little line of hair that dips down from his navel, disappearing into the towel.

"Want me to do a twirl?" he asks, lifting a brow.

"Why are you in the living room half dressed?" I ask tightly.

"Because I need to get my clothes." He saunters over to his case, lifting it up easily and putting it on the sofa. He unzips it and pulls out a shirt and some pants.

"You're still looking," he says, even though his gaze is on the case.

"You had a message while you were in the shower," I tell him, ignoring his taunting.

"You been checking my phone, Carmichael?"

"Your phone was buzzing. I was trying to turn it off. And then I decided not to touch it, since I don't know where it's been."

His gaze lifts to mine. "You don't know where it's been," he repeats. "Where do you think it's been?"

"With two women named Catriona and Liliana?" I reply.

His smirk widens. He says nothing as he picks up the phone to read the message. Then he turns it back off.

"Aren't you going to reply?" I ask. I don't know why I'm so annoyed right now.

"I'll do it later," he says. "Now I'm going to get dressed. You want me to leave the door open so you can watch?"

"I wasn't watching you," I protest.

"Sure you weren't." He winks and turns around.

"I wasn't," I say loudly, as he closes the door.

Aggravated, I sit down and let out a loud sigh. I'd drop my face into my hands but I don't want to smudge my makeup.

We've been together less than twenty-four hours, and I already remember why I don't like him that much.

It's going to be a very long few days.

CHAPTER
SIX

LINC

I wouldn't call myself highly sexed. Medium, maybe. I don't know. Healthy. Whatever. All I know is that I like sex very much. And I make sure whoever I'm with likes it too.

But it's been the only thing on my mind ever since I overheard her categorically telling the person on the other end of the line that she was never going to have sex with me.

And it's stupid, because I don't want to have sex with her. Not really. She's been a pain in my ass ever since I started working at Hampshire PR.

Some guys love a challenge like that. The ones who think that sex is some kind of transactional relationship where they win every time.

But not me. For me, sex has to be mutually pleasurable. I don't want to win. I want to make her win.

Okay, I want to make her come.

I take a deep breath and try to forget that thought. Not just because it's inappropriate – so highly inappropriate I don't even know where to start. But because I think that sex with Carmichael could only end in tears.

For both of us.

"Would you like to start with a cocktail?" the server asks.

Tessa and I are sitting under a thatched roof held up by wooden columns. Lights are hanging from every rafter, the soft, yellow kind that make everything and everybody look better. We're sitting next to the beach, giving us the perfect view of the darkening ocean as the sun slowly slides beneath the horizon. In the corner a band is playing what sounds like a slow version of an Ed Sheeran song, and a couple are on the dance floor, swaying together and laughing.

"What cocktail do you recommend?" I ask.

"The Bahama Mama, of course," she tells us. "It's everybody's favorite."

I catch Tessa's eye and she nods. "Two of those please."

Five minutes later we're sipping at our pink frothy cocktails. They're made with crushed ice, and the first mouthful gave me a brain freeze.

Tessa insisted on taking photographs and videos of the cocktails first, and now she's recording me. I lift a brow before I take a sip of the cocktail.

"You want me to take my top off for the video?" I ask her.

She wrinkles her nose. "I'm not one of your yacht girls."

Oh, she's still salty about that. "You shouldn't dismiss it until you try it," I tell her, smirking because she has no idea what she's talking about. And if I'm being honest, I like winding her up.

"The yacht or your girls?" she asks, giving me a smile that looks like danger.

"They're not my girls," I say. "I'd have thought a feminist like you wouldn't demean women that way."

That makes her frown. She takes a long sip of her cocktail. "You're right," she mutters. "I shouldn't."

I take a deep breath, because it's going to be a long night if we keep annoying each other. I decide to take some videos as well, pretty much to try to keep up with her. I start with a panoramic, my eyes on my phone screen as I slowly twist around and video the beach, the now inky-black sky, the illuminated rafters of the hut we're sitting in.

And I finally get to her. She fills the screen as she looks at me, a strange expression on her face. Beneath the lights, her hair is shining. Her skin is too. It's pale and lustrous, the complete opposite of nearly everybody else here.

"You don't need to video me," she says.

"You took some shots of me."

"Because you're the kind of guy we want to appeal to in our pitch."

"I am?" I tip my head, putting the phone down so I can look at her directly. "What kind of guy is that?"

"Rich?"

"I'm not rich."

"You're not poor," she says softly. It doesn't feel like a jibe this time, just an observation.

"No, I'm not. But most of that is thanks to my family, not me." Or more specifically my dad. He was a financier. Made a lot of money in investments. And as a beneficiary of the family I get to share some of it. And I live rent free, which is a big deal in New York City.

"You have disposable income. You're a good looking man. Discerning…" she trails off.

"You think I'm discerning?" I ask, confused because a second ago she was railing about my yacht girls.

"I think you could be."

For a moment, neither of us says a word. I just look at her, trying to work her out. We've been working for the same company for almost two years now, but I know so little about her.

Hell, I didn't even know she was divorced until she told me the other day. She's more impenetrable than Fort Knox.

And now I'm thinking about fucking penetration again. Why does my mind do this? Why can't it be normal? I knew I should have whacked myself off in the shower.

I was going to do it, too, until she heard me drop my damn bottle of shampoo and I realized that the walls in the cottage were so thin she could hear everything.

Including me touching myself and groaning, if I were to do it.

Which I didn't. Because I'm a gentleman.

"I think you don't know me at all," I say softly. Her gaze doesn't waver. Christ, she's pretty. Especially when her hair is down which I know is a fucking cliché but it's true.

"Can I take your food order?" the server asks, cutting through the silence. It's almost a relief to pull my eyes away from hers as we give our orders and the server assures us the wait won't be long.

Which is good. Because we need to get back to the cottage and she needs to go to sleep so I can take care of something very important.

Without her listening. Because that would kill me.

———

TESSA

Our food arrives ten minutes later. We decided to skip the appetizers and go straight for the main course, which turns out to be a great plan, because I've already got my heart set on one of the amazing ice cream desserts I've seen them bringing out to other guests.

I chose the Mahi Mahi tacos, which are glorious. Tiny handmade wraps, filled with flaky white fish, a rainbow of vegetables, and the most exquisite salsa I've ever tasted. Linc looks equally enamored with his meal – Bahama Curried

Chicken, served with coconut rice and a charred side of flat-breads. He closes his eyes and groans as he swallows a mouthful and I realize again just how attractive this man is.

I wasn't lying when I said he's the demographic we're trying to appeal to. I know enough about his background to understand his life has been extremely different than mine. Not that I blame him for that – we don't get to choose who we're born as.

"Would you like a taco?" I ask, magnanimously, because this food is too good not to share. He takes one eagerly, and then offers me a forkful of his chicken, and I get why he let out an orgasmic groan when he tasted it.

"Why does food always taste better on vacation?" I ask.

"The same reason everything else is better. Because you're relaxed." He tears off a piece of bread and offers it to me.

I'm getting full. And I want to leave some space in my stomach for dessert, but it feels churlish to refuse. It feels more like a peace offering than a piece of bread. So I take it.

"What else is better on vacation?" I ask.

He smiles and I roll my eyes.

"Do you think about anything other than sex?" I ask him.

"Not really, no."

At least he's honest.

I clear my throat, because I'm blushing. And I'm thinking about sex, too.

Thanks, Ange.

"Can I ask you a question?" he says, breaking the silence. He's actually cleared his plate.

"You want my last taco?" I ask. "Because have at it. I can't eat anymore."

"That wasn't my question, but I'll take it anyway."

He eats the taco like he consumes life. Like it's the best thing ever. When it's gone, he's still looking at me.

"Okay," I say. "Ask me your question."

"Why do you hate me?"

Oh. That's not what I was expecting. I blink, trying to think of how to respond.

"I don't hate you." What a great response. Especially when it's been clear that I really dislike him. Or I did. For a while.

Okay, until today when I tried to broker some peace.

And maybe I still do. Maybe this third – yes third – cocktail is responsible for my mellowing out.

"Yeah you do." There's a look of amusement on his face. "Maybe we should make an agreement. We don't lie to each other while we're on this island."

"Why would I agree to that?"

He lifts a brow. "Because I'd have to agree to it, too. And you could ask me anything you want."

"What makes you think I want to know anything about you?" I ask tartly.

He grins. "Because you're as nosy as I am. You're just better at hiding it."

I let out a long breath. "I don't hate you."

He looks stupidly pleased about that.

"I'm not the easiest person to get along with," I admit to him. "And you might have started working for Roman right as I was going through the worst part of my divorce. My best friend called it the 'We Hate Men' phase."

"It definitely felt like your 'I hate Salinger' phase."

"I'm sorry." I shrug. "But you also seemed to delight in riling me up."

"I'm going to tell you a secret," he says, leaning in.

"Is this part of the being honest thing?" I ask warily.

"Yeah. You just told me the truth, so I'm going to tell you one. Quid Pro Quo."

"Isn't that what Hannibal said to Clarice?" A shudder snakes down my spine. I hated that movie. I remember watching it as a kid and not being able to sleep for days.

"Who's Hannibal?" he asks, frowning.

"It doesn't matter. Tell me your secret." Because I'm stupidly invested in this honesty thing now. At least until it's my turn again.

"You're the first person I've met who doesn't like me," he says.

It takes a moment for the words to sink in. And when they do, I shake my head. "That's not your secret."

"It is."

"Lots of people must hate you." The words slip out before I think them through. But luckily he throws his head back and starts laughing. "Wait, I didn't mean it like that," I protest.

He can't stop laughing, though. His face starts to redden and I'm starting to worry he's going to choke.

"Are you crying?" I ask him.

"I think so," he manages, spluttering out the words.

When he gets his breath back I try to explain again. "You can't go through life without people hating you," I say. "Some of them do it for no reason at all."

"Like my brother and his wife." Linc nods, sagely.

"They hate each other? Are they getting a divorce?" I ask him.

"No, they're horribly in love. But they started out hating each other. Worked at the same company actually."

"Well isn't that a lovely lawsuit waiting to happen?" I grin.

"But seriously," he says, his eyes catching mine. They're a striking blue. "Nobody hates me."

"That's not possible. You must have an ex or two with little Linc mannequins full of pins," I say.

"Nope. I'm friends with all my exes. Was the chief bridesman to one a couple of years ago." Now he looks smug.

"What about at work? It's not just me who finds you…"

"Finds me what?" He looks like he's enjoying himself a little too much. He smiles over at the bar and nods at somebody before bringing his gaze back to me.

"Challenging," I say.

"Nobody finds me challenging," he says, as the server brings us over two more cocktails. Our fourth round. I shouldn't drink anymore, my words are starting to slur. Even worse, I'm starting to like this man. Rum has a lot to answer for. Still, I thank the server and take a long sip of the glorious cocktail.

"They find me charming," he says, winking at the server. She blushes and grins back at him. "Not challenging."

I shrug. "Okay, so it's only me. I've ruined your unblemished record."

"You're right." He nods, looking thoughtful. "But I'm winning you over, aren't I?"

"The cocktails are winning me over," I tell him. "You're just basking in their glory."

He laughs again. "By the end of this week, I guarantee you'll be putty in my hands."

"You're very sure of yourself," I say, gazing at him coolly.

"I just know who I am. Don't get me wrong, you're my toughest win yet, but I'm going to do it."

"Good luck with that," I say, finishing my cocktail.

Damn, I really am feeling drunk.

CHAPTER
SEVEN

TESSA

My head is banging. My mouth feels like it's an arid desert, and my stomach isn't feeling much better. I grab the smartwatch that's charging next to my bed and check the time.

It's three am. I groan. Mostly because I'm not going to get back to sleep without going to the bathroom.

And going to the bathroom means walking past Linc on the sofa bed.

This is why it's so much better to be a man in the middle of the night. If he was in this situation he'd almost certainly walk out of the double doors at the far end of the bedroom and pee off the deck.

He'd probably make friends with the damn birds while he did it. For a minute, I picture him as a peeing, male Snow White, singing "With A Smile and A Song".

Everything starts to spin as I roll over and plant my feet firmly on the floor. I'm too old for hangovers like this. I thought I'd gotten over drinking too much while still in college, but no, apparently I now have a thing for Bahama Mamas.

When I reach the door to the bedroom I hear a noise.

A groan.

It's deep and low and it makes me freeze. Is that Linc? What's he doing?

Oh god, he's not…

He groans again. It's louder this time. My face heats up and I'm completely torn between walking to the bathroom and running back to bed. I stand at the door for a minute, wondering how long that kind of thing takes him.

Does he take his time? He's the kind of man who savors life. I don't think he'd hurry anything. He'd wrap his hand around his big shaft – because let's face it, I know he'd be big – and slowly and surely tug until he reached the edge.

Why am I thinking about Linc Salinger's masturbation style?

And then the world twists again as he lets out a scream.

It's like an ice cold bucket of water over my head. What the hell?

There's whimpering coming from the other side of the door, and I know this isn't him touching himself. He's having a nightmare.

My heart is hammering against my chest as I pull at the door handle, softly enough not to make a noise. I thank the god of oiled hinges as it opens without a creak, then pad into the living area.

Linc is thrashing about on the bed. The sheet he pulled over himself earlier has worked its way down to his ankles, kind of binding them up so he can't get loose. He's wearing a pair of shorts and nothing else. And he's still groaning.

I pad over softly, trying to remember what we used to do with Zoe when she was little and had night terrors. All I can remember was that I wasn't supposed to wake her.

"Please!"

My heart almost breaks from his plea. It's so plaintiff it hits me right in the chest. I drop to my knees next to him. I touch his brow. It's clammy. His whole body is shining with sweat.

"It's okay," I whisper. "Go back to sleep."

He whimpers as I stroke his hair. Then his hand reaches out toward me and I don't know what to do.

So I take it. Squeeze it. And somehow that calms him.

"It's just a bad dream," I whisper, hoping that somehow my words are making it through to his unconsciousness. "It's okay. You're okay."

His hand grips mine so tightly it hurts. But I don't try to pull away. He starts to calm, but as he tries to roll over his legs get stuck in the sheets again. So with my free hand, I have to stretch hard to loosen them and my spine does a little crack.

Because he won't let go of my hand.

Once it's loose enough to pull away from his ankles, he calms down even more. Once he lets go of me, I'll cover him up again. Not that it will help much. This sofa clearly isn't made for a man his size. He dwarfs it.

No wonder he got all caught up in the sheets.

I immediately feel bad, because I'm small enough to fit on the sofa without a problem. Sure, it wouldn't be the most comfortable night's sleep, but it would be better than the one Linc is having.

He turns onto his side, one leg on the sofa, kind of folded up, the other slung out toward me.

"I'm sorry," he whispers. And for a moment I think he's woken up. Startled, my eyes scan his face, but his own are still tightly closed.

"It's okay," I tell him again. I reach out to cup his jaw. The roughness of his beard growth tickles my palm. He leans into my touch, his breath warm against my skin.

"Go back to sleep," I say. "It's okay."

It takes another ten minutes before he's asleep deeply

enough for me to untangle our fingers and stand up. There's a crick in my neck, and my legs feel achy after crouching beside him for so long, but by some kind of miracle the hangover is gone.

I take the sheet and smooth it out over him, leaving it loose so he doesn't get caught up, before I hurry to the bathroom, because things are getting desperate now.

He's snoring softly when I come out, and I start to relax. I fill two glasses of water, leaving one on the table next to him before I take a long sip from the other. A wave of exhaustion washes over me, because it's a stupidly early hour of the morning.

"I'm just going to bed," I whisper, even though he can't hear me. And then I walk back to the bedroom, taking one last glance back at him.

He's still fast asleep. Looking calm, like the last twenty minutes never happened.

It doesn't stop me from wondering about his nightmare, as I walk through the bedroom and put my glass by the bed. What was his dream about? Does he have nightmares often?

Or was it just induced by too many cocktails followed by having to fold his body on the too-small sofa.

As I climb under the covers and relax into the pillow, I find myself thinking about how strong his grip was. How his chest rose and fell rapidly as he screamed out.

In the day time he's strong. Laid back. Attractive as hell if you're into that kind of thing.

But right now he seemed like somebody completely different. Somebody vulnerable. And I hate that it makes me like him more. There's a chink the sexy Salinger armor. But instead of making him weaker, it just makes him more interesting.

———

Linc doesn't mention last night at all as we eat breakfast the next morning. William brought a continental selection down to the cottage, and we sit out on the deck at the little table with a view through the trees to the ocean, sipping on coffee and watching as the waves crash into the shore.

Reaching behind him, he uses his fingers to rub at what I assume is a knot in his shoulders.

"How was the sofa bed?" I finally ask him, desperate to see if he can remember his dream.

"Fine, I think." He shrugs. "Apart from it being too little and me being too big."

"You could still have the bed," I say, shrugging. "I'm little and that's too big."

"No thanks, Goldilocks," he says wryly. "I kind of like waking up and feeling like an old man."

I rip off a piece of pastry and put it into my mouth. Okay then, neither of us are talking about last night. Which is fine, because I'm not nosy at all.

Okay, only a little bit.

"Do you want to go over the itinerary for the next few days?" I ask him.

He shrugs. "Sure. What's up first?"

"Today we're exploring the hotel," I tell him. "I've written down the videos I want to take."

He picks up the piece of paper I've scrawled all over, lifting a brow as he reads it. "Why have you written the clothes I should be wearing on here?"

"Because when I take videos of you in the business suite I need you in a suit," I tell him. "And when you're in the gym you'll need workout clothes. I thought you could bring them all up to the main hotel and that'll save you having to come back here and change between shots."

He narrows his eyes at me. "I thought you were just going to give an outline of the kind of videos we're planning to produce."

"If we're here, I'm pretty sure Gold will expect to see mock ups." I shrug.

"So why can't you be the one wearing business clothing?" he asks. "Surely we want to be equal opportunity here."

"Because I'm taking the footage," I say. "And I thought we'd already established that you're our target audience."

His eyes catch mine as he tops up his coffee. "I am. And I want to see women in the business suite."

I roll my own eyes at him. "Just put on a sexy suit and shut up, Salinger."

He shakes his head. "Since you ask me so nicely, I will."

We spend the first part of the morning taking shots of the exterior of the resort, working our way from the beach, past the cottages, to the main hotel building itself. The white walls reflect the golden light of the sun, and I have to try a few different angles to get the right exposure.

"You're good at this," Linc murmurs as I play back some of the video I've made. "But why are you using your phone?" He glances over at the digital recorder I've set up on a tripod. "Surely that will have better results."

"I want to make it look authentic." I shrug. "The kind of video an influencer would make. Portrait style, a little jolty."

The corner of his lip curls up. "I guess you're the expert."

It almost sounds like a compliment.

We spend an hour in the business suite, having to stop regularly as people come in to use the video conferencing office in the corner, or to print out documents with the huge machine that makes way too much noise.

When everybody finally leaves I walk over to Linc. "Lose the jacket," I tell him. He does as he's told and then I loosen his tie. He looks at me, those thick lashes sweeping down as I smooth out the creases on his shirt.

"I thought you wanted me to look business like," he murmurs.

"I want you to look relaxed. Like you can make millions while on vacation."

He starts to laugh. "You've got it all worked out, haven't you?"

Yes, I have. Gina and I worked on our plans for the last two weeks. Having to refocus the pitch to include location filming was a curveball, but I need to go with it. "Sit in that chair," I tell him, pointing at a leather swivel chair in front of a desktop computer. "Pick up your phone and look like you're having a great time talking to somebody on the other end."

To my shock, he does as I ask him. I lift my phone up and look at him through the screen. He really is very attractive.

I let out a long breath.

"Can you run your hand through your hair?" I ask him.

He tips his head to the side. "Seriously?"

"Yes please."

"You want me to put the phone down?" He holds it up.

"No, keep pretending to talk. Use the other hand to touch your hair. Think sexy businessman."

"I'm starting to feel objectified," he murmurs.

Oh god, that's not what I was aiming for. "We can stop."

He starts to laugh. "I'm toying with you, Carmichael. If you can take the heat of me being a sexy businessman, then let's do it."

An hour later we make it to the gym. This time he insisted that we both change into workout gear. I pointed out I didn't have any, so he marched me over to the boutique in the hotel lobby and made me try on a pair of calf length leggings and a crop top. I feel horrendously exposed in them as we walk into the – thankfully empty – gym.

"You go first," I tell him, pointing at the treadmill.

"How fast do you want me to run?" he asks.

Truth be told, I have no idea. I think I might be allergic to gyms. I certainly haven't stepped foot inside of one in years. I do a yoga class at our local YMCA on the Saturday mornings when Zoe isn't home, but apart from that most of my energy goes into renovations.

"How about ten?" I say, sounding uncertain., because I have no idea what a good speed is.

He starts to laugh. And then he gets on the treadmill and presses the start button. Before long, his legs are a blur as he runs faster than I can focus on him.

And the man is barely breaking a sweat.

"Can you run faster?" I ask him.

"Fuck off, Carmichael."

I start to laugh, which makes the shot go completely shaky.

"Okay, your turn," he says when I finally tell him he can stop.

"Oh no." I shake my head. "I'll just stand here and look pretty."

He takes the phone from me and marches me over to the treadmill. "Get on."

"I can't run," I tell him honestly.

"Of course you can run. Everybody can run."

I lift an eyebrow at him as I hit the start button.

Within a minute tears are rolling down his face as I attempt to keep a seven mile an hour pace. My lungs feel like they're about to explode, my whole body drenched in sweat.

"Did you get it?" I puff out, my throat burning.

"Get what?" Linc asks.

"The shot?"

"Oh. I forgot to tell you, the screen locked." He holds up the phone to show me the black screen. "Let's try again."

"Let's not." I hit the stop button on the treadmill, but I don't expect it to stop so quickly. I nearly end up face down on the belt.

And he still can't stop laughing.

"I'll get you back for this," I tell him, grabbing a towel to mop my sweat ridden face.

"Sure you will." He grins and passes me back the phone, before grabbing a bottle of water from the refrigerator and throwing it to me. "Drink, Carmichael. Before we end up taking shots of the Grand Exuma Hospital."

"There's no Grand Exuma Hospital," I tell him. "There's a mini healthcare place and after that you have to go off-island."

His eyes catch mine again. "Of course you'd know that."

"I like to research a location thoroughly before I make a pitch," I say, defensively.

Linc lifts a brow. "I'm beginning to notice."

CHAPTER
EIGHT

LINC

The sun is beating down on us the next morning, as the boat speeds through the sapphire blue water. I'm wearing a pair of swim shorts and aviators, my body warm and glowing. And I'm trying not to smile because Tessa keeps looking over at me then quickly looking away.

I work hard to keep myself fit. Traveling all the time for work is great, but it means I have to eat out a lot. Which means I have to hit the gym a lot more.

Plus I'm vain. And I like to look good.

There are twelve of us on the boat. All couples, apart from Tessa and me. We were picked up at seven this morning and taken to the little pier at the end of the beach, where we climbed onto this boat and were given coconut and melon for breakfast.

Carmichael is sitting next to a couple who can't keep their hands off each other. I'm pretty sure the rings on their fingers weren't put on by each other. He's too old and she's way too interested in him for them to be married to each other.

Yeah, I'm cynical, but I'm also a realist.

She's got that stupidly adorable hat on again. And it took us an extra twenty minutes to leave the cottage because she insisted on covering every single inch of her body with factor thirty, while I just sprayed myself with whatever sunscreen I had in my wash bag. She's also wearing one of those floaty short dresses over her swimsuit. And she's holding her phone up, taking videos of the ocean, the boat, and the fish that swim up to the surface of the water every time we stop near a shoal.

So far we've seen stingrays, barracudas, and something called a drumfish, with black and white stripes that make it look like a relative of a zebra. And every time we look overboard, the woman next to me pushes herself against me. Her name is Maya and her husband has been constantly on his phone as we glide through the ocean. Even in his shorts and white starched polo shirt he looks like he's in the office.

I guarantee he works on Wall Street. He just has that air about him.

"How long have you two been together?" Maya asks, shooting Tessa an interested look.

"We're not together," I say. "We're co-workers."

"You came on vacation with your co-worker?" Maya asks. "What does your girlfriend think about that?"

Tessa is pretending not to listen. She's still filming but her eyes keep darting from the screen to us.

"I don't have a girlfriend," I say, more to see Tessa's response than anything else.

"You don't?" Maya asks. "What's a gorgeous man like you doing alone?"

Tessa clears her throat. I try not to smile. There's a tightness to her jaw that's delicious.

Why is it I enjoy annoying her so much? I've no idea.

She's kind of softer than I realized. Yesterday's filming marathon around the resort was actually more fun than I thought it would be. I'm not used to getting involved in the nitty gritty of a campaign. I mostly wine and dine clients, and when they're in trouble I get them out of it.

Seeing this side of our work is fun.

"My last girlfriend couldn't keep up with me," I tell Maya, and Tessa lets out a huff.

"Sexually?" Maya purrs.

I nod, trying to look sad. "She couldn't take the pleasure."

Tessa coughs loudly. Our gazes catch and she's glaring at me. I shoot her a smile and she rolls her eyes.

"What a silly woman," Maya says. "But she set you free to find somebody who appreciates your… skills."

Her hand moves down my arm, tracing the lines of my biceps. And her husband doesn't even fucking notice.

It's not like I'm interested. Nor am I looking for a fight, though I'm pretty sure I'd hold my own against Mr. Wall Street.

I'm just wondering why the hell he's come to the most beautiful set of islands I've ever seen for a vacation when all he's doing is glaring at his phone.

And enjoying Carmichael's frowns, of course.

"There it is," the driver calls out, and we all follow the direction of his finger as he points at an island. A Cay, actually. The Exumas are surrounded by tiny cays and islands. According to Tessa's research – which yes, I have read – there are three hundred and sixty-five of them. One for each day of the year.

The one we're looking at is special. It's called Big Major Cay, and like the others we've seen, it has pale golden sand that borders a green forest full of tropical trees.

But this island is different. Because it has swimming pigs that live there. I didn't even know pigs could swim, but apparently these ones can and they're a huge tourist draw.

The boat pulls up as far as it can, and one by one we climb down into the warm ocean. The water reaches my hips, the waves lapping at them as a couple of us help the ladies down.

I notice Maya's husband doesn't even bother to get off the boat, even though she's stripped down to the tiniest gold bikini that hugs her every curve. So I help her down, and she hangs around me as I reach for Tessa.

And for a moment I'm struck dumb, because she's taken off her cover up and looks hot as hell.

She's wearing a two piece swimsuit. And though it's no where near as skimpy as Maya's bikini, she looks more beautiful in every way. Her skin is pale and glowing from the sunscreen she rubbed all over herself. And her hair is up, revealing the soft curve of her neck.

I try really fucking hard not to look at her chest. But I fail miserably.

Fuck, she has perfect tits.

Not too big, not small either. Just right. And I know they'd be soft, because there's nothing about Carmichael that's artificial. She's so real she forgets who she is sometimes.

Fuck, I'm getting hard.

I swallow quickly, thankful for the ocean right now. Because if anybody sees me staring at her, I'm in trouble. Thankfully Maya seems to have gotten bored and is now talking to her husband.

Tessa lifts a brow as I offer her my hand, then takes it, looking a bit sullen. She climbs over the side of the boat and I steady her as she slides into the water.

"Okay?" I ask her. My hand is still on her waist. Water is lapping over it.

Her eyes flicker up to mine. "Don't worry about me. Go spend some more time with your new friend."

"Are you jealous?" I ask. Weird that I'm kind of hoping she says yes.

"Of you and a married woman?" she asks, looking over at

Maya who's currently hissing something at the guy she's married to. "No, not at all."

I tip my head to the side. "You sound very judgmental."

Tessa shakes her head. "Affairs hurt people."

It's weird how her words feel like a bucket of cold water, even though we're surrounded by the warmth of the Atlantic. "I'm not having an affair. I'm just talking to somebody who's being ignored by the man she traveled with."

Tessa lets out another huff. "I know how she feels."

"Is that directed at me?" I ask, frowning. "Because you were the one ignoring me."

"I wasn't ignoring you. I was filming," she says tartly, but there's something more than that annoying her. I can tell. I can read people. It's my superpower.

She pulls that stupid hat on and I fight the urge to throw it far, far into the ocean.

Before I can say anything else, there's a squeal of excitement from a woman in front of us. And that's when we see them.

What looks like forty hairy, massive pigs, all swimming toward us.

Maya screams, and runs away from the boat and through the water, jumping into my arms.

———

TESSA

My jaw tightens at Maya's overreaction. Everybody knows there are swimming pigs here. They're exactly the reason we all got in the boat and have sat in it for over an hour, so her screaming seems over dramatic.

But Maya is still clinging to Linc, who looks stupidly amused as I glare at him.

"It's okay," he says to her. "They're veggie sauruses."

"They're what?" she asks, not getting his *Jurassic Park* reference at all.

His eyes meet mine again. And now he looks like he's about to laugh. Against my will, a smile forms on my face.

And just like that, we're on an even keel again. Or something approaching it.

The driver gives us carrots to feed to the pigs, which actually aren't vegetarians. Like us, they're omnivores, though their diet consists mostly of fruit and vegetables.

Linc puts Maya gently down into the water, then puts a couple of feet between them, but I'm too busy watching a huge pig swim up to me. He must weigh as much as Linc, and he's got black and white hair, but his snout is perfectly pink as he eyes the carrot I'm holding.

He lifts his head out of the water expectantly, and I feed him the carrot, which he half-swallows between his teeth, before turning and swimming back to the shore with his prize.

And instantly, I'm in love.

Now that they know we have food, more pigs approach. I look over at Linc, who's feeding a baby pig, and he looks just as enchanted as I am. Maybe Maya doesn't like pigs, because she's hanging onto the boat talking to her husband, who looks like he's barely listening to her.

Another pig comes to me and I feed it, remembering the research we did about them when we were preparing our presentation. My phone is in a waterproof pouch around my neck and I lift it up to start recording the miracle taking place before me.

Nobody really knows how the pigs came to live on the island – which is uninhabited by humans. There's a theory that they swam here after a shipwreck a hundred years ago, and learned to take care of themselves when all the sailors had died. Others say that a group of sailors brought them to the island to kill and cook them, but sailed off, leaving the pigs behind.

Whatever brought them here, they're clearly thriving. And locals make sure they're well fed and taken care of. They're one of the most popular attractions in the Exumas and I can see why.

They're enchanting.

When the pigs are fully fed, they swim to shore, their little legs paddling like crazy as they glide through the water. We follow them in, and sand coats my wet feet as we walk up the beach.

Most of the pigs trundle across the sand to a copse of trees and lay in the shade. A few of them are still huddling around us, clearly hoping for more carrots. And then I look over at Linc, who's walking through the surf toward me.

The piglet he fed earlier is swimming beside him. He turns to look at Linc, as though to make sure he's still there.

"Go in," Linc says to him. "Go find your mama."

But the piglet ignores him. And when Linc emerges from the water, the piglet continues to follow him like he's Linc's shadow.

"Seriously, I have no more food." Linc holds his hands up, like he's talking to a baby. "Shoo."

I bite down a smile, because the little piglet has obviously taken to him. He slides his wet body against Linc's legs, looking pleased as punch.

"Get off," Linc mutters.

I grab my phone from the waterproof pouch hanging around my neck. Because some things have to be recorded for posterity. The pig gazes up at Linc, and I swear he has the same expression on his face that Maya had earlier.

Speaking of Maya, her husband has finally gotten out of the boat and the two of them are having a furious argument down the beach. Which is only adding to my good humor.

Linc walks away from the piglet. And the piglet follows

him. Then the piglet starts scrabbling his paws against Linc's legs, like a puppy wanting to be picked up.

"Can you help me instead of filming?" Linc asks, catching me holding my phone up.

"Nope, sorry." I grin. "I'm busy. And you're adorable."

"I'm not fucking adorable," he mutters, his jaw tightening.

"Language," I say, really trying not to laugh now. "The pigs have ears."

It's his turn to roll his eyes, and I enjoy it way too much. Linc reaches down and picks the pig up as though he's going to walk him back to his family in the trees. He cradles the tiny pink thing against his chest, and I swear everything inside of me combusts.

And then two seconds later, there's a squeal and a huge pig thunders toward him, making Linc jump.

"Put the baby down. That's the mama coming for you," our captain shouts at him. "She's angry at you."

Linc's eyes widen in fear. And I have to admit, I zoom in on his face for a moment, before zooming out to see him gently putting his new best friend on the ground, before he starts running for his life as the angry momma pig chases him down.

He races to the shoreline, his feet splashing in the ebbing waves as he attempts to evade the pig. As he turns around to check if he's put enough distance between himself and the pig, one of his feet gets caught beneath the other and he does a magnificent face plant into the shallow water.

The pig, sensing she's won, grunts and turns around, ambling back to her little piglet, who follows her as they walk to where the rest of their gang is sunbathing.

I can't help it. I double over in laughter, because if I don't bend I'm almost certainly going to pee myself. Through a veil of tears, I watch as Linc slowly gets up, his face crusted with sand that he tries – and fails – to wipe off.

At least I have the evidence recorded in case I need a future laugh.

————

LINC

"Seriously, I'm going to need you to delete that video," I tell her. She hasn't stopped grinning since I fell face over ass into the sand. She showed everybody in the boat on the way back to Grand Exuma, too. The only one who looked sorry for me was Maya.

"I'm sorry, I can't do that." Tessa puts her phone into her beach bag and turns to me with an eyebrow raised. "I'm keeping it as leverage."

"Leverage for what?" I ask her.

"Any time you annoy me at work, just remember that video is one fingertip away from being sent to all of Hampshire PR." Her smile widens. "Although I think they'll be impressed by how fast you can run when you're being chased by a mad mama pig. Thank goodness you went to the gym yesterday."

We're sitting in a cabana overlooking the ocean. She's still in that bikini, which is very distracting, with her laptop on her knees as she looks through the shots she took yesterday and today.

Thankfully the hat is off. She's put it on the sand next to her because the brim kept hitting the back of her sun bed. I keep willing a breeze to come along and spirit it away.

"I'll find a way to delete it." I know a few tech geniuses. Or is it genii? Whatever, they can probably break into it if I ask them nicely.

"My phone only opens with my fingerprint," she says smugly.

"There are ways around that."

"Like what?" She looks at me, interested.

"I guess I could chop your finger off," I say, pretending to be serious. She rolls her eyes. "Or your phone could take a short walk off a long pier."

"You wouldn't."

I lift a brow. "Wouldn't I?"

Fact is, I wouldn't. Growing up with five brothers, I've learned that being humiliated isn't as bad as it sounds. Hell, I can easily swing it back my way if the whole office sees that video. Within five minutes of it being released, I'll spin a story about me saving the others from the pig, and then get the sympathy vote from at least half of our co-workers.

But I'm not telling Tessa that. Because she's more relaxed than I've seen her in years. Sitting with her laptop on the sun bed, her long legs in front of her.

Her phone starts to buzz.

"What's that alarm for?" I ask.

"Time for more sunscreen," she says.

"You just put some on."

"An hour ago." She reaches over to take the huge ass bottle out of her bag, dolloping a huge blob onto her palm.

"You're gonna end up with a vitamin D deficiency," I tell her, watching from the corner of my eye as she slowly slides the white lotion down her arms, on her chest.

On her stomach.

Fuck, I want to turn around and watch her fully.

"Better than looking like my skin has turned to leather," she tells me. "You're gonna regret not using more when you're looking like Yoda when you're forty."

I start to laugh. "You think I'm gonna look like Yoda?"

She shrugs, sliding her palms down her thighs. I'm entranced by her movements. I can see the way her skin undulates beneath her touch.

"If the cap fits."

I tip my head to the side, watching as she finishes applying it. "Okay then, if you're so worried, put some on me."

"What?" The corner of her lip quirks up as she looks at me.

"Lotion me up," I tell her turning around so I'm facing her.

"Lotion yourself up."

"But you do it so much better." And yes, I want her to touch me. Her eyes catch mine and she narrows them, as though trying to decide whether she'll win this little battle by saying no or saying yes.

"Lay back."

I'm trying not to grin as I do as she's told. Her shadow passes over me as she stands and before I can say another word a dollop of lotion falls on my chest.

Followed by her soft hands.

I didn't think this through at all. Because she's rubbing her fingers all over my skin. Starting on my shoulders, making her way to my pectorals.

Her fingertips brush my nipples and I have to bite my tongue not to let out a groan.

I'm tense as fuck as she puts another glob of lotion on my stomach, rubbing it in gently. Her fingertips brushing the waistline of my shorts.

"Do my back," I grunt out, turning over onto my front before she can see that I'm getting turned on.

"You'll rub off the lotion," she says. "You're supposed to let it sink in before you touch the towel."

"It's fine," I say tightly, as she slowly starts to massage the lotion into my back. If I thought I was hard before, I'm fucking painful now. I start to think of everything unsexy. The dollar rate against the euro. The way Roman always picks his teeth after he's eaten steak.

The way my brothers threw me in the lake a few years ago

before it had had a chance to heat up and I started worrying my balls would never drop again.

Thankfully I get myself under control before she reaches my calves. I let out a low breath.

"Your girlfriend's here," she says, her voice low.

"What?" I look up to see Maya walking along the beach, in another bikini – this one white and, if possible, tinier than the last one. A cabana attendant follows quickly behind her, carrying towels, a bottle of water, and her beach bag.

I sit up and shoot Carmichael a dirty glance. "Not my girl-friend," I murmur.

"Sure." She smiles at me, like she knows the effect she just had on me. "Whatever you say.

"I'd like this one," Maya says when she reaches us, pointing to the cabana next to ours. "Oh, hello Linc." She smiles at me, completely ignoring Tessa.

"Hi." I nod.

"Are you going to the dance party tomorrow night?" she asks. "We have to have a boring dinner with one of David's clients first. But after that, I'm letting my hair down."

"Dance party?" I ask, trying to buy time. I'm so aware of Carmichael watching us. And I can still feel the way her hands felt on me.

I want to feel them again. Shit.

"At The Shack," Maya says. "The next beach down. They have a dance party every week. There are prizes for the best dancer," she says.

"We probably have to work," Tessa says, looking at me, a frown pulling at her brows. "Though I might have to stop by to take a few shots at the start of the evening. When the light is still good."

"Yeah, sorry. We have to work." I flash Maya a smile. Because I really don't want to dance with her.

"Oh come on, all work and no play makes Linc a very boring boy," Maya says flirtatiously. Then her eyes land on

Tessa. "Unless there's something going on between you two and you want to be alone?"

"There's nothing," Tessa says so quickly it makes me blink. She looks at me. "If you want to go, then go. You can take some video and I'll stay here and finish our presentation."

Oh, I know that tone. I've heard it way too many times in my life not to hear the danger in it. My mom was the queen of it.

"Do you want me to go?" I ask her. Truth is, I like dancing. Almost as much as I like teasing this woman. And I'm still a little horned up after her touch.

"If you like." She shrugs, doing her best to look nonchalant. But I grew up surrounded by people. Spent my life studying their moods. This woman is definitely not nonchalant.

"Come with me," I say softly, my eyes catching hers. And the stupid thing is, I really want her to. I have no idea why, past the way she can put on lotion. "Your video skills are way better than mine."

There's a noise from the cabana beside us. Maya's making the attendant roll all the sides up.

"I don't really like dancing," Tessa says.

"Why not?" I ask her, genuinely curious.

She shrugs. "I just don't."

"Like you don't like running?" I ask her.

"Something like that. I don't have the best coordination."

"Practice makes perfect. And anyway, we'd get better footage between the two of us," I point out. Because now I really want to dance with her. I bet she's never had the right partner. "You should come."

She lets out a long breath, but says nothing.

Maya is looking at Tessa again. "Are you sure there's nothing going on between you two? Because I could go for a threesome if needed."

"Oh my God," Tessa whispers, laying back on her lounger, covering her face with her hat. "Give me strength."

Maya shrugs and asks the attendant to order her a cocktail, then proceeds to oil herself up, shooting glances our way. I lift the corner of Tessa's hat up to catch her eyes.

"You okay there, Carmichael?" I whisper.

Maya's phone starts to ring. She answers it then lets out a huff, standing up and walking away as she starts talking rapidly to whoever is on the line.

"I'm fine," Tessa mutters.

She doesn't look fine. She looks sweaty and uncomfortable. I know that feeling well.

"Is it about the threesome thing?" I ask her.

Her face reddens more. "Can we stop talking about threesomes please?"

"I wasn't the one who started this." For once.

"Oh my God," Maya shouts down the phone. "I can't believe this. Surely nobody's that stupid. The pool is saltwater, not chlorinated." She looks over at us. "I have to go. Our new pool boy at home is an idiot. I'll see you at the dance party tomorrow."

She flounces off, still shouting into her phone, and I lift Tessa's hat brim higher. "You can come out, she's gone."

"I think I like it under here," Tessa mutters. But I take the hat from her face anyway, frowning at her.

"I don't think she was serious about the threesome," I say consolingly.

Tessa looks at me. "You think I'd have a threesome with you?"

I blink at her tone. She sounds seriously annoyed. "No."

"Would you have a threesome with me?" she asks.

I open my mouth and shut it again. What kind of question is that? Whichever way I answer I'm fucked. So I don't answer.

"I wouldn't have one with Maya," I say instead. Tessa frowns.

"I wouldn't have one with anybody," she tells me.

"Why not?"

"Because I'm a mom." She says it as though it explains everything.

"Moms have sex, right?" I reply. "They have to. Otherwise there'd only be single children in this world. As much as I hate to think about it, I have a younger brother. I'm pretty sure he wasn't born via immaculate conception."

Stop thinking about sex with Carmichael.

"Can we stop this?" Tessa asks.

But I'm on a roll now. "And Queen Victoria, look at her. She had to be doing it constantly. Didn't she have about a dozen kids?"

"She probably lay back and thought of England," Tessa says, shaking her head. There's a hint of amusement in her voice and it feels like a victory. From salty to happy in a few sentences. "Anyway, I'm pretty sure Queen Victoria never had a threesome."

"I'm guessing from your tone that you've never had one either," I say.

Her whole face has turned red. "No. Have you?"

"You want to know?" I ask.

"Yes."

"At college. Yes. Not since then. And that one was kind of alcohol fueled. And completely consensual." I blink. "In fact, I was so drunk I was seeing double. It was kind of like a fivesome."

"What about that text you got from those girls on the yacht?" she asks.

It takes me a minute to remember what she's talking about. Then I start laughing. "Catriona and Liliana? They're old friends from college. And happily married. To each other." I run my thumb along my jaw. "Not that it matters. Sex is good. It's designed to make you feel good. We shouldn't judge people who have sex with two others. Or five others. Whatever…"

She looks embarrassed. "You're right. And I'm sorry if you felt judged."

I shrug. "I didn't really." I'm not easily offended. Even by her.

She starts to laugh.

I roll onto my side, facing her.

"Can you do me a favor?"

"I'm still not deleting that video," she tells me.

I'd completely forgotten about that. "I know. I'm not asking you to. But will you come to the dance party with me?"

Her clear gaze catches mine. "Why?"

"Because I need somebody to protect me from Maya," I say, though it's a lie. Truth is, I want to dance with Carmichael. I want to feel her hands on me again, this time with my eyes on hers.

I want to hold her in my arms. Consensually.

She lets out a long breath. "Okay, but I can't guarantee I'm going to dance."

I grin at her, because it feels like I've won a prize. "I'll take it." And she is going to dance with me.

Even if it takes all my charm to persuade her.

CHAPTER NINE

TESSA

"I need to call my daughter," I tell Linc when we arrive back at the cottage. "Then I think I'll get some food delivered. I want to work on the pitch some more." I still haven't rewritten the script yet. My chest feels tight at the thought of all the work I still have to do.

It looks easy, taking videos and loading them to social media. But there's a reason why influencers get paid so much. There's an art to it.

But if I'm being truthful with myself, it's not work that's making me feel edgy.

It's him.

Ever since I put lotion on him earlier, all I can think about is how his body felt. Hard. Warm. And completely enticing. I hate that I'm attracted to him, but I am.

Stupidly attracted.

"You sure you don't want to go out to eat?" he asks, his brows dipping.

"I'm tired," I tell him honestly. "It's been a long day. And

I'm getting worried about seeing James Gold. I want this presentation to go perfectly."

"It will," he tells me. "Because we've got it under control."

"Under control doesn't mean leaving it until the last minute," I remind him. Even the thought of doing that sends a shiver down my spine.

"I know. But dinner will take an hour, tops."

"You go," I tell him. "I know you hate being cooped up."

He blinks, as though I've found a truth about him that he doesn't want me to know. But it's obvious he doesn't like being in one place for too long. If he's in the cottage for more than an hour he starts to pace the floor.

At first I wondered if he suffered from claustrophobia, but then I realized it wasn't the enclosed space, per se. It's not moving. He likes to move. Never be in one place for too long.

He's like the littlest Hobo. No wonder he loves his job so much. All that traveling would make me shiver, but it makes him thrive.

"I'll go for a walk," he says. "Pick us up some food. We can eat and work tonight."

"Seriously?" I ask him. "Because I don't mind if you go out."

"Yeah you do." There's a hint of a smile on his face.

"No I don't."

"I'll be back in an hour," he tells me. "You want anything in particular?"

"I wouldn't mind those fish tacos again."

"On it."

As soon as he leaves I head for the bathroom, taking my shorts and t-shirt off, then my bikini before I step under the perfectly pressurized shower. The water feels like a massage on my shoulders, washing away all the stress and anxiety that I can never quite shake off.

I've been tense since Maya asked Linc about the dance

party. And yes, mostly because I can't dance and he's going to find that out. But also, because I don't like her at all.

I can't believe she suggested we have a threesome.

I try to push it out of my mind. Because it's none of my business. If he wants to sleep with somebody that's his call.

So why is there a weird pull in my chest at the thought of another woman touching his body the way I did when I put the lotion on. Of him smiling at somebody else the way he smiles at me when he's not thinking about how annoying I am.

I squeeze a handful of shower gel out to wash away the lotion I have on my own body. My skin is warm, soft, and my nipples are so hard they tingle.

I slide my hand between my legs, thinking of Linc's touch there and then pull it away because that's so wrong.

We're workmates. Without the mate. And yes, I think we're warming to each other. But I shouldn't be thinking about how easily he could lift me against the tiles and slide inside me.

How good he'd feel. How strong he'd pump against me until we were both breathless.

I reach back and turn the shower knob until the water is freezing, because I need a damn wake up call.

When I get out of the shower, I pull on my pajamas, because there's no point in getting dressed again if I'm not going out. And then I dry my hair enough so I can twist it into a bun before I sit down at the table and pull my phone out, determined to stop thinking about him.

It only takes two rings for Zoe to pick up. And as soon as her face appears on the screen I relax into mommy mode, thankful to have my girl to concentrate on.

"Hey sweetie, how's things?" I ask her. It looks like she's in the bedroom at her dad's house. Her hair is down, the thick strands falling over her face. The curtains must be closed because she's surrounded by gloom.

"Boring," she says.

"Oh." I blink. "What's up?"

"Dad and Melissa are having a date night. Her mom's here and she's brought some friends around."

"What kind of friends?" I ask.

"A group she plays some kind of card game with. They're drinking cocktails and eating some kind of horrible pasta. It stinks of garlic."

I give her a sympathetic smile. "You hate garlic."

"Right? I suppose I should be grateful," she huffs. "At least I get to avoid the PDA for a night. Dad and Melissa are disgusting."

It's funny, because nobody tells you about this part of divorce. You've moved on, you've accepted it, but you can never truly walk away. Jared and I used to have disgusting PDA. And I don't miss him, not at all. But for a minute, I find myself missing being wanted.

"It's better than them arguing," I say, trying to cheer her up.

"Oh they do that too. And other stuff."

"What stuff?" I frown.

Zoe frowns, like she's realized who she's talking to. "It doesn't matter," she says. "I just hate it. Please come home."

"I'll be home for the weekend," I promise her. "And we'll go out to the diner. You can eat anything you like, as long as it doesn't have garlic on it."

She looks slightly mollified. "I want a burger. Melissa doesn't like red meat. She says it's full of toxins. Even dad's turning into a health freak."

I'd love to see that. Jared never did anything that involved breaking a sweat when we were married. And he loves burgers, the same way Zoe does.

If she was at home, I'd order her Door Dash, get her a burger. But one thing I promised myself after the divorce was that I'd respect her dad's wishes when it was his parenting time.

I've seen too many kids torn apart by the parents they love to do it to her. No matter how hard it is sometimes.

"How's school?" I ask her, changing the subject.

"Boring. We're doing algebra in math. I hate it. And Ella's having a sleepover on Friday but Dad says I can't go, because it's family game night."

"Family game night sounds fun," I say, encouragingly.

"About as fun as getting your fingernails pulled out one by one," she mutters.

I'm about to reply when the door behind me opens. I turn to see Linc walking in. He takes his sunglasses off and looks over at me.

"Oh, you're still on your call," he says. "Sorry."

"Who's that?" Zoe asks. Because when I turned, I must have angled the phone at him.

"It's my co-worker."

"I'll go," he mouths at me. I nod.

"Hi co-worker. What's your name?" Zoe asks, her voice echoing through the speaker. She sounds more animated than she has since I called.

"His name is Linc," I say. "We're working on the pitch I told you about."

"Hi Linc," she says.

"Hi." He looks so relaxed as he walks over and smiles at her. The smile she gives him back is huge. "It's Zoe, right?"

"Yeah." She can't hide how pleased she is that he knows her name.

"Hey, is that a Linebackers t-shirt?" he asks her. I lift a brow, surprised he knows who they are.

"It is," she gushes. "They're my favorite band."

"Mine too. I know the lead singer."

Her mouth drops open. "You do?"

"Yep. I think they're coming to New York next month. I could probably get you a backstage pass if you're interested."

"Oh my God!" she squeals, and for the first time since I called her she looks like an overexcited teenager. "That's amazing. Mom, did you hear that?"

"Yeah, I heard." I give her a smile because it's nice to see her happy. I know the past few years have taken their toll on her. Jared and I both took her to family counseling when we first told her about the split, and she's had some individual counseling since.

But I know the upheaval has been hard anyway.

"I'll send Ryker a message. See what we can do."

"That's amazing. Thank you so much," she says.

"No problem." He glances at me. "I'm going to get changed. I dropped in on the restaurant. They're going to send food over at seven. That work?"

"It works great. Thank you." I smile at him.

"Bye Zoe," he says. "I promise you'll have your mom back soon. Thanks for lending her to us."

"Any time," Zoe says. And if she wasn't thirteen years old, I'd swear her voice was all breathy.

Even kids get entranced by Linc Salinger.

"Has he left?" she whispers, after he's grabbed some fresh clothes from his suitcase and headed into the bathroom.

"Yeah." I'm not going to explain that he'll be back. Or that we are, in fact, sharing a cottage. Sure, I like to be truthful with my child.

But there are some things she doesn't need to know.

"He's kinda cute. And he knows Ryker. How cool is that?"

"Very cool," I agree.

"Can I go now?" she asks. "I want to tell my friends that I know somebody who knows the Linebackers."

"Sure," I say, because it's so good to see her smile. "I'll call you tomorrow. I love you."

———

LINC

We eat dinner outside the cottage as the sun sets. They sent over both fish and chicken tacos, along with some chocolate desserts that we've stashed in the refrigerator for later. And a jug of cocktails – Bahama Mamas of course. We've only had a glass each. Enough to relax but not get drunk.

Because I know Tessa wants to get some work done. And I'm okay with doing some work, too.

"Your kid seems pretty cool," I say, loading some tacos on her plate before filling my own. William said to leave the dishes on the deck when we're finished and he'd pick them up later. I make a note to leave a huge tip with them, because the man deserves it.

"She has her moments," Tessa says, though her cheeks pink up with pride. And I like that a lot. "She's excited about meeting her favorite band though." Her eyes meet mine. "Unless you were kidding."

"I wasn't kidding," I tell her. I'd never let a child down like that. I've been let down too many times myself. "I sent Ryker's manager a message after I took a shower. He's agreed to organize some tickets. Said Zoe could bring a couple of friends with if she wants. And I'm assuming you'll want to go with her too."

"Someone will have to," she says. "They're too young to go alone."

"I guess teenage hood isn't what it used to be," I muse. "I went everywhere alone."

"Me, too."

I take another bite of the fish taco and groan. "I could seriously live on these for the rest of my life."

"You should start up a blog about hotel food," she tells me. "It could be your side hustle."

"Now that sounds like a lot of work I don't need. Ever notice that once something starts earning you money it's not fun anymore?" I ask her.

"Never become a sex worker then," she says, lifting a brow.

And I start to laugh because it's so unexpected. Christ, I like her, and that's so weird to me. And yet it feels completely natural, too. "Damn, that was my back up plan. Now you've put me off."

"I doubt anybody could put you off something you want to do," she says.

"What makes you say that?"

"You have the silver tongue thing going on. You can persuade anybody of anything. It's disconcerting."

"It is?"

She nods. "Yeah. And annoying because I wish I had the silver tongue."

I shift in my chair, because now I'm thinking about tongues and Carmichael and it's a pretty distracting combination.

"Not like that."

"I know." I smile. "And I don't have a silver tongue, or whatever it is you think I have. Because if I did, you wouldn't hate me."

"I don't hate you." Her voice is soft.

"Okay, then you did. Until you realized I'm a good guy."

"The jury is still out on that." She's smiling. "But I think you're good enough to sleep in my bed tonight."

I choke on my mouthful of taco, and Carmichael starts to laugh.

"I didn't mean it like that," she says. "I meant it's your turn for the bed. I saw how achy you were again this morning."

"It's fine. I'm getting used to sleeping like I'm folded in two." I take a sip of the cocktail to wash down the errant taco.

"No, I insist. You need to be on top form for dancing tomorrow night. I'll take the sofa."

"You're not sleeping on the sofa," I growl.

She tips her head to the side, the corner of her lip quirking. "Careful," she says. "If you keep on like this I'm going to start thinking there's a gentleman inside you."

"I can categorically state there's never been a gentleman inside me," I tell her, lifting a brow.

"Is that a euphemism?" she asks.

I shrug. "Nope. And I'll take the sofa."

"We can share the bed." She says it quickly. Enough for me to do a double take.

"What?" My brows pinch. I must have misheard her.

Her cheeks pink up adorably. "It's a big bed. I tried to starfish in it last night but I still ended up almost falling out. I'm a compact sleeper."

I pull my lip between my teeth, because I'm still not totally sure she's serious. But I'm totally sure that sleeping in the same bed as Carmichael would be unwise.

Yes, I know she's not into me. And at any other time I wouldn't be into her either. But here, in Exuma, I feel like I'm finding out about the real her. You lose your inhibitions on vacation in a way you never do elsewhere.

And seeing Tessa without inhibitions is kind of enticing.

The thought of us being under the same covers, her warm body close to mine, makes my blood heat up.

"It's not a good idea."

"It's that or I sleep on the sofa," she tells me. "Take it or leave it."

I run my finger around the rim of my cocktail glass. "It's funny, because you're more of a gentleman than I am."

"I don't think so," she says, rolling her eyes. "I'm just sick of seeing you walking around like an old man every morning. We can build a pillow wall between us if you'd like."

"A pillow wall?" I try not to smile. But she's so fucking cute I'm not sure I can handle it. "You think that will keep me away from your side?"

"No. I trust you to stay on your side without a barrier," she says, and it just about slays me. "The pillow wall would be there to make you feel better. Come on, let's both get a couple of good nights sleep and then we can go home and pretend that none of this ever happened.

I pretend to muse her offer over. "It's a deal," I say.

"It is?"

I nod. "If you promise you'll delete that fucking video, then yes."

CHAPTER
TEN

TESSA

"Are you going to stand there all night?" I ask Linc. We've spent the evening working on the presentation, and I'm feeling so much more relaxed. He pretty much wrote the voiceover while I carried on editing the video and I'm starting to realize it's not just his easy way of talking to people that's made him get as far as he has in this business.

He's astute. He understands people. He knows what makes them tick.

And in our world, that's dynamite.

He walked into the bedroom a minute ago, and did a double take when he saw I was already in bed. On the left side, because when I was with Jared I always had to sleep on the right side and I hated it.

"I'm just wondering if we should have the talk now," he says. "Because if you want my body, we should at least exchange health details."

"Shut up and get in." I roll my eyes and lift the cover. He

walks over, pulling his t-shirt off so he's just in a pair of shorts and I really try not to look at him.

But dear god, it's not fair. This man has everything. The easygoing nature, the flair for getting what he wants and the world's most perfect body.

"You okay, Carmichael?" he asks, smirking.

"I'm a little warm," I say huskily, because I know what he's doing. Trying to rile me up again. But two can play at that game.

I pull the covers off my own body, revealing the short pajamas I bought at Bloomingdales. Ange had insisted I needed something lighter than the flannel I wear in New York.

His eyes dip to my thighs and he lets out a long, low breath.

"Might want to cover up," he tells me. "I turned the air conditioning up."

"Then you should probably put your t-shirt back on," I tell him.

"I never sleep in a t-shirt."

"And I usually sleep naked. So let's compromise."

His eyes darken and I like it a little too much. It's been a long, long time since a man looked at me like that.

"You're playing with fire," he mutters, climbing into the bed beside me. The mattress dips deliciously.

I shimmy down the bed and roll onto my side, facing him. He does the same.

"So this is weird," I say. "I can't remember the last time I had a sleepover."

"Want me to paint your nails?" he asks, and I grin.

"I could do yours."

"I have a manicurist for that."

Of course he does. The man is perfectly polished.

"What else do girls do at sleepovers?" he asks, blinking slowly. He has the most delicious thick eyelashes.

"Not what you think," I say dryly.

"I wasn't thinking about sex." He runs his thumb along his jaw. "Though now I am."

"It's hard to remember what we did," I say, quickly changing the subject. "I guess we talked about our other friends. The boys we liked. Our parents."

"Where did you grow up?" he asks.

"In Texas."

"Your parents still there?"

"No, they moved to California."

"That's a long way from New York," he says and I nod. I don't see them that much anymore.

"Truth or dare," he says.

"What?"

"Isn't that a game that people play at sleepovers?" he says, a half-smile pulling at his lips. Blood rushes through my ears.

"I guess." I nod. "What would the dare be?"

"Putting some real clothes on. But I'd rather you chose truth."

My chest tightens again, the way it seems to do a lot when he's around. I'd never realized how much this man could get under your skin if you let him.

"What truth?" I ask.

He presses his lips together, as though trying to think of the most excruciating question. "Okay, tell me the most embarrassing thing that happened to you as a kid."

My eyes meet his, and I feel my cheeks flush.

"Oh, Carmichael. Do you have a juicy secret?" he asks me. "Because now I need to know."

"I can just take the dare," I remind him.

"Tell me your secret. Go on."

I have no idea why I'm entertaining answering him. Maybe it's the way he's looking at me with the softest expression I've ever seen from him.

"I walked in on my parents having an orgy," I say quickly, my words mashing together.

For a minute he says nothing, his mouth agape as he stares at me.

"No way," he finally responds. "Seriously?"

I nod, remembering how mortifying it was.

"I'm gonna need all the juicy details," he tells me.

"You have to promise not to tell anybody."

He touches his brow. "Scout's honor."

And it's weird, but I trust him to keep it to himself.

"I was fifteen, just a bit older than Zoe," I tell him. "I was supposed to be staying at my friend's house for a sleepover but I got sick and her mom dropped me off at home.

"Did her mom see?"

"No. Thank God. She could tell there was somebody home from the inside lights. So she dropped me off and drove away." I pinch the bridge of my nose. "I can't believe I'm telling you this."

He gently pulls my hand away. "I'm touched that you are. I thought you were going to tell me you got your skirt stuck in your panties at school or something. So what happened next?"

I let out a long breath. "I walked in and saw my dad…" I shake my head. "I can't. It's so mortifying."

"Your dad was balls deep in somebody not your mom?" he asks.

"Something like that," I squeak.

"And your mom?"

My cheeks are burning. "Was in the kitchen."

"Not cooking?" he asks.

"Not cooking," I agree.

"Jesus, Tessa. I think you just won the game. What did you do after that?"

"I snuck out. Slept in the summerhouse in our backyard. Then pretended to come home the next morning."

"Nobody noticed you were there?"

"No, I don't think so. At least I hope not." I wrinkle my nose. "And I never mentioned it to my parents."

"So they don't know you know?" he asks.

"No. But I've never looked at them the same again."

"I bet."

"So I guess that's why I was a bit uptight when you mentioned threesomes. I just…" I shake my head. "I want to be a good parent for Zoe."

"You're a great parent. Anybody can see that."

I give him the smallest of smiles.

"Carmichael?" he says. And I relax, because we're back to Carmichael and Salinger. I can deal with that.

"Yes?"

"You want a hug?"

I open my mouth to say no, but then I realize that I really do want one.

I think I need one.

I nod. "Yes please."

And it turns out that as well as being sweet talking, successful, and annoyingly good looking, Linc Salinger also gives the best hugs.

Go figure.

———

LINC

I wake up in the morning with a hard on that's precariously close to Carmichael's ass. Okay, it's touching it. So I shimmy back because if there's one thing she doesn't need it's the dirtiest part of me touching her the morning after she pretty much bared her soul to me.

Truth is, I found it difficult to go to sleep after her confession. I felt bad that I'd pretty much wrenched it out of her. And felt even worse that once I pulled her into my arms all I could think about was kissing her.

Inappropriate much?

Absolutely.

Did I want to do it anyway?

Absolutely.

Weirdly enough, she passed out about five minutes after I pulled her into my arms. And when I finally drifted off, about an hour later, I actually slept better than I have in a while, too.

And now I get to watch Carmichael wake up.

She does it in fits and starts. First of all she groans and stretches her arms, then kind of folds in on herself. Then she groans again and opens one eye, before closing it like she doesn't like what she sees.

"Are you staring at me?" she asks.

Okay, so she's grumpy, too. This is delicious.

"Just admiring your bed head," I tell her and she groans again, reaching up to touch her long, thick locks.

Her eyes spring open, and this time they stay open. "What time is it?" she asks.

"Ten."

She sits up so fast my eyes can't keep up. "You're kidding."

"Yes, I am. It's seven."

"You're an asshole."

"Thank you." I smile at her. "You slept well, by the way."

"So did you. For once."

"What does that mean?" I ask. Because I'm pretty sure I didn't tell her about my nightmares.

"Nothing. Just that when I woke in the middle of the night you were snoring like a baby."

I sit up too, running my hands through my hair. "Well I guess this bed is good for both of us."

"So it seems."

"Want to sleep with me again tonight?" I ask, wiggling my brows. She laughs and it warms me.

"Yeah, sure." She shimmies to the side of the bed and climbs out, treating me to a delicious view of her ass. Christ, it's perfect. Round and full, but with a lift to it. No wonder my dick liked it so much.

"Salinger?"

"Yeah?" I clear my throat and drag my gaze away from her backside up to her turned face.

"Thanks for being so sweet last night."

I smile and she smiles back at me. "You're welcome."

CHAPTER
ELEVEN

TESSA

"You slept with him?" Angela's voice rises an octave. "Oh my God, girl, I'm so proud of you."

"Not like that," I point out, trying not to laugh at her over-the-top reaction. "We didn't do anything that wasn't PG."

"You spooned."

Okay, so there was a little spooning. And yeah, I'm almost certain that I felt some... enthusiasm... poking into my ass this morning. But I'm almost certain it was a physiological reaction and nothing to do with me.

"It was just a friendly thing," I tell her. "He keeps waking up all twisted and achy. The bed is huge. Like double the size of my one at home. It felt wrong not to offer to share."

"Sure it did." Amusement still tinges her voice. "So are you going to do it again tonight?"

I let out a long breath. We have two days until the presentation and then we fly home. I'm almost certain that this... detente, or whatever you want to call it between me and Linc, will be long forgotten by the time we touch down on the tarmac at JFK. Yes, we get along well here, but our lives are so different.

And now I'm starting to get homesick for Zoe. I let out a long breath. "Probably," I say. "But not the way you're thinking."

"Why not?"

Her question is simple yet so complicated I don't know where to start.

"Because I'm older. A mom. I should know better."

"You're a woman, Tessa. A beautiful woman. And you've had a shit couple of years. And from what I've seen this guy Linc is pretty hot. Has he made it clear he's not interested?"

I think of last night. The way he hugged me. The gentle touch of his hands as he stroked my hair.

"I don't know," I admit. "I think he might be."

"Of course he is." Angela says. I can picture her rolling her eyes at me. "What guy wouldn't be?" Then she lets out a cough. "Ignore that. What guy other than a dick with no sense wouldn't be?"

I start to laugh. "When you put it like that…"

"Seriously, honey. You only have two nights left to have fun. What happens in Exuma stays in Exuma. Enjoy yourself. Let your hair down. Stop worrying about the future so much and enjoy things as they are."

"You make it sound so easy."

"That's because it is. You overthink things. And I know you've had to for the last few years. But that's history. This is your new start. Just be open to things, that's all I ask."

The cottage door opens and Linc walks in, his face lighting up into a slow smile when he sees me.

He's been in a meeting in the business suite. A zoom call with Europe, I think. We've spent most of today working. The pitch is almost ready. He made me promise that tomorrow afternoon we will go to the beach to relax for the last time before we give our presentation the following day.

"I gotta go," I say to Angela. His eyes are still on me. I feel myself start to blush.

"Is he there?"

"Yes. And you're on speaker."

Linc's smile turns into a smirk, because now he knows we were talking about him.

"Goodbye, Ange," I say, hanging up before she can reply because I have no idea what she'll say next. All I know is that it'll almost certainly be embarrassing.

A moment later a message flashes up.

Spoilsport. – Angela

"How was your meeting?" I ask Linc, trying to ride out the embarrassment.

"Not as interesting as your conversation, obviously."

I shake my head, but I can't stop the smile from pulling at my lips. "We have two hours before dinner and then the dance party." Which I still don't want to go to, by the way. "Do you want to shower first or shall I?"

———

We arrive at the party just after nine. The Shack is a small wooden bar on the beach, and there are people everywhere, standing at the counter, drinking on the sand, hanging around the DJ who's set up his decks on a wooden stage to the left of the bar.

We talked nonstop over dinner. He told me stories about growing up with his brothers and then asked me a hundred questions about Zoe. He knew a lot more about Manga than I thought he would. And of course he's an encyclopedia about the Linebackers, her favorite band.

And then he held my hand as we made our way to the party.

It's weird, but it feels like we've really become friends, and I like it. That's why I've pushed Angela's words to the back of my mind, never to be thought of again.

I don't think I've ever had a friend like Linc before. But it has its advantages because he manages to sweet talk his way to the front of the bar within half a minute, and within three he's carrying two glasses back to the two sun loungers I managed to snag us on the beach.

"There you go," he passes me a glass, sitting down on the bed beside me, but twisting his body so his feet are on the sand in between the two of them. He clinks his plastic glass against mine. "Cheers."

"Cheers," I say, taking a sip.

"Ouch. This tastes like a hangover waiting to happen."

"We still have some last minute work to do tomorrow," I remind him. "We can't drink too much."

He winks at me. "It's a proven fact that dancing prevents hangovers."

"Not if you have to drink a bucket of punch to get the courage to do it," I mutter.

"Why would you need liquid courage to dance?" he asks me, looking genuinely curious.

"Because some of us have two left feet."

He looks down my legs, as though he half believes me. And I'm so glad I decided to touch up my pedicure today. No chips, no hard skin, just pretty feet.

A half smile pulls at his lips. "I'll take it easy on you," he promises me. "At first."

His eyes catch mine and it doesn't feel like we're talking about dancing anymore. "It's not my first time," I say.

"I know. But it's your first time with me. That's different."

Okay, we're definitely not talking about dancing. Or are

we? It's hard to tell with Linc. "Don't take it easy on me just because I'm an amateur compared to you."

His smile gets wider. This damn punch has a lot to answer for. "You have to learn to walk before you can run, Carmichael. We'll start with something easy. Slow. Then we'll work up to the crescendo."

"You're calling me Carmichael again," I say.

"I always call you Carmichael."

"Last night you also called me Tessa."

His gaze softens. That smile is still there but it feels less of a challenge, more of a prize. "Did I?"

"Yep."

"It didn't feel like a Carmichael moment, I guess."

"What's a Carmichael moment?" I ask him, because I can't even imagine what he means by this.

"A Carmichael moment is when you're being you. Challenging. Fighting me." He tips his head to the side, his eyes scanning my face.

"And a Tessa moment?"

He presses his lips together, as though he's assessing his answer before he responds. "A Tessa moment," he says, "is when you need kindness."

"Maybe I need kindness more than you think."

"Yeah," he says, nodding. "I think you do. So are you gonna come and dance with me or what?"

"Just one," I tell him. "And you have to be gentle with me."

He shouts out a laugh and pulls me up, taking me to join the others dancing in the sand.

———

LINC

. . .

She feels different tonight. And yet weirdly the same, too, in the best kind of way. It reminds me of that time I had a full body scrub in a Turkish bath. Having your top layer of skin scraped off by an angry looking man with a hand full of what felt like glass shards wasn't exactly my favorite experience of all time.

But the result was amazing. For a few days, my skin was as soft as a baby's. It also gave me a little insight into the 'beauty is pain' mantra my mom always uses.

Fuck that. I like pleasure. Especially the pleasure of dancing with this woman.

She was right, though. She isn't exactly the best dancer. I'd go as far as to say she's one of the worst I've seen. She has absolutely no rhythm. It's like her ears and her body are completely disconnected. She misses the beat every time.

"Can I sit down yet?" she asks, as the DJ spins another disc. This one has a slower beat than the last. Smooth, sensual.

Her body does not respond to the change in rhythm. Not at all. I bite down a smile as she dances way too fast for the new song. And I realize something. I like her more when she's not perfect at everything.

Because nobody is perfect at everything.

A beautiful woman in a short, white dress with dark flowing hair walks behind Carmichael. Her eyes catch mine, before she looks at Tessa and rolls her eyes.

It pisses me off.

It pisses me off even more when Tessa steps back, not knowing she's there, and steps on the woman's bare toes.

"Watch where you're going, bitch," the woman growls.

Tessa blinks, stunned.

"Don't stand so close then," I say, taking Tessa's hand and pulling her into me.

"Your girlfriend sucks at dancing. If you want to find

somebody who knows how to use her body, I'll be over there," tall, dark, and mean says, nodding over at the bar.

I put my arms around Tessa and I can feel how stiff she is. And I'm even more pissed than ever. We were having fun. Nobody needed to say anything.

"Just fuck off," Tessa says, turning around to look at the woman behind her. "This one's mine."

I don't know how I hide my laugh, but somehow I manage with a cough and a quick cover of my palm across my mouth.

Okay, so Tessa isn't a shrinking violet. She's pissed.

I'm not sure I could like her any more than I do right now.

As soon as the woman disappears and we're alone again, Tessa rolls onto her tiptoes to whisper in my ear.

"I'm going to need some more of that punch."

"One more dance," I urge her. "And then we'll take a break."

The song is slow and sensual. I squeeze her hand that's in mine and she takes the hint, stepping into me until our bodies are pressing against each other.

I dip my head to smell the sweet floral notes of her shampoo as she rests her face against my chest. Then I slide my free hand down to the dip of her spine, moving us together, this time to the rhythm of the song.

Last night, we slept together. In the literal sense of the word. But this feels even more personal. Like another layer of skin has been removed from us both.

"Salinger," she murmurs. I hardly hear her voice over the music.

"Yeah?"

"Do you have a hard on?"

"Not yet."

"I think I do."

Jesus, what did they put in that punch? I'm starting to think I should have asked them.

"Women don't get hard ons," I say, trying not to smile.

"What do they get then?" She looks up at me. There's a dazed look on her face.

"Wet."

As soon as I say it I'm wondering if she is. Fuck, I want to touch her. She's still looking up at me goofily.

"Tessa," I say.

"Carmichael," she corrects me.

"Whatever. I just want to make sure you're okay. Do you feel sick? Dizzy?"

"Because I'm talking to you about sex?" she asks.

I mean, yeah. "I'm just worried that somebody might have spiked your drink."

"You got me the drink. You're the only one who could have spiked it." She looks up at me. "Did you spike it?"

"No." I shake my head. "I'd never spike your drink."

"I know you wouldn't." She rests her head against my chest. "I'm not drunk, I'm just…"

I hold my breath as I wait for her to tell me what she is. But then there's a tap on my shoulder. I turn my head and Tessa looks up.

Fucking Maya.

I almost groan, because I'm desperate to hear what Tessa thinks.

"Can I steal him off you?" Maya asks. "For one dance."

Tessa steps back, and I immediately miss the feel of her body against mine.

"Have at him," she mutters.

"Actually," I say to Maya, "we were busy."

"No, honestly." Tessa smiles at Maya, though I notice it doesn't reach her eyes. "Go ahead. I'm going to grab some water."

Before I can say anything else, she's weaving through all the bodies undulating on the sand.

"I love this song," Maya says, grabbing my now free hand.

But I shake it off. Because no, Tessa's not getting away from me just when we were finally getting real.

I want to know how she feels. I want to fucking kiss her.

I want to find out if she's as turned on as I am from dancing together.

"Sorry," I say to Maya. "Got things to do. Have a good evening."

And then I'm pushing my way through the crowds.

———

TESSA

I hear him calling my name as I stride along the beach, but I don't slow my pace. He catches up to me within thirty seconds though, reaching for my hand.

I let him take it.

"Where are you going?" he asks, sounding confused. He's matching my pace easily, the sound of the music and the people becoming more distant with every step.

"Back to the cottage," I say. "I'm tired."

"You were going to leave without saying goodbye?" He sounds annoyed.

"I was going to text you."

"You were supposed to stay with me. You promised," he reminds me. "You said you'd protect me from Maya."

I finally stop walking and look up at him. The moon is almost at full splendor, and the light reflects against his face.

He looks angry at me. Good. I prefer that I think.

I know angry. I know how to deal with him when he's pissed with me.

The problem is, I don't know how to deal with my feelings for him.

And yes, I have feelings. Way too many of them. And

every single one is confusing. I like him. He makes me laugh. And of course he's stupidly attractive. But I also know that he's way above my league. Younger, richer, and definitely not long-term material.

But he makes me feel like a woman again. Something I haven't felt in a long time.

Ange's words echo in my head. And I realize that I'm not scared of being with Linc. I'm scared of what happens after.

"You don't need me to protect you from anyone," I say softly, the thoughts still rushing around my mind.

His eyes narrow. "Are you annoyed with me?" he asks, looking confused.

"No, not at you. At me," I say honestly. "I'm sorry. I shouldn't have said that."

"Said what?" he asks. We slow our walking to a normal pace. There's a breeze wafting in from the ocean. It rustles against the trees.

"Asked you if you were..." I trail off. "You know."

"If I was hard."

"Yeah."

"You were having fun, Carmichael. So was I. We're allowed to have fun. We're allowed to dirty talk if we want. We're grown adults."

"We work together," I remind him.

"And?"

"And it's not a good idea."

He stops walking. And I stop too. He reaches for my shoulders and turns me so we're looking at each other.

"What are you afraid of?" he asks.

"I'm not afraid of anything," I lie.

"You're scared of me."

Oh, he knows. And it makes me feel more vulnerable than ever. I'm supposed to be a grown up. In charge of my emotions. But right now I feel like I'm lost at sea.

I let out a long breath. "I just know this isn't a good idea." I'm not sure if I'm trying to persuade him or me.

"What isn't? Tell me." He leans in closer. I can feel the warmth of his hands against my shoulders. "Are you wet right now, Carmichael?"

My heart rate speeds up. "Yes."

"Good."

"Why's that good?" I ask him, because it doesn't feel good to me. Okay, yes, it does feel good but...

"Because I'm hard. Have been for days. For you."

Oh.

I look up at him. He has a dark expression on his face. It makes my heart pound against my ribcage. It dances faster than I ever could. Has more rhythm, too, thank goodness.

"I've wanted you since I met you," he continues. And damn, he's such a sweet talker. I don't know what's real and what's not. I want it to be real.

Maybe I need it to be.

"No you haven't. You thought I was stuck up."

"I like a challenge," he tells me. "And anyway, now I know why you were like that. You were in the middle of a divorce. That messes with people."

My chest tightens. Those early days of the divorce were the worst. The fear of the future. The knowledge I needed to take care of Zoe, but not knowing how to.

The realization that I wasn't good enough for the man I loved.

Linc cups my face as he smiles at me. "Why do you keep fighting this?"

"Because I don't want to get hurt again," I finally admit. "And we're not... compatible."

He blinks. "What does that mean?"

"It means you're you, and I'm me."

Linc shakes his head. "You're gonna have to spell it out for me."

"You're a man that every woman wants. You're sexy and gorgeous and you can sweet talk everybody you meet. I'm…" I take a breath. "A single mom. I work all the hours god sends. And I haven't had sex in two years. I really don't think I'm the kind of woman you're looking for."

"Two years?" His eyes widen. "Jesus."

"See? We're like oil and water."

"I love oil and water."

I start to laugh, because this man has that effect on me. "Shut up and let's go home."

CHAPTER
TWELVE

LINC

We walk silently along the shoreline. It's more than a mile back to the bungalow, but when I suggest I call the hotel to have somebody pick us up, Tessa shakes her head.

And that's okay with me. It's a beautiful evening and we've both taken our shoes off to walk on the sand. The moon is shining down on us, the water is gently lapping against our bare feet, and there's a breeze lifting the end of Tessa's hair, making it dance against her skin.

I'm still thinking about what she said. No sex in two years. What kind of fucking idiot was her husband to let her go?

Yes, she can be challenging. But in the kind of way that makes me want to work harder. Do better.

If we were living in medieval times, I'd want to prove myself to her so she'd give me her damn handkerchief.

At some point during our walk, she's let me take her hand. And it feels like a win. Her palm is flat against mine, our fingers intertwined.

I like it more than I fucking should. It's just holding hands for fuck's sake.

"Carmichael," I say, because I've noticed she relaxes more when I call her that.

"Yes?"

"How about kissing? Have you kissed anyone in two years?"

"You're weirdly fixated with the two year thing," she says. "And no. For the record, I haven't kissed anybody either. Not the way you're talking about anyway."

"Is there another way?" I ask.

"I've kissed my daughter."

Oh. Yeah. For a moment there, I forgot she had a kid.

"What about orgasms?" I ask her. She frowns up at me adorably.

"I'm not telling you that."

"So yes, you've had orgasms."

"Salinger..." It's a growl and I love it.

"How often do you touch yourself?"

Her cheeks pink up.

"How can you be so fucking together about work and your kid and everything else, yet get embarrassed by orgasms?" I ask her. "They're just sneezes to the power of eight."

"What?" She looks at me, trying not to smile.

"Orgasms are like a powerful sneeze. Seriously. I read it somewhere." I frown, thinking about it. "Though the ones I give are probably more like thirty times a sneeze."

"Of course," she says dryly.

I drop my shoes then take hers and let them fall to the sand, too, before taking her face in my hands. I drop my head until our brows are touching and she doesn't pull away. Her skin is so fucking soft it's making me even harder.

Her eyelashes flutter and then I start to throb.

Wait. Why are eyelashes making me hard? They're just tiny hairs. I push the thought away, because right now my brain is between my legs.

"Carmichael," I murmur. "I'm going to kiss you now. Unless you stop me."

She doesn't move. Just looks at me with those big, wide eyes. And I want them to be looking at me as I make her come.

It's all I can think about. Nobody but her has made her come for two years.

That's a long fucking time. An eternity. And yes, touching yourself is good. It fills a need. But coming with somebody else?

That's heaven.

I want to give her that. I want to have it.

She tips her head up almost imperceptibly. But it's enough for me to feel the warmth of her breath against my lips. Every part of me is tingling. But I resist the urge to close the gap between us.

I want her to do it.

I want her to want me. The same way I want her.

Her breath hitches. Her head tips back a little more.

Damn it, I can't wait anymore. That's it. I lower my head until our lips brush against each other.

And I'm lost in her.

And I don't want to be found.

———

TESSA

He releases my face as I kiss him back, his hands sliding down my shoulders, fingers feathering my arms, until his palms curl around my waist. His tongue softly slides against mine as he pulls me against him.

And I can feel just how much he's enjoying this kiss.

I wrap my arms around his neck, and he grunts approvingly against my lips. I can feel the breeze against my back, his hands sliding down to my ass, pulling me even closer.

Until I'm breathless and needy against him.

He's an expert kisser. Just the way I knew he would be. His fingers knead my skin, his lips plunder mine. And hot blood rushes through me.

Right to my core.

And all I can think about is how much I need this. His touch, his mouth.

To feel the way he wants me.

He slides his hand down my thigh, hitching my skirt up until his fingers are touching my bare skin.

"Fucking hell, Carmichael," he murmurs. "Where have you been hiding this body?"

I smile against him. "Shut up and kiss me."

"Wouldn't you rather do this somewhere more comfortable." His thumb is rubbing against my outer thigh, making every part of me clench.

"I don't know…"

"I mean kiss. In private. We're not going to do anything you don't want to do."

My eyes lift until our gazes are locked. And I nod because yes, I want to kiss him again. Preferably horizontally. My body aches to feel the weight of his.

We're not going to do anything you don't want to do.

I'm not sure if that's a threat or a promise.

It takes us ten more minutes to get back to the cottage. Linc carries both our shoes, practically marching us along the beach like we're in boot camp. Every now and again, he looks at me and smiles.

And my body flutters in response.

When we climb up the steps to our room, I can feel my heart thumping. When we get inside, I don't know what's going to happen.

Liar. You know exactly what you're doing.

"You still with me?" Linc asks as he unlocks the door. He's still holding my hand. I don't know if it's because he suspects I might run again, or if he's trying to reassure me.

Maybe both. And I get it. It's been more than a decade since I kissed somebody new. And I'm scared. I really am. If I stop this now, I know he'll understand. Or at least I hope he will.

But I don't want to stop it. I'm too fired up. So I try to push the fear away, though I'm not as successful as I'd hoped.

"I think so."

He drops our shoes, pulls me inside, and closes the door behind me, turning around so I'm sandwiched between his body and the wall.

"That's not good enough," he murmurs. "I need a yes, Carmichael."

"Are you going to call me Carmichael when you're inside of me?" I ask him. The words surprise me as much as they shock him. Did I really say that?

Yes. Apparently I did.

"Am I going to be inside of you?" His voice is low as he looks at me.

"I think so."

"Then why do you look so scared?" He sounds genuinely concerned.

"I'm not scared I'm just... you know."

"I don't know. I need you to say things. Vocalize them. I don't want to mess this up. So you're going to have to tell me."

I take a deep breath. "Can we see where this goes?" I ask.

"Yes, we can do that." He dips his head until his lips are

touching my neck, just where it curves into my shoulder. "Is this okay?" he murmurs against me.

"Yes," I breathe.

He kisses his way up, finding the sensitive spot just beneath my ear.

I start to giggle.

His lips curl against my skin. "Are you ticklish?"

"A little."

"Where?" He runs his fingers down my side. I don't laugh this time. "Not here," he says.

"Nope." I like the sensation though. Every time he touches me it's like he's trying to learn the lines of my body. How to make me feel good.

"I'm just going to have to kiss you all over then," he says, standing up until he's towering over me again. I look up into his eyes and feel a little giddy at the intensity in them.

I have to grab onto his arms to steady myself.

And yes, I squeeze them a little. Because he has the best biceps. I never knew that arm muscles could be attractive on a man but every time I see Linc in short sleeves I feel like he's melting my insides.

His mouth captures mine again, and I sigh against his lips. Why have I waited so long to kiss somebody?

Because you didn't want to kiss anyone until Linc.

A little danger alert sounds inside of me but I ignore it.

I've spent the last two years doing everything by the book. Being the good parent while Jared went off for a rerun of his youth. And I don't regret it. I don't regret anything I've done for Zoe.

But she's not here. This won't hurt her.

"Stop overthinking," Linc murmurs, sliding his hand down my back. His palm cups my behind and squeezes causing me to arch into him.

"I'm not."

"Yes you are. You went all stiff on me." His gaze softens. "And I believe that's my job."

I giggle again, because it's impossible not to when he's around. Despite the nagging deep inside me, I know that he's not going to hurt me. Linc likes pleasing people.

It's his superpower.

And right now I'm the beast in his sights.

His lips are soft, barely there as he brushes them against mine again. His hand moves up, his thumb gentle as he strokes it against the underside of my breast, before the pad presses against my nipple.

The sensation is so strong I jump in his arms.

"What was that?" he asks.

"I just… nobody's touched me there in a while."

He squeezes his eyes shut, looking almost pained. "Nobody's touched you anywhere in a while," he says as though reminding himself of the fact. "Fuck."

"Is that a problem?" I ask him.

"Only for my dick. It's kind of enticing, you know?"

My brows dip. "What do you mean?"

"The thought of touching you for the first time. Of reminding you how pleasurable this can be." His lip quirks up. "With another person."

"What are you planning to do? Give me a presentation?" I tease. "The full PowerPoint experience."

He starts to laugh. It's like he realizes I need a moment to catch my breath. "I'll start with my health status. Clean at my last checkup. You?"

I lift a brow.

"Okay, so you're clean, too."

"I mean, it's been two years. And of course I had all the tests after Jared…" I trail off. What's the protocol for mentioning your ex-husband to the guy you are pretty much throwing yourself at?

"Jared's a fuck up. And he's not going to be mentioned in this room again, okay?"

Ooh, he actually looks annoyed. That's interesting.

"Works for me." I nod solemnly.

"Good." He smiles at me. "Want to take a bath with me, Carmichael?"

"I thought you said you were clean," I say and he rolls his eyes at me.

"I am. But I want to see you naked and I figure wet and naked is even better."

And that's when I realize, that he's going to see everything. The stretch marks on my stomach. The ones on my breasts. I'm pretty sure every muscle in my body tightens, and not with pleasure.

Yes, he's seen me in a bikini. And yeah, I'm kind of average for my age. But holy schmoly, I'm probably the oldest woman he's ever been with.

"Maybe we should just go to bed," I say, my voice small.

He's silent for a moment. I feel his gaze on my face, but I can't bring myself to look at him.

"We don't have to do anything, you know that, right?" he asks.

"I know." I nod. "I just..."

"What?" There's a frown in his voice.

"I'm scared." There, I've said it. He wanted me to say how I feel. But I don't feel any better. I feel like an idiot, because he's almost certainly going to laugh at me.

But miracle of miracles he doesn't. Instead, he looks almost sad when I finally gather the nerve to glance at him.

"What the fuck did he do to you?" he asks.

"What do you mean?"

"The man who won't be mentioned," he continues, softly stroking my hair. It feels good. I close my eyes and let the sensation wash over me. "I don't know what he did to you to make you feel like you're not the most beautiful woman on this fucking island, but you need to know you are, Carmichael. You're gorgeous and you should know it."

I look up at him, and there are tears in my eyes. "I'm not twenty-five."

"Thank fuck. Because I'm not either."

Oh god, this is stupid. I should be under him right now. In the throes of passion. But instead a tear begins running down my cheek.

"Oh fuck." He brushes his thumb against my skin, scooping the tear away. "Don't let him ruin this for you. Hasn't he done enough?"

"I'm sorry. I…"

"You don't need to be sorry. You don't ever need to be sorry." His voice is soothing. "I just hate that he's made you feel this way."

"Have you ever made a woman feel this way?" I ask him.

"I try not to," he says, honesty radiating from him. "My mom, when I was younger. She watched my dad leave her for somebody else. It was hard."

My stomach tightens. "I'm sorry."

"I hated seeing her go through that. Promised myself I'd never do it to anybody else."

I let out a ragged breath. How did I not know this about Linc? How did I not realize just how sweet he can be?

"I've had a few longer term relationships," he tells me. "But we parted amicably."

"And shorter term ones?"

"I always make sure we both know what we're getting into."

I blink. "So what is this?" I ask him.

His lip curls up into a smile. "What do you want it to be?"

"I don't know." I frown. "I just… I wanted this. Want you."

"I want you, too." His voice is still so soft it's like a feather.

"But not if it makes you cry. I'm not into sleeping with weeping women."

That makes me laugh and he smiles. "Let's take the pressure off this. I'll pour us a drink, you go run the bath. Get in and get relaxed, then call me when you're ready."

"What if I'm never ready?" I ask, more to myself than him.

His eyes catch mine. "No pressure, Carmichael. I'll still hug you all night no matter what."

CHAPTER
THIRTEEN

LINC

I hear the bath starting to fill up as I pour out two glasses of champagne from the minibar and set them on the kitchen counter, then I sneak over to the mirror to make sure I look presentable.

And then I scroll through my phone because I meant it about giving her some space. I'm not the kind of asshole who would try to hurry her. Luckily my brothers' messages in our Bachelor party chat do that perfectly.

HOLDEN: I thought we said the bachelor party was going to be calm.

BROOKS: We didn't say that. You did.

. . .

HOLDEN: Well I'm the groom so what I say goes. One night, that's all I wanted. Then I see this.

Ah, I guess he's gotten my email with our flight details.

LINC: It is one night. We fly, we play golf, we have an evening of debauchery, and then we fly home.

LIAM: What kind of debauchery? I'm going to need to run it past Sophie.

I roll my eyes. Liam used to be my wing man. Or maybe I used to be his.

ELI: Golf I can do. Debauchery I can't. I need to be in bed by ten or I wake up cranky.

MYLES: Ava asked if she can join in the debauchery, too?

HOLDEN: THERE'S NOT GOING TO BE ANY FUCKING DEBAUCHERY

LINC: Calm your tits. It's all good. The debauchery involves a private meal in the casino, a few hours in the high rollers room, and a concert. That's it.

. . .

I send the message off and lock my phone because my brothers are pissing me off. You don't ask somebody to do something for you, then criticize it.

Brooks and I have got it sorted. We've arranged the rooms and the entertainment in Vegas. We'll fly together from JFK. Then Myles, Liam, Eli, and Holden will fly up together on a private jet from Yeager Airport, and will be met by a limo that will bring them to meet us for golf.

It's literally everything Holden asked for. But for some reason, none of them trust me to get it done.

Yeah, now I'm pissed off.

"Linc?"

Her voice brings me out of my thoughts. I let out a long breath, because the last person who needs to know I'm pissed is Tessa.

Not when I've spent the whole evening trying to relax her.

"Yes, baby?"

"That sounds weird. No babies."

I start to laugh. "Okay," I agree. "I can go with that."

"Are you coming in then?" she calls out.

"Thought you'd never ask."

I grab the champagne glasses and balance them in one hand while I push the door to the bathroom open with the other. The steam hits me immediately, and it takes a moment for me to be able to see through it.

And *holy fuck* when I do, I think I'm about to combust.

She's naked. In the tub. No bubbles or anything to hide herself. I go hard instantly.

Because she's beautiful. Every fucking part of her. I pass her one of the glasses, my eyes almost popping out.

"Don't ever let anybody tell you you're not perfect," I say, my voice thick. "Because I don't think I've ever been so hard in my life."

"Show me," she whispers. And because I love to please

people – no scratch that, because I love to please Carmichael – I down the champagne in one go and put the glass on the sink counter. Then I start to unbutton my shirt, my fingers deft, my gaze never leaving hers.

And when I shuck it off and throw it to the floor she lets out an audible sigh.

"Can't you at least have some imperfections?" she asks me.

I glance down at my chest, frowning. "What do you want me to do? Punch myself, leave a bruise?"

She giggles. "No. Come on, take the rest of your clothes off. I'm thinking your dick must be tiny to compensate for the rest of your body."

I roll my eyes at her but still do as she asks, unbuttoning my pants, pulling them down over my hips, revealing the thick ridge of my hard-on pushing against my boxers.

"Damn," she mutters. "Not small then."

I grin at her. "Stop with the compliments. You're only making it harder."

"I can see that." She takes a sip of champagne and puts the glass on the counter beside the bath. "Are you getting in or what?"

Here's the thing about baths. Unless they're the size of a small swimming pool they're not exactly comfortable for somebody of my height. Something always has to give, my knees, my feet, or possibly my whole legs.

So it takes a little while for us to get comfortable in there.

I end up lifting Tessa up, and planting her on my lap, and she laughs the whole time. And I realize, that laughter soothes her. It relaxes her.

And fuck, I love it when she's relaxed.

"This is nice," she murmurs, her back against my chest, her hair tickling my face. She wriggles and her ass presses harder against me.

"Baby, if you keep doing that, this bath is gonna get dirty very quickly."

"You called me baby again."

Oh shit, I did. "Sorry."

"It's okay. It's growing on me."

I kiss the curve of her neck. "You're growing on me."

She lets out a contented sigh.

"Want me to touch you?" I ask her. Because I'm desperate to get my hands on her body. I want to feel every part of her. Make her breath catch. Watch her cheeks flush. I want to see what she's like when she comes.

I twitch hard against her and she giggles again.

Fuck, I want to be inside of her.

But I can't. I know that.

She turns to look at me. There's so much trust in her eyes that it makes me feel a hundred feet tall. "Yes, I'd like that," she whispers.

I'm fucking throbbing now. I kiss her neck again, then the line of her jaw, before she twists enough that our mouths connect.

Her tongue is soft as it slides against mine. Her body lifts up and down with the soft movement of the water as I move my hands down, cupping the weight of her breasts in my palms.

Her nipples tighten and I pinch them between my thumb and fingers. Putting just enough pressure on them to make her gasp.

"Okay?" I whisper.

"Yes." Her voice is ragged.

I alternate between hard and soft, plucking then stroking, our mouths fused together until she's moaning. She's fucking delicious as she arches against me, her ass pressing against my dick.

"Touch me," she whispers, her mouth still melded to mine.

I smile against her, enjoying how much she's enjoying this. "I am."

She lets out a little frustrated sigh, so I kiss her again, then slide my hand along her stomach, the other still teasing her nipple. I trace the seam of her thighs, moving up until she's breathing raggedly against my mouth.

"Please…"

When I touch her, I can feel the slickness between her legs and it's so damn enticing. Gently pushing the pad of my finger against her, I find her clit, giving it the lightest of touches, before I start to circle it over her, again and again.

She shivers against me, despite the heat of the water surrounding us. I kiss her again. "You're such a good girl."

She shivers and I like it. My girl enjoys praise.

And the way she's moving to the touch of my finger, she fucking deserves it.

"Linc," she whispers. "More. Please."

Her wish is my fucking command. I slide two fingers against her then push them inside. She arches her back as I move my other hand down to the bundle of nerves that has her gasping. I'm kissing her, fucking her with my fingers, teasing her with my thumb, and then she stiffens against me, a long drawn out cry vibrating against my lips as I hold her tightly, slowing my movement to draw out her pleasure.

Christ, this woman is hot. What kind of man wouldn't want this all the time? Wouldn't want to please her. To feel her come apart in his arms. I'm as hard as steel here.

When she finally catches her breath, she twists in the bath until she's straddling me. We kiss again, her breath warm against my lips, her body pliant as I steady her hips as she faces me.

She rocks and I feel the tip of myself against her. It feels so good it's almost painful.

"Carmichael…" I warn, because we're so slippery and I'm a breath away from being inside of her.

"I was wondering when you were going to call me that." She leans forward to kiss me again. Her eyes are shining.

"It's that or baby," I mutter, my brain firmly between my thighs. She squirms again and fuck.

I'm inside her. My eyes roll into the back of my head.

"Don't make me think about it," she whispers against my mouth. "I need you, Salinger."

The way she says my name does something to me. I squeeze my eyes shut and groan. "Condom," I whisper.

"Oh shit," she says. "I forgot about that."

When I open my eyes our gazes connect. There's so much heat in hers, I want to combust.

"I have one in my wallet." I try to stretch but I can't reach my pants. And I don't want to let go of her.

Maybe I'm afraid she'll change her mind if I let go. But also, maybe she needs that.

The right to change her mind, I mean. So I let her go and she grabs at me, and I laugh, because she clearly isn't changing anything.

"I can't reach," I tell her. "Give me one second."

I climb out and grab a towel, stepping on it as I reach for my pants. The little foil packet is in there.

"Can you use condoms in water?" she asks.

"Of course you can." I look at her quizzically. But she's not looking at me. She's staring right at my hard dick.

"Haven't you ever done it in the bath?" I ask.

"No. Have you?" She sounds almost tremulous.

I let out a long breath because now is not the time for that conversation. "Not with you. And for future information, it's fine to use a condom in the bath."

"Noted." She grins at me.

I rip the tip of the foil. "Are you sure, Carmichael? It's not too late to change your mind."

Her smile is huge. "And lose my opportunity to enjoy your monster dick? Yes, I'm sure."

I laugh as she reaches for me, and I'm lost as her fingers curl around my length. The feel of her palm against me makes my legs want to buckle.

"Can I put the condom on you?" she whispers.

"Have at it," I manage to say.

It takes an act of will not to move my hips as she softly rolls it on. Her touch is so fucking perfect it makes me want to growl. I climb back in, and this time I'm the one hovering over her, staring into her delicious eyes.

"Just so you know," I tell her. "This is my first time. So be gentle."

She cracks up laughing and I kiss her, swallowing her giggles. She's still grinning as I push myself against her, feeling her slowly open to me. My knees are pressing too hard against the porcelain, and I'm hunched over her in a way that will make my muscles hate me in the morning, but fuck it I'm inside Carmichael and it's everything.

"Jesus Christ are you in all the way?" she asks.

"Not yet. Want me to stop?" I'm really not as big as she's making out. More than average, sure, but not porn star big. Still, my ego loves her for the praise.

"No, just give me a minute."

The way she's staring up at me with wide, trusting eyes makes my dick twitch inside of her. Her breath catches in her throat, so I kiss it. Then her jaw, moving my lips upwards until they're against hers.

"Okay?" I murmur.

"Okay," she breathes.

Still kissing her, I slowly push the rest of the way, until I'm buried in her. It feels so damn good I let out a low growl and she giggles again.

I like it. I want her to laugh constantly while we fuck. So I whisper in her ear.

"I'm going to nickname your pussy the Lincoln Strangler."

She laughs and my eyes roll back into my head. I need to

concentrate because there's no way I'm going to come before she does. I move my hand in between us, finding the bundled part of her that I know rocks her world, moving my fingers softly over it as I slide inside of her again.

"Oh my God," she whispers in my ear and I try not to grin. "Lincoln."

"I like it when you call me that." I'm panting now. Trying to think of anything but coming inside of this delicious woman.

I capture her nipple between my lips and she lets out a gasp. I feel her tightening around me and I start to think she really is strangling me. What a way to die. Cock asphyxiation. Explain that one to the coroner.

"Linc!"

"Stop fighting it," I tell her.

And she does. This time when she comes there's water everywhere. She's splashing around as her body lets go and then I'm coming, too. She starts laughing and I come harder, then I'm laughing too because what a fucking mess.

Water is pooled on the tiles next to us. Her hair is in wet ropes underneath me. And I'm pretty sure if I pull out of her, my cock will hate me.

"Jesus, Carmichael," I manage to grunt out. "Where have you been hiding all my life."

"In your hate list," she tells me.

"I never hated you. You're the one who hated me." I reach down between us again, putting my fingers around the condom before I move. "I'm gonna pull out now," I warn her.

She gives me the prettiest pout.

"Condom," I remind her.

"Oh, yeah." She nods and watches as I dispose of it, then I get back into the bath and pull her on top of me, so her legs are straddling my thighs and our chests are firmly pressed together.

"How was your first time with me in the bath?" she asks, her eyes shining. I love a happy Carmichael.

And yeah, I blink that thought right away.

"Middling," I tell her, trying not to laugh at her outraged expression.

"Careful," she says as I kiss her neck. "You might end up back on my hate list."

CHAPTER
FOURTEEN

TESSA

I wake up the next morning in a Linc Salinger induced sex haze that makes walking feel like I'm bouncing on marshmallows. It's all his fault. I barely got any sleep, thanks to his beautiful body pressing against mine the whole night.

I'm sitting in the business suite at the hotel, going over our presentation in preparation for tomorrow morning. We fly out in the afternoon, which I'm worried is too soon because I'd like to stay to answer any questions James Gold might have.

But I also want to see Zoe. And I need to talk to Angela. Because I can't tell her over the phone that I've finally broken my post-divorce cherry. All of Manhattan will hear her shout of victory.

Linc is in one of the break out rooms, talking on his phone as always. He looks at me through the glass and smiles and I feel it in my stomach.

Of course I smile back. It's almost impossible not to, especially after last night.

The man made it his personal mission to give me as many orgasms as possible. Frowning isn't really an option.

We didn't have much time for talking this morning. He had to rush out for a zoom meeting first thing, and I had to call the office because my schedule for next week is already filling up and I need to get my staff working on things in advance of my own meetings in New York.

And just like that it feels like I've burst my own bubble. Because that's what this is, a lovely sexy little bubble with the two of us inside. But after tomorrow reality will bite.

We'll go back to being Salinger and Carmichael. My chest does a weird little twisty thing at that thought.

"You okay?" Linc asks, making me jump. I didn't even notice him coming out of the side room.

"I'm fine." I force a smile onto my face. "Everything okay at work?"

"That one wasn't work. It was a conference call with my brothers."

After all of our conversations I feel like I know them. There are six brothers including Linc, and their baby sister from their dad's third marriage. I haven't seen a photograph of them yet but I'm desperate to see if any of them look like him.

"Is everything okay with them?" I ask.

The corner of his lip quirks. "I like it when you're being nice to me," he says. "I think I'll demand it at all times."

I lift a brow. "Demand all you like. When we're back in the office everything changes."

"Why?" he asks, as though he's surprised by that.

"Because…" my voice trails off. "You're you and I'm me."

"I've no idea what that's supposed to mean." His phone starts to ring again, and he looks at the screen, groaning. "Hold that thought," he says. "We haven't finished talking about this."

"Sure," I say sweetly, as he walks back into the other room

again. Truth is, I think we'll be nice to each other. And the fact is, I won't have to see him that much since he's out of the office almost all the time.

It's weird how that thought feels like a bad taste in my mouth. My brain has obviously been overstimulated by the hot man shouting at his phone in the glass booth.

———

"Tonight I'm taking you out to dinner and then we're coming back here and I'm fucking you until you forget your own name," Linc announces casually that evening, when he walks into the cottage.

He's been out most of the day. He's a workaholic, just like me and it's one of the things I'm finding stupidly attractive about him.

He comes from money. He's made more. And yet he never lets up. He just keeps on going.

"We have the presentation first thing," I remind him. And right now I'm packing because we won't have time in the morning. My heart is already racing thinking about going home. I'm feeling stupidly torn between wanting to see my daughter and wanting to spend longer here with him. Every time he looks at me my body responds.

"Okay, I'll let you remember your own name. But you'll have to scream out mine." He walks over and presses his lips against my throat. "Hello, darling."

I smile, because he's so ridiculous. And so ridiculously handsome. He's wearing a pair of dark gray dress pants and a white shirt, the sleeves rolled up. His aviator sunglasses are hanging from the v of his shirt where the top buttons are undone.

"How was your day?" I ask.

"Busy. Stupid. How was yours?"

"I got everything finalized," I say proudly.

"I'm sorry I left you to work alone." He genuinely looks it, too. "There's a problem with a client in Paris."

"The one you always sweet talk?" I ask. I try to keep my voice light, but yeah, there's a hint of jealousy there. Not that there should be. Because this thing is clearly physical. And when we go home it's over.

"She's fifty," he says. "No need to go all green eyed over her."

"I'm not green eyed," I protest.

"Sure you're not." He gives me one of his trademark heat-inducing smiles. "Come on, take me through the presentation. Then it's dinner and bed for us."

He pulls me off the chair I've been sitting on, then lifts me onto his lap. I can smell the warm depths of his cologne. Feel the heat of his skin from the sunshine on his walk back from the hotel. He kisses my neck again, just where he knows I'm the most sensitive, and I let out a sigh.

"The presentation, Carmichael," he reminds me.

I lean forward and start up the slide show, talking him through each one. He asks me questions – pertinent ones, and I answer them as though he doesn't already know what I'm about to say. Because he's just as on top of this as I am.

And at the end, there's a last slide. On top it says *The Blooper Reel*. In the center is a video and it starts to play.

It's of Linc running along Pig Beach, being chased by the biggest, hairiest angry mama pig you ever want to see.

As he lands face first in the sand more words come up over the video.

"Hampshire PR will run the extra mile to make sure you're happy."

"Not funny, Carmichael," he growls into my ear. But there's amusement in his voice and it makes me grin.

"I think it's hilarious."

"I thought we agreed you'd delete that video," he says, pushing the hair away from my neck so he can kiss it again.

He has a thing about my throat. I'm starting to think he might have been a vampire in another life.

Except then he'd still be a vampire, because they can't die. Well that's confusing.

"I never said that," I point out.

He moves his hand down to where my skirt meets my thighs, lifting it higher, feathering his fingers against my skin. Until he reaches the apex, and slides them into my panties.

"Linc…"

"Tell me you'll delete it," he says, his voice all low and sweet as he starts circling the pad of his finger against me.

"That's bribery," I gasp. But all I can think of is the delicious warmth he's creating between my legs.

"Promise me." He cups me with his palm and slides one finger inside. I gasp as he pushes a second one in, then moves the heel of his hand against me where I need it most.

"I…"

He kisses my ear, my jaw, the corner of my lips. "It'll be our little secret, right?" His voice is turning me on as much as his fingers. He has this way of putting you in a trance.

A sex trance. I'm pretty much a zombie for this man.

And then he stops moving his hand entirely. Pulls his fingers out until I'm empty.

"What's happening?" I ask as he lifts me from his lap and pulls my skirt back down.

The next moment there's a knock at the door and I realize that Linc must have seen whoever it was walking up the steps to the cottage.

A blush steals up my face, but I'm also stupidly grateful that he made sure I was looking decent before our unexpected guest could see me through the window.

My thighs are still shaking as he strides over to the door and opens it. "William?" he murmurs.

Oh, our concierge. I wave over at him, and he smiles back.

"Sorry to interrupt, but the phone isn't working," he says.

"What phone?" Linc asks.

"The hotel phone. Mr. Gold has been trying to call you. He'd like you both to join him for dinner tonight. At his house."

"James wants to see us tonight?" Linc asks. He looks almost pissed off. "Is he here already?"

William nods. "He arrived an hour ago. His business was wound up early. He asks that you be ready for dinner at eight. I'll be here at seven-thirty to pick you up."

I glance at my watch. It's already six.

"Okay." Linc glances over his shoulder at me and I shrug.

So much for practicing our presentation tonight. But if the client wants us, then the client gets us.

The customer always comes first.

———

It's three a.m. and we should be asleep but Linc is currently holding my hips, staring up at me like I'm the most beautiful thing he's ever seen. I'm straddling him and he's inside of me, his hands moving me up and down in a rhythm that's making both of us gasp.

We didn't get back to the cottage until an hour ago. James Gold was absolutely delighted to see us – well mostly Linc – and spent the whole night regaling him with stories of mutual friends and acquaintances. He was charming to me, too. But it felt like the longest of nights not being able to touch each other.

Every time our eyes met all I could think of was how much I wished we could be alone together.

As soon as we got back to the cottage he swung me over his shoulder and carried me to the bedroom, while I laughed, tapping ineffectively at his back and demanding he put me down.

"I've been waiting all fucking night to touch you," he told me. "Don't tell me to let you go again."

And there he was. Sweet Salinger. The man who knows how to make me feel good in every way.

Right now he's making me see stars as he flutters his tongue against my nipple and thrusts into me, his hands still grasping my hips as I fall into another pit of perfect oblivion.

"Tessa," he rasps, surging inside of me. This is the second condom we've used since we came back from dinner. We're like two kids at an all-you-can-eat buffet, with a timer hanging over our head.

Because tomorrow we have the presentation and then we go home.

When we both manage to catch our breath he pulls me into his arms and kisses my cheek.

"You called me Tessa again," I say sleepily against his chest.

"Did I?" he says. "Must have been mixing you up with somebody else."

"Shut up." I curl my hand into a fist and softly punch his chest.

"There's this hot chick at work I keep fantasizing about," he tells me. "I was kind of imagining you were her."

"You're such an idiot." I smile against his skin. God, it's so comfy here.

"All staff meetings are never going to be the same again now that I know what it's like to be inside you." He strokes my hair. "I'm going to be presenting with a hard on."

"You'd better not. The entire female population of Hampshire PR will faint."

He chuckles, his chest lifting and falling. "Yeah, but only you will know what I'm thinking about."

I let out a long breath. I don't want to think about being back at work right now. The only thing I'm looking forward to is seeing Zoe. There's a little hole in my heart that only gets filled when I see her.

But apart from that, I could seriously live in this little bungalow on this beautiful island forever.

It's hard to believe it's only been a few days since I stepped on that airplane with Linc. It feels like a lifetime.

His lips brush mine. "You have that little frown again," he murmurs. "The one you get when you're overthinking."

My brows dip. "I don't frown," I tell him.

"Sure you don't, grumpy." There's a smile on his face as big as an ocean as he reaches up to smooth the lines. "I want to see these in our next meeting," he tells me. "So I know you're thinking of my monster cock."

I start to laugh and he kisses me again, then he gets up to dispose of the condom in the bathroom. I hear the running of water and the flush of the toilet, before he walks back in looking like a God in a tiny towel.

When he climbs back into bed he pulls me into his arms, so my head is resting on his chest.

And I'm worried, because I could so easily get used to being taken care of like this.

"You're still frowning," he tells me.

"Shut up."

He laughs softly. "Go to sleep," he tells me. "We have to get up early in the morning."

"You're the one talking," I murmur, loving the feeling of his skin against my cheek.

He chuckles and it makes his chest rumble against me.

CHAPTER
FIFTEEN

TESSA

"Carmichael?"

A warm hand touches my cheek. I push my face against it, liking the way my jaw fits into his palm.

"Wake up," Linc says. I open my eyes right away. He's kneeling on the bed, his face inches from mine.

And he's fully dressed. Wearing a white shirt and a gray and navy striped tie. It's perfectly knotted. I can smell the aroma of his shower gel. I know it well because I might have used it on myself.

"What time is it?" I ask, my voice groggy. There's the palest of sunlight creeping through the gaps in the curtains. Did he close them? I'm sure they were open last night because the moon was shining in.

"It's six," he says. His voice is low and even.

"The presentation isn't until nine," I say. "Why are you dressed?"

"I have to leave."

His words are like a bucket of cold water on my face. I sit

up, holding the sheets to my chest because I feel so damn naked next to him.

"Where are you going? When will you be back? We have the presentation in a few hours?"

"Paris," he tells me. "The trouble I thought I'd sorted yesterday has escalated. The press has gotten hold of it. Roman needs me to fly in today."

"But the presentation…" I say again.

He runs his thumb along my jaw. "You've got the presentation," he says. "It was always yours. You can do this, Carmichael. You don't need me hanging around."

Yes, actually I do. I do need him. "What time is your flight?"

"Gotta leave in ten minutes."

"Why didn't you wake me earlier?" He must have gotten the call at least an hour ago. He would've had to arrange his flights, his transfer, and somebody to drive him to the airport.

"Because one of us should get some sleep." He leans forward to brush his lips against mine and I'm confused. "I'm sorry," he whispers.

There's an invisible wall coming up between us. I can feel him building it, brick by brick. And I want to laugh, because I'm the expert at walls. I always thought it would be me ending this.

Not Linc. Not him.

I want to cry. Because despite my misgivings I've had the best time here with him. He makes everything come to life, brings it into glorious color. And I realize that for the past couple of years I've been living in black and white.

I've changed. Even in a few days. Thanks to him.

His phone buzzes. "That's my car." He kisses me again. "I'll call you when I get to Paris."

"When will you be back in New York?" As soon as the words come out I hate them. I sound so stupidly needy and I hate that. I'm not a needy person.

"I have to fly straight to Vegas after Paris," he says. "But soon. I'll call you."

I nod as his phone buzzes again. He presses his lips to my brow. "You're beautiful and you're amazing," he tells me. "You'll ace the presentation."

And just like that he leaves. And I'm laying naked in the bed, the sensation of him being inside of me already feeling like a distant memory.

My head starts to pound. And though it's only six, I decide to take a shower and spend the morning working on the presentation. I need to adapt the parts Linc was going to take the lead on.

Because he won't be here.

———

Less than three hours later I find myself walking to the business suite alone. James Gold and his team are waiting for me in the meeting room, and I shake each of their hands, giving Linc's apologies, though it appears he's already messaged James.

And then I open up my PowerPoint slides. I've practiced this presentation so many times I know it by heart. The adrenaline helps, pushing me through almost on autopilot. It's a relief when I hit play on the final video and let it run.

It's the mock up we've made with some influencers. If we get the go-ahead, we'll fly them into the resort and spend a few days taking social media videos and stills. Better ones than I've been able to mock up while we've been here. We'll have traditional media there, too. I have a lot of contacts with travel writers. Liaising with them is part of my job.

The final wording comes up on the screen.

. . .

Gold Resort, Grand Exuma. The time is now. And it's all yours...

I turn to look at Gold and his team. We're sitting in the main business suite at the resort. It's light and airy and the air conditioning is caressing my skin, keeping me cool.

There are smiles on their faces and I let out a long breath full of relief. "Do you have any questions?" I ask them, ready to answer whatever they have. And yes, apparently they do, because I end up talking for another twenty minutes before their inquiries run out and the room is silent.

"Well, I think you know we're impressed," Gold says. "Coming here was the right thing to do. You've really understood the essence of the place. It's different, right?"

I smile and nod. "Yes, it is." And that's what I'm going to take away from this. That there is more to life than juggling work and home and renovations. That there's a part of me that needs to be free.

No, I'm not running out on Zoe. She's my absolute priority. But she's getting older. One day she's going to fly the coop and it will be just me.

I need to work out what kind of life it is that I want to live.

"Okay," Gold says, clapping his hands together. "It's a shame Salinger isn't here, but he called to explain why. And I don't think it will come as any surprise to tell you that Hampshire PR has hit it out of the park. I'm going to think on it, but right now you're very much my preferred option."

———

My airplane lands on the tarmac at JFK later that evening and I finally relax. People start to turn on their phones. I look at my own. There are a few messages. One from Zoe, asking me if I've landed yet – because we arrived ten minutes late.

Another from Angela telling me that more people die on the toilet every year than on an airplane. I have no idea if this is true, but I laugh anyway.

And then Linc's name comes up on the screen. I'm stupidly excited to see it, in a way that is so unlike me.

I press my finger on the screen and open it up.

Glad it went well. L x

I stare at it for a moment. I'd sent him a message after the presentation to let him know that it went well with Gold and that we should hear back from his team within a week.

But then I had to hurry to catch my flight to Nassau and didn't hear back from him until now.

And if I'm honest, I'm disappointed.

I don't know what I was expecting. Not a declaration of love or anything, that's for sure. But maybe thanks for a great trip. Or great sex.

Maybe part of me was even hoping he'd send me some dirty texts.

But seriously, is that what I want? This week has been fun. More than that, it's what I needed. But I can't see how any of this would work when we're back in the real world.

I don't think he'd want it to anyway.

The seatbelt sign goes off and everybody stands and starts to gather their carry-ons from the overheads, jostling for a position to be the first ones off the plane. A child in the back starts to cry.

I slowly gather my things, as the pilot welcomes us to New York and tells us that it's raining outside.

I guess that's it. Exuma's over.

It's time to get back to real life.

CHAPTER
SIXTEEN

LINC

"For fuck's sake," Myles mutters as his ball stops short of the green. "This is stupid. Why didn't you arrange for strippers instead?"

I shake my head, because Myles will bitch about anything. I don't know how his wife puts up with him. Ava's a damn angel.

I flew into Vegas last night after a week in Paris, and I'm in the worst kind of mood. Part of it is jet-lag, but a lot of it is because I'm an asshole.

I haven't called Carmichael. I wanted to, but I didn't. And I know that makes me the worst kind of douche, but I have no idea what to say to her.

Liam and Brooks are already at the club house, no doubt trying out all the finest whiskeys behind the bar. Eli and Holden are ahead of us, the two of them talking about the next green I think.

And Myles is pouting like a baby at his club.

"I don't know why you're grumbling," I tell him. "I'm the

one who just crossed two continents and then came straight here to watch you miss every hole on the course."

"One continent. You crossed one," Myles corrects.

"Europe and North America. I make it two." I hit my ball easily into the hole and Myles groans.

We've all been playing golf since we were kids. It's our dad's favorite sport, and the one thing he knew how to do when it was his custody time. Golf, dinner, then back to our respective moms. All those Saturdays made us experts.

Or some of us, at least.

"So how was Paris?" Myles asks when he finally pots his ball.

"Busy. Tiring. I feel like I'm in a plane more than I'm on the ground." And I didn't sleep a fucking wink. Which isn't like me.

Maybe I shouldn't have gone to Paris. I know Tessa was pissed that I left her alone at the last minute. But if Roman tells me to jump, I fucking leap. So I flew to Paris, schmoozed some journalists and our client, then flew straight here to Vegas for Holden's bachelor party. We're playing golf today and tonight more of his friends arrive for a private dinner in the casino followed by a private gambling room.

No strippers at all. Because I'm a good brother.

"I forgot you were in the Bahamas before Paris. How did it go?" Myles picks his ball up and dusts it off.

"Good." My reply is short. Because I don't want to talk about the Bahamas.

"What were you there for again?"

Okay, so we're talking about the Bahamas. Great. "A presentation," I say. "Gold Leisure."

"James Gold?" Myles asks.

"Yep. He wanted us to go to Exuma to experience the place for real."

"It's a hard life," Myles says dryly. "Wait, who's us? Did Roman go?"

I wince at the thought of it. "No, a colleague."

And now I'm thinking about Tessa again. Not Carmichael. I've started to divide them in my mind. Tessa is Bahamas. All floaty dresses and sun-kissed skin. Carmichael is the haughty co-worker who hates my guts in New York.

"I slept with her," I tell Myles. He stops walking and turns to look at me.

"What?"

"My co-worker. We had sex."

Myles eyes scan my face. "And why are you telling me this?"

Because I need to talk to somebody. Somebody who'll actually listen. Maybe even understand.

And yeah, Myles and I haven't always seen eye-to-eye but he's my oldest brother. He's fucking wise beyond his years. He loves me, I know that.

And I love him.

"Because I messed everything up," I say. "I left her a week ago in Exuma and I haven't called her."

"Why haven't you?"

"Because I'm an asshole.

"Of course you are," Myles says smoothly. He's cheered up immensely now that the focus is on me and my fuck ups and not his terrible golf technique. "Get in the golf cart, you can tell me all about it."

So I do. Sitting next to my brother while he peels a banana and eats it in the slowest, most excruciating way, I tell him all about Tessa, including that she's a divorced mom, and our week together leading up to the way we ended in bed.

"And that's it?" he asks, swallowing down a mouthful of banana.

"Yeah, that's it."

He puts the peel into the little plastic baggy they've put in the cart to serve as a trash can. "I still don't get why you're telling me it. You had sex with your colleague. Okay, that's a bit stupid since you have to work together. But she sounds like she's got her head screwed on. She won't say anything if you don't."

I frown. "But…"

"Not that I want to talk about it, but you have sex with a lot of women, don't you?"

My face wrinkles even more. "Not that many…"

He lifts a brow. I shrug. "Average," I say. "Maybe slightly above."

"Do you know what average is?" he asks.

"No, do you?"

"We're getting off the subject," he says huffily. If there's one thing my brother loves, it's a problem to solve. He lives for it. "So you had sex while traveling with a co-worker. It happens all the time all over the world. Just chalk it up to experience and move on. Maybe send her some flowers or something."

"I haven't slept all week," I tell him and he winces.

"Shit."

"I think I like her."

He actually fucking winces.

I frown. "Is that a bad thing?" I ask him. "Me liking somebody? Shouldn't it be a good thing? Shouldn't you be happy for me right now?"

"You're the one boo-hooing because you fucked everything up royally," Myles points out. "And I'm mostly reacting like this because I think you might have chosen the wrong person."

"What do you mean?" I frown. "Why's she the wrong person? What do you have against her?" The need to defend Carmichael rises up inside me. "She's fucking perfect. Beautiful, funny, clever as hell. And she's renovating a wreck of a home all on her own."

Myles starts the cart up, an electric whir rising through the air. "I mean you picked the wrong person because she sounds too good for you. Plus there's the big thing."

"What big thing?" My blood begins to heat up. Myles is supposed to be on my fucking side, not telling me I'm not good enough for her.

I mean I'm not, but still. That's for me to say, not him.

"You just told me she's a single mom. You've never dated a single mom. Not ever."

There's a silence. Because he's right. I never have. It's not a choice I made. It's just that all the women I've been with previously have been single and probably younger than Tessa.

"You can't fuck around with them," Myles says. "Because if you walk away, you don't just hurt them, you hurt their kids."

"I'm not planning on hurting anybody," I say. "I've spoken to Zoe. She's a nice kid. I've got her tickets to see the Linebackers."

Myles taps his fingers against the wheel, looking ahead at the path as we drive. Holden and Eli are at the next green, and we slow down to join them. But neither of us gets out of the cart.

"Nobody thinks they're going to hurt anybody at the beginning of a relationship," Myles says patiently. "You think your mom thought dad would hurt her?"

"No." My chest tightens.

"My mom didn't either. And yet he hurt them both. And can I point out something else?"

"If you have to." I'm starting to feel sick and I have a feeling whatever Myles has to add is going to make it worse.

"I'm just trying to be the voice of reason here. You walked out with a hasty goodbye. And you've not spoken to her since. That's not how you treat somebody you care about. And it's definitely not how you treat a single mom."

Yeah, I feel worse. About a hundred times worse. "Can we

just head back to the clubhouse?" I ask him. "I need a drink. Now."

————

TESSA

I'm sanding the living room walls when there's a knock at the door. Zoe's at her friend's house. It's Maisie's birthday and they decided to have a last minute sleepover, even though Zoe spent most of the last week telling me how much she missed me.

I still remember what it was like to be a kid and being excluded from parties. So I agreed that she could go as long as we have lunch out together tomorrow.

The knock comes again. I put the sander down and run my hands through my hair to put it in some kind of order. I jump over the hole in the floor that the electrician insists has to stay open for the next couple of weeks while they finish rewiring and make my way to the front door.

Angela's standing on the stoop and as soon as she catches sight of me she starts to laugh. "Loving the dusty hair," she says. "Did you get it done in the Bahamas?"

I look at the hand I just used to push my hair back, and sure enough it's covered in drywall dust. Ugh. "Come in," I tell her. "But look where you're going."

"I know the holes in your floor like the back of my hand," she tells me. She's carrying a brown bag that smells suspiciously like my favorite takeout, along with a bottle of sparkling wine from a California vineyard that we both love.

"Zoe called me," she says, following me inside and closing the door behind her. "She told me she's stood you up on a Saturday night and begged me to come over to entertain you."

"You didn't have to do that." Though my stomach is glad she did. We walk into the kitchen and I grab some plates and glasses from the formica cupboards. She pulls out silverware from one of the boxes and starts to set the tiny kitchen table.

"Yes I did," she says, opening up the wine. "A chance to talk to you all alone without little ears listening? Who would turn that down?"

"Zoe's ears are big," I say and Angela grins.

"I know. That's why I can't ask you about sex with your co-worker while she's around. When did she get to be so perceptive?"

"I don't know." Angela's brought my favorite Thai food from the restaurant two blocks down. I open the lid and groan when the aroma wafts up. I swear my stomach does a little happy dance.

I serve out our dinner, then carry the plates over to where Angela is sitting, already sipping at her wine. "Don't drink too much," I warn her. "After this you're going to help me with the sanding. I want to finish it tonight."

Angela forks up some noodles and puts them into her mouth. "Dear God, I'd marry the chef if I could eat this every day."

"He's about eighty," I remind her.

"That's why there's Viagra," she says. Then she catches my eye. "Speaking of which…"

She knows all about my days with Linc, because she was the first person I called when I got back.

"He hasn't called," I say softly. And the truth is, I'm still not sure how to feel about that. I really thought he'd at least check in with me after I arrived back home. Even a 'Hi, how are you? Thanks for the great sex but it's not going to happen again' would have been better than radio silence.

"That rat bastard." She takes a sip of wine. "It doesn't get any better than this, does it? Let's just give up on guys and eat and drink ourselves to oblivion."

"Sounds good to me." Except it doesn't. I hate to say it, but as much as I love eating and drinking, having sex with Linc was no comparison.

It was out of this world. I take a sip of the wine and remind myself that he's not the only man who can give good orgasms. There are plenty of men out there.

"Maybe he's just really busy," she says hopefully. "You did say he had to fly to Paris then Vegas, right?"

"Mmhm."

"And you said he was nice." She's talking with her mouthful now. Not that I blame her. This food is too good not to eat.

"He is. Or was. I don't know." Nice. Sexy. All consuming. "But I guess it was like a vacation fling."

"Seriously?" She frowns.

"Yes." I've been thinking about this a lot. We had a good time. We didn't make each other any promises. And yeah, him ghosting me is a little dickish, but I haven't messaged him either since his reply.

And right now I think that's for the best. I don't need drama in my life. I've had enough to last me until I retire. I just want fun and happiness. I'm not going to let his lack of communication get me down.

"But the sex…" She pouts, looking completely disappointed.

"Was great. But that's it. He's not interested, and I'm glad about that. There's no way he could fit in here." I gesture at the kitchen, the broken cupboards, the old fashioned stove. He must be used to everything shiny and new.

Including his partners.

"Seriously," I tell her. "I'm good." Or I will be.

"What about making that dating profile?" she asks me, hope tinging her voice.

"When the renovations are finished," I tell her. "I promise." Ange is right. I don't want to be alone forever.

"Ugh. This is so disappointing." She grabs her phone and starts typing.

"What have I told you about phones at the table?" I tease. "I don't let Zoe do it."

"I'm just checking his Insta to see if he's posted." She pauses. "Damn, he's on private." She peers over the top of her phone. "Are you friends on there?"

"No." I hadn't thought about it. I'd barely used my phone when we were in Exuma, apart from calls the office and Zoe. And before then I wouldn't have touched any friend request he sent with a ten foot pole.

"Wait. I'll see if he's tagged by somebody who isn't private." Her eyes light up. "Yes! Yesterday. Let me look."

And I watch as the smile slowly falls from her face.

"What is it?" I ask her.

"It doesn't matter." She goes to put her phone back in her purse.

"Of course it matters," I say. "What did you just see?" I reach for her phone and she hesitates.

"Okay but don't get mad," she says, handing her phone over. The screen has already locked but I know her passcode the same way she knows mine. I tap it in and the screen lights up with her Instagram account.

Linc's name is in the search bar. And below that are three possible Linc Salingers, followed by a grid of photographs. I press on the first one, and there he is. Looking devastatingly handsome in a tuxedo. Wherever he is, it's at night and his skin is lamplit and golden. There's a half smile on his face, but I'm not looking at that.

I'm looking at the woman he's standing with. His arm is around her and she's nestling into him, her face against his shoulder. My eyes go to the caption. It's in French and I have to press the translate button.

Lincoln Salinger and Celine Duchamps attend the gala of the year. Don't they make a cute couple? The date on it is from last week.

I hand her the phone back, forcing a smile onto my face. "There you go," I tell her. "It was just a fling."

"You're much prettier than her," Ange grumbles and I shake my head. "And younger," she adds.

"And we're both older than him," I say pointedly, taking a large mouthful of wine. "Now can we change the subject, please?"

CHAPTER
SEVENTEEN

LINC

"I thought we said no strippers," Eli says to me as the door to our private room at the casino opens and five women walk in, their dresses barely skimming their upper thighs.

"Where's the groom?" one of them says, her voice low and sultry as she scans the room.

"Linc?" Holden looks at me, panicked. "You promised no women."

"I didn't organize this," I tell him, staring over at Brooks who shrugs in a "nor did I" kind of way. Liam is talking to Myles about something, and I gotta be honest neither of them would have done this. They're too scared about their wives cutting their balls off.

"If Mac finds out about this..." Eli trails off, shaking his head. "Linc, you're a fucking idiot."

"It wasn't me," I say again. But I stand up anyway. Because I'm the organizer of this damn bachelor party and it's my neck on the line if any of these admittedly beautiful women so much as touch Holden.

The man used to fight to keep his stress under control. God only knows what he'll do if he has to deal with them.

"Ladies," I murmur, walking over to them. "You all look beautiful tonight. But I think there's been a mistake." I nod at the door. "Can we discuss this outside?"

"This is the Salinger party, right?" tall, dark, and pretty next to me says. "Are you the guy getting married?" She puts her hand on my chest and I sigh loudly. I pull it away and she giggles.

There's a security guard at the door. All part of the package I arranged. He's wearing a black suit, with a wired earbud like he's keeping the president alive rather than looking after a group of idiots losing money at poker.

"Where's your boss?" I ask him.

"Head of security?" He frowns. "I think he's probably in the monitor room."

"No, I mean the head of the casino," I tell him. "I need to speak to him about…" I gesture at the women who are all talking and laughing. And showing no sign of leaving.

"Mr. Lindy is in his office. Would you like me to have you escorted there?" he asks.

"I'll escort him," the handsy chest-toucher says. "Just say the word and I'll take you to heaven, baby."

I roll my eyes. She seems like a sweet girl.

"Can you get Lindy to come here?" I ask the security guard. There's no way I'm leaving these women. If I go, they will be back in the private room like a shot.

And my brothers are nowhere near as diplomatic as I am. It'll end in tears. Or in violence. And I'll get blamed.

And I'm pissed because I don't even want to be here. I want to go home. Or at least to my bedroom in the penthouse suite we've rented. I want to call Carmichael again. See if she picks up this time.

Because she didn't the five other times I called her after

my talk with Myles. I'm such a fucking idiot. I should have called her last week.

It takes five minutes for Lindy to arrive. We shake hands. I've known him a while. I used to bring clients to this casino in my previous job.

"We have a problem," I say, leaning so I can whisper to him. "I didn't order these ladies."

Lindy looks surprised at my words. "Yes you did."

Oh shit. No I didn't. I really didn't. My stomach starts to tighten because if he says that to my brothers...

"I didn't ask for them," I say again, my voice lifting an octave.

"They're part of the package you ordered." He lifts a brow. "Evening entertainment," he says. "That's what you asked for."

The blood drains from my face. "I meant a fucking singer or something." Jesus Christ. I'm dead meat. I pinch the bridge of my nose, trying to ignore the racing of my heart. "We need to get them out of here now."

"Of course," Lindy says smoothly. "There's just one small problem..."

"What is it?" I snap, because it's a matter of minutes before at least one of my brothers comes out to find out what's going on. And with my luck it'll be Myles. He'll hear Lindy saying I ordered women and I'll never hear the fucking end of it.

"They usually make... extra money." Lindy clears his throat. "Tips, if you will. Because I booked them out for the evening for your entertainment."

I stare at him for a minute. "So you want me to pay them tips for services I haven't even asked for?"

Lindy shrugs. "I just think they deserve to be compensated."

My mouth drops open. I'm about to argue with him, but then the door to the private room opens and I panic. "Add it to my bill," I tell him, and he nods affably. I'm a fucking chump, but at least I'm not going to be the butt of my brothers' jokes for the next god knows how long.

"Everything okay?" Brooks asks, popping his head around the door. "Myles wanted to come out but I think I held him off."

"Everything is fine," I tell my younger brother. "Thanks."

"No problem. You coming back in?" he asks.

"I'll be there in ten minutes. I just gotta make a phone call." And calm the fuck down.

"Okay."

He disappears, as do Lindy and the ladies, who all blow me a kiss as they walk away. I turn to the security guard. "Nobody is allowed in there without my express permission," I tell him.

"Fine by me." He shrugs.

"Good. I'm just going to make a call. I'll be back in five minutes." I give him a glare. "Nobody."

"Sure."

Striding across the lurid carpet I make my way to a quiet corner and unlock my phone, pulling up Tessa's name on the screen.

It goes straight to voicemail this time, not even ringing. Jesus, I need to talk to her. The only thing that's stopping me from getting on a flight to New York right now is my brother and the fact that I love him to fucking heaven and back.

"Carmichael," I say into the phone. "It's me. Stop ignoring me. Call me back."

But she doesn't.

CHAPTER
EIGHTEEN

TESSA

"So is everybody clear on what we need to do?" I ask, looking around the team. We're all seated around the large oak table in the boardroom of Hampshire PR. There are donuts and coffee and everybody's in a good mood because we've received the official notification that the Exuma contract has been signed by all parties. Which is great, but I need them to concentrate now because winning the contract was easy compared to the work ahead of us.

"Of course," Gina murmurs, smiling at me. "And I'll send out a reminder to everybody in an email. With a tracker they need to update daily."

"Thank you." I give her a smile because she's such a life saver. "And remember that drinks are on the business this Friday night." Roman has already given me the go-ahead to put money behind the bar. I won't be going but Gina will arrange it, then type up the invoices and make sure everything's done properly.

I go to shut down my laptop, and suddenly everybody

stops talking. The sudden hush makes me frown, and when I look up Linc is standing in the doorway, his eyes on me.

He doesn't look happy. Which is good, because I don't need anybody in this room knowing what happened while we were away. He tried to call me a few times over the weekend but with my newfound decision to move on I ignored them all.

Everybody starts to crowd around Linc, the conversation starting up again. But he ignores them, opting to walk over to me.

"Can I have a word, please?" he says.

There's an edge to his tone that sends a shiver down my spine. "I'm busy," I tell him, because I'm a coward at heart.

"You've just finished a meeting," he says, his gaze still on my face. "I heard you."

"You were waiting outside?" I frown.

"I would hate to interrupt you," he says. And I know in my heart he's talking about all those ignored calls. And messages. Okay, so there were more than a few. But I'm also kind of annoyed because he doesn't get to call me like all is fine after radio silence for over a week.

"Give me a minute," I say. "I need to go to the ladies' room. I'll come to your office."

"Oh no." He shakes his head. "I'll come to yours."

"Yours is more private." Whatever he wants to say to me, I don't want my staff overhearing.

"And if I go to mine, you won't come. So I'll be waiting for you in your office."

"Fine." I sigh. "Whatever."

I turn to the left, heading for the ladies' room, while he turns to the right, presumably heading straight for my office. I should have told him to take my laptop, because I'm going to have to put it on the bathroom counter.

Making a note to clean it thoroughly with one of those handy wipes that Gina keeps in her drawer, I set it down and stare at my reflection in the mirror, wanting to silently scream.

Because everything about him feels electric. Like he's lighting me up after being dark for so long.

He ignored you for days, I remind myself. And that's all I need to get calm again.

I won't go through this again. I won't let myself be second best. I'm way too old to be playing games, even if they do make my blood heat up. I square my shoulders and check my makeup, adding a little more lipstick. Then I wipe it off because I don't want him to think I put it on for him.

He isn't in my office when I get back. He's sitting on the corner of Gina's desk, and they're both laughing at something.

"Go on in," I say to Linc, nodding at my office door. "I'll be in there in a minute."

He winks at Gina and she grins back.

"Et tu, Brutus," I mutter to her.

"Do you mean Judas?" she asks, still smiling as though I just said the funniest quip ever. And she knows exactly what I mean.

"No. I mean the one who stabbed Julius Caesar in the back."

She tips her head to look at me, still smiling.

"It doesn't matter. Can I borrow a wipe please? Actually, make that two." Because I'll wipe down anything Linc touches when he leaves. I don't know where he's been. Meow, I am testy today.

Gina whips out two little packets and passes them to me. "Thank you," I tell her, then I walk into my office, taking a deep breath.

"Salinger," I murmur, carrying my laptop over to my desk. I may as well clean it while he talks to me. It'll give me something to do with my hands. But before I can put it down, he's taking it from me.

"I wouldn't do that..." I say and then I trail off. If he wants germs from the bathroom all over him, then have at it.

He opens it up and looks at the screen. "Hmm."

"What are you doing?" I ask him.

"Just checking to see if it's working. I wasn't sure if you had a problem with all your devices or just your phone."

"Haha." I take it from him. "And by the way, that was sitting on the counter in the ladies' bathroom a minute ago. You may want to wash your hands."

He rolls his eyes at me. "My face was between your thighs last week and I didn't wash that either."

My eyes widen. "Lincoln." I glance at the door. It's shut, thank god, but I wouldn't put it past my team to be listening with a glass held up to the door.

"So I'm Lincoln now," he says. "Not Salinger. Not Linc."

"Can we stop this?" I ask him, feeling pained. "You're the one who walked away and didn't call me. So don't be an ass about it."

"I called you all weekend."

"After a week of nothing," I point out.

"I'm sorry," he says. "I should have called you earlier. But I'm trying to make up for it. And you didn't call me either," he says and I roll my eyes.

"I've been busy," I tell him. He raises a brow to let me know he isn't buying it. "Okay," I continue. "I just don't think there's anything left for us to say to each other."

"What the hell does that mean?" He's leaning on my desk. Something else I'm going to have to clean. "Didn't we have the best time in Exuma? And now you're like this." He waves his hands at me. "What's wrong with you?"

"You haven't exactly been lonely since you left the island," I counter. "I saw the photograph."

He frowns. "What photograph?"

"The one of you and your friend in Paris."

He blinks, not understanding. And now I'm the one feeling annoyed. With myself mostly, for caring.

"It doesn't matter anyway," I say. "I think we can both agree that what happened in Exuma stays there, right?"

"You know that's Vegas, right?"

I look at him. "And you were in Vegas for the weekend." Not that I was stalking him. I know because he told me about his brother's bachelor party.

"Yes. And for the record, nothing happened there either." He lifts a brow. "Apart from the strippers that I didn't order and sent away."

"You were with strippers?" My voice raises. And he immediately clamps his hand over my mouth to stop the office from hearing me.

I pull it away, grimacing. "Your hand is covered in germs."

"So's yours," he points out. "And when did you get to be such a germophobe?"

I let out a long breath. "This is stupid. Can't we just pretend that Exuma never happened?"

Linc blinks. "Is that what you want?"

My chest feels so tight it hurts. "I just don't want to deal with drama," I tell him. "I have so much going on in my life right now. The last few years have been full of it."

"You think I bring drama?" he asks.

"Yes. And I'm too old for it. I'm not a starry eyed kid. I've got a child. A good job. A home that looks like it's a bomb site. I don't need this, too."

His brows pinch as he listens to me. "I don't understand what you're saying."

I don't either. Not really. "I'm saying that Exuma was..." I sigh. "It was everything. And I'm so grateful for all you did for me. You made me feel special. Made me feel alive." I give him a watery smile and his jaw tightens. "But you're a playboy. Younger than me. And I have Zoe to think of. I need my life to be stable, secure. Drama free."

"Are you breaking this off?" he asks, his voice thick.

"There's nothing to break off," I breathe. "We're not an item. We're just two people that had sex." Mind blowingly delicious sex.

His expression changes. He looks hurt and I hate it. But I made myself a promise that I'd always be honest. After Jared's lies, it's the one thing I can do.

No matter how much it hurts.

He lets out a long breath. "If that's what you really want."

"Thank you," I whisper again. "We'll always have Exuma, won't we?"

He blinks, those thick lashes of his sweeping down. "Don't quote fucking *Casablanca* to me, Carmichael," he growls, turning his back to me.

"Linc…" I call out, but he's already halfway out of the door. He slams it behind him and I take a deep breath.

I should feel better but I don't. I've done nothing but think about this all weekend, and I know it's for the best. So why does it feel like I've just stabbed a knife in my own heart?

———

The knife gets twisted even harder the following week when a courier arrives at the office with a manilla envelope containing four tickets to the Linebackers concert. I haven't heard from Linc at all. There's been no sign of him in the office and I don't ask anybody where he is.

It doesn't stop me from feeling sick when I see four all access passes, along with a printout of what time we need to arrive and directions to the stage door at the arena.

"Oh my God," Zoe squeals when I arrive home and show her the tickets and passes. Her face is pink with excitement. "How many are there?"

"Four. You can bring two friends. I just have to get them the details before hand." I received an email from somebody who works with the band earlier. I'm guessing Linc passed on my email.

He didn't have to do this. He could have been churlish and walked away with the tickets after the way things ended.

But he didn't. And he's made Zoe so happy. I need to thank him somehow.

"So they can run a security check, I bet," Zoe says. "I can't believe I'm going to meet them. Do you think they'll let us take pictures?"

"I'm pretty sure that's part of the meet and greet," I tell her. I'm so happy she's happy, I really am. But I haven't stopped feeling sick since Linc walked out of the office. And it had nothing to do with all the germs I had to clean up.

And everything to do with the fact that I feel like a bitch.

"Can I go and tell my friends about these?" Zoe asks, picking up the tickets again.

"Of course. Who are you inviting?" I ask, only mildly interested because I'll be the one responsible for them.

"I don't know yet," she admits. "I'm going to let them audition for them. If they want to come meet the band they'll have to impress me first."

"Zoe," I say, a warning tone in my voice. "That's not a nice way to treat your friends."

"I'm joking." She rolls her eyes as she stands up and blows me a kiss. "I'd never treat my friends like that."

No, she wouldn't. But I did. I think I'm getting a headache.

———

LINC

. . .

"Why are we getting drunk again?" Brooks asks me as the server comes over and pours another glass of G. Scott Carter's finest whiskey into our glasses. I motion at her to leave the bottle.

Because I want to sink myself into oblivion tonight. I've spent another week in Europe – London and Rome this time, sorting things out for Roman. Staring at my phone and wanting to call her. I saw her today for the first time since our argument in her office. She was in a meeting and I could see her through the glass windows of the boardroom.

She didn't see me.

"Because it's been a long day," I sigh. "And I don't want to go home alone."

"As flattered as I am," Brooks says, lifting his glass. "You'll still be going home alone. Or at least not with me." He looks around the club. Even though it's early in the evening, it's full of Manhattan's finest. Rich men, beautiful women.

And us.

There's a blonde in the corner who keeps looking over at me. Our gazes catch as I down my glass of whiskey, letting the liquid burn my throat.

I pull my eyes away. I'm not fucking interested.

And isn't that one for the books?

"So Vegas went well," Brooks says, as I pour myself another glass.

"Uh uh."

"Apart from the escorts." He grins.

I finish up my glass of whiskey and put it on the table, saying nothing.

"Well this is scintillating conversation," Brooks mutters, crossing his legs. "Why don't you go hit up that killer blonde? She can't take her eyes off you. Then I can go home and get some sleep."

"You're supposed to be cheering me up," I tell him.

"How? You won't tell me what's wrong even though

you've had a face like thunder ever since we walked in. You won't talk to anybody else. And that," he says, pointing at the bottle. "Is gonna cost you five hundred dollars when you could have drunk one of your bottles at home for free."

The music changes and I wince. The fucking Linebackers. This song is everywhere right now and I hate it with a passion. The blonde is swaying to the sound of the lead singer – Ryker – telling the girl that he'll never settle down.

Wise fucking man.

"I got tickets to see this band later in the week," I tell him. My voice is slurring. Shit, I'm more drunk than I thought. I swallow another mouthful anyway.

"The Linebackers?" Brooks asks. "Oh yeah, you did something with their music, didn't you?"

They provided the soundtrack to an advert I was involved in. "Yeah. But I'm not going."

"Why?" Brooks looks like he's going to laugh. Which is all I need. I took care of this kid since the day he was born. I've spent my life protecting him.

I'm just gonna need him to return the favor tonight.

"Because *she's* going."

My brother lifts a brow. "Oh this is getting interesting. Who is she?"

"Tessa Carmichael."

"Right." He smiles. "The woman you went to Exuma with?"

"How do you know about that?"

"Group chat," he says. "Myles mentioned you'd taken the trip with some woman."

"I didn't see it." I frown.

"Because you flounced out of it after Holden got all pissy with you when you were in Exuma."

"Did I? Can you invite me back in?" I ask.

He holds his phone up. "Done. So let's go back to the subject. You and this Tessa chick…"

"She's not a chick," I tell him. "She's a woman." Every single inch of her. I won't let him dismiss her like she's not important. Because she's important in every way.

His lip curls. "I bet she is."

And now I'm annoyed because he's paying attention to her. Christ, I'm need some sleep. The combination of jet lag and expensive whiskey isn't making me feel good.

"She thinks I'm full of drama," I say, stumbling over the last word. It comes out half formed.

Brooks burst out laughing. "Of course you are. But women throw themselves at you anyway. Like that blonde over there."

I follow the line of his stare. Yeah, she's still looking.

And for a minute, just a minute, I consider going over to talk to her. To make me feel better.

But then that'll prove Carmichael right. Because I've definitely decided she's Carmichael. She hates my guts again for some reason.

I liked it better when she liked me. Really liked me. When she came on my mouth and my dick and my fingers.

"Linc?" Brooks says.

"Huh?" I open my eyes, not even realizing I'd closed them. But I'm so damn tired. Of everything.

"You have company." Brooks says, tilting his head my way. The blonde is standing next to me, looking down at me with a smile on her face.

"Hi," she says. "I'm Sapphire."

"Of course you are," I reply. "But no thank you."

CHAPTER
NINETEEN

TESSA

"No." Zoe shakes her head vehemently. "You're not wearing that. We're going to a rock concert not a corporate event."

I look down at my outfit. A pair of black pants and a white top. "What's wrong with this?" I ask her. She huffs, grabbing my hand and dragging me back into my bedroom, being careful to avoid the holes in the floor. I think we could avoid them with our eyes closed. I imagine that even when it's all repaired we'll be jumping over where they used to be.

"Sit," she says, pointing at my bed. "You need to start dressing your age."

"I do dress my age," I protest. I think I have good style. "I just don't go to concerts very often."

She rifles through my closet and pulls out a pair of black jeans. They're old. Like super old.

"Vintage," she murmurs, and I wince, feeling ancient.

"I thought you wanted me to dress young?" I say, frowning.

"I want you to dress cool," she tells me. "And boot cuts

are back in. Put them on." She throws the jeans at me then turns back around, muttering to herself as she goes through my tops.

"This might work," she says, tipping her head to the side. "No, too mom like."

"I am a mom," I remind her. And tonight I'm a mom to three over excited teenage girls. I'm not looking forward to it.

"You're never gonna get a guy if you don't make an effort," she says. "Here we go. Perfect." She pulls out a sequined top, though it looks more like a handkerchief. It's stretchy and cropped and I think I wore it before I even met Jared.

"I didn't know I had that anymore," I say, shaking my head.

"Put it on," Zoe says again. I roll my eyes at her but I do as I'm told. The jeans are cut low at the waist, so the buttons hit just above my hipbones. And the top doesn't start until above my navel.

"Zo, I'm not wearing this out," I tell her. "I haven't bared my stomach in years."

"But you have a tan," she points out. "You look fabulous."

"Let me change the top, okay?" I say, looking to compromise. "I'll keep the jeans." To be honest, I'm surprised they even fit me. The divorce diet did it's thing, I guess. I lost over ten pounds after Jared left me. And with the renovating keeping me fit, it's stayed off.

"Okay you can change the top," Zoe concedes. "But I'll choose it. And you have to let me do your hair.

An hour later we arrive at Madison Square Garden, where Zoe's friends are waiting with their parents. Thank god I changed my top, they'd probably have dragged their daughters back home if they'd caught sight of how I looked earlier.

But right now, I have to admit, I feel good. Zoe did a great job with my hair, curling it using some kind of YouTube tutorial so it tumbles over my shoulders. And after a fierce debate I put on some natural looking makeup. I'm wearing a cute bustier style top that I bought eight years ago and only wore once, because Jared hated it. And a jacket with rolled up sleeves, because when I'm out here I feel better covered up.

Slutty chic, Angela called it when I sent her a photo. It made me laugh. Something I haven't done in more than a week. I needed it.

I arrange to meet the girls' parents at the parking lot at the end of the show, and then we head to the crew entrance, where we're scheduled to meet Sondra, the band's PA. I give our names to the security guard, who radios through, and within a minute Sondra's at the door, ushering us inside.

There are people everywhere. Crew rushing around, security guards looking serious as they talk to each other through their radios, and then we hit a line of people, talking excitedly. Sondra ushers us past them. "That's the line for the meet and greet," she tells us.

"Do we need to join it?" I ask. "At the back?"

She shakes her head. "Backstage pass means you go straight into the room.

Zoe grabs my hand and squeezes it. I look at her and I can see how tight her facial muscles are. She's vibrating with nervous excitement.

"You're going to be fine," I tell her.

"But this is the Linebackers." She looks at her friends. They all look as panicked as she does.

"Just imagine they're all naked," I say, then immediately regret it. "No scrap that. And don't tell your parents I said that."

The room is bigger than I expected. And fuller, too. The five band members are standing in front of a banner, having their photographs taken with fans. Sondra waves at one of them who waves back, as she ushers us into another, smaller room at the side.

"Help yourself to food and drinks," she says, then glances at Zoe and her friends. "The non-alcoholic stuff."

"They won't be touching anything alcoholic," I tell her, following the three teenage girls into the room. As soon as the door closes behind us they squeal and run into each others' arms, jumping up and down.

"Did you see Ryker looking at us?" her friend Maisie asks.

"Oh my God, he's so sexy," her other friend, Alice, agrees.

"If he talks to me I'm gonna die. I swear to God." Maisie's face looks pale.

A minute later more people start to pour in. They're all different ages, and after talking to one kind looking lady a little older than me I discover they're family members. A few more fans with backstage passes come in, then finally the band walks in and everybody cheers.

When I look over at Zoe she's actually shaking. Sondra leads the band over to her and her friends.

"This is the Salinger's group," she tells them. "And they're kids, so no swearing."

"Pinky fucking promise," the guy whose name I think is Ryker says. Zoe and her friends collapse into fits of giggles.

Sondra walks over to me. "You want your photo taken with them too?" she asks.

I shake my head. "I'm here for Zoe."

"Not a fan?"

There's only one answer to that when I'm here on their dime. "I like their music. I just don't want to take their time up when so many others are here."

"It's okay," Sondra says. "You don't have to love them. It'd do them some good to know that not every woman would throw themselves on the floor when they're around." She motions over at them. "Hey Ryker?"

He lifts his head up. "Yeah?"

"Come over here."

"No honestly," I say quickly. "I don't need a photograph."

He saunters over with all the confidence of a man at the top of his game. The slight swagger to his walk reminds me of Linc.

"I need to introduce you to somebody," Sondra says, grinning. "A woman who doesn't think you're hot."

My cheeks flush. "I didn't say that," I tell him quickly. My eyes meet Ryker's. "I'm sorry, I just…"

"She just thinks you're not all that." Sondra blows him a kiss and Ryker grins back.

"Ignore her," he says to me. "Ryker." He holds out his hand.

"Tessa," I say, taking it. His fingers curl around mine.

"I'll dedicate a song to you," he says. "See if you'll change your mind and want me after the concert."

"I'm going home straight after the concert," I tell him, knowing it's just some banter. I'm pretty sure he has his post-concert entertainment already lined up. "But thanks anyway."

"Who are you with again?" he asks, looking around.

"She's one of Salinger's," Sondra tells him.

"You're Salinger's girl?" he asks. And I start blushing again. It's so hot in here. I'd take my jacket off, but I'm not showing this bustier off in here. It's for the darkness of the concert only.

"I can't remember the last time anybody called me a girl," I tell him, and he laughs. "And I'm definitely not Salinger's."

"Where is he, anyway?" He looks over my shoulder.

"He couldn't come," I say, and my throat tightens.

"Shame. Next time you see him tell him I said hi."

He moves on to another group, and before too long the band leaves the room altogether, and the rest of us are led to the special VIP area in front of the stage, where there are seats and a standing area.

"Can we go to the front?" Zoe asks, her face as flushed as mine.

I nod. "Yes, but don't leave this space without me." I'm pretty sure they can't anyway. It's carefully guarded. Plus there's only one way in and one way out and if I stay where I am they'd have to walk right past me to get to the bathrooms.

"We're not going anywhere," Zoe promises. She and her friends walk to the front of the stage, the three of them talking and giggling. I can't remember the last time I saw her this happy. And damn it, I'm going to send Linc a text. Right now.

Thank you for the tickets. We're here right now. You've made three teenage girls very happy. – Tessa

There's no reply, but I didn't expect there to be. He's probably out wining and dining a beautiful French woman. More people start to arrive and the temperature in the auditorium rises about three degrees. I'm starting to sweat. The lights are low enough for me to take off my jacket, so I lay it on the seat behind me, and glance over at Zoe and her friends again.

They haven't moved an inch.

"Carmichael."

The low voice sends a shiver down my spine. I recognize it instantly. My body does, too. It's like every cell stands to attention. The way they've all been starved of it since I came back from Exuma.

I turn to look at him. He's wearing a pair of jeans and a black t-shirt. He looks stupidly sexy.

"I didn't think you were coming," I say. A big cheer erupts as the opening band comes out and takes their places. More people file into the VIP area and Linc is forced to step closer. He's immediately behind me, so close I can feel the warmth of his chest against my back.

"I wasn't going to," he says. "I changed my mind."

"I sent you a text," I tell him.

"I saw it." His voice is soft against my ear. "Where's Zoe?"

It makes my heart feel a little full when he says her name. He remembered it. "Over there." I point at her and her friends. They're so close to the stage they could climb on it.

Dear God, I hope they don't.

"Why aren't you with them?" he asks.

"I figured I'd let them have a little fun without me. Nobody likes their mom all up in their business."

He gives a little chuckle. "I guess not." There's a pause. "I like your top."

I look down at the bustier. It's laced at the front, with little capped shoulders. It clings to me like a second skin. "Thanks. This was the second choice. You should have seen the top Zoe tried to make me wear. It was like a handkerchief."

"I would definitely have liked to see that," he confirms. I roll my eyes but I like it anyway.

Here's the problem. I like him. Despite the drama and the way things ended. It's stupid, but I've missed him.

"I'm glad you came," I say.

"Are you?" He sounds surprised.

"Yes. They're your friends. I would have hated for you to miss it because of me." I let out a breath. "And I kind of missed you."

The biggest smile pulls at his lips. "I kind of missed you too, Carmichael."

Somebody pushes past us, and I stumble backward, into his hard chest. Linc puts his hands on my bare arms to steady me. His fingers are soft, but I still shiver at his touch.

"Careful," he murmurs. But he doesn't let go of me.

Before I can reply the opening band begins. The sound is almost deafening in the VIP area. I'm glad I insisted the girls wear ear protection for the concert, despite their protests.

The band is playing an upbeat number. The female singer is telling us she's never gonna stop fighting. People are dancing around us, and Linc is still holding my arms.

I lean back against him, and for a moment he tenses.

Then he slides his arms around my waist.

"This okay?" he shouts in my ear.

"Yeah. Just move if Zoe looks." But she won't. She and her friends are dancing like crazy, screaming along with the words. Linc places his flat palm against my stomach, pulling me closer.

Every part of me clenches.

My nipples are hard against the bustier. My skin is heated. He dips his head and presses his nose against my throat, as though he's breathing me in.

"Fuck I've really missed you." He brushes his lips against my neck and I start to feel unsteady.

"Linc."

"I know. I'm keeping it PG."

He starts moving me to the rhythm of the music, his hands still on me. Each song fades into the next, and all I can think about is the way he makes me feel.

Like I'm alive again. Like I'm special. And maybe I like the drama a little. Isn't it a part of life, along with the tears and laughter? I feel like I'm at a crossroads, having to choose between the dull, straight road ahead of me, and the twisty one that winds into a forest and gets lost in the hills. I can't see where it ends up but it looks so much more enticing.

I want that. I want him.

He lets me go when the band comes to the end of their set and there's a little break as the crew sets up for the Linebackers. Zoe runs over to me. "Mom, I need the bathroom."

I look over at her friends and then back at Zoe. "We all go together," I remind her. "I can't leave your friends unsupervised and only take you. Go get them."

"But we need to save our spot," Zoe says. "For the Linebackers."

"I'll go save your spot."

Zoe looks up, surprised at the sound of Linc's deep voice.

"Zoe, you remember Linc," I say. "He organized all this."

"Oh my God, Mom said you weren't coming." She throws her arms around him. "Thank you, thank you."

He holds his arms out to the side like he's being patted down at an airport, and I smile at him, because Linc is never taken by surprise like this. Then he listens intently as she babbles on about how this is the best night of her life.

"Zo, go get your friends," I remind her. Because the crew looks like they're almost done setting up.

There's no line for the VIP bathroom, so we're back in the auditorium before they dim the lights for the main act. Linc has patiently saved the girls' spot. He's also sweet talked the people around them to make sure they take care of the girls.

He's pretty much a celebrity as far as the front row is concerned.

And when he comes back to me, the lights dim. His hand touches the curve of my spine and electricity sizzles between us.

I've no idea what's happening here, if I'm honest. But I want to enjoy the moment. Because I really am happy he turned up.

The band appears on stage and the screams are deafening. Even Linc frowns.

"I got told today that not every woman would take her panties off for me," Ryker says into the mic, and all the women start screaming again. His eyes scan the VIP area and I shrink back into Linc, hoping he can't see me.

Shit.

"So this one is for Tessa. Apparently the only woman in the world who prefers Victoria's Secret to Ryker Wakefield."

He strums his guitar and the drums kick in and fifty thousand fans start to throw themselves around the sound of their favorite band.

Even in the VIP area it's getting a little violent. Linc slips his arms around me protectively.

"What was that about?" he asks. I can't tell from his voice if he's annoyed or amused.

"Just something I said in the VIP room."

"Well I'm glad it's not only me who gets the brush off." His voice tickles my ear.

I turn to look at him. "You didn't get the brush off in Exuma."

He grins. "No I didn't."

Then he slides his lips down my neck to the dip of my shoulder, and I spend the rest of the concert in some kind of messed up haze.

CHAPTER
TWENTY

TESSA

"I'm taking you home," Linc says after the show as we walk through the sultry evening air. Zoe's friends are with their parents now, so I only have to keep an eye out for her. There are people everywhere. A group of girls walk past us singing a Linebacker song. They're wearing Linebackers football jerseys and giggle all the way.

"Don't be silly." I smile at him. "We can take the subway."

"My car is right there," Linc says, pointing to the corner of the parking lot. "The trains are gonna be jammed. It'll take you hours to get home."

"Mom," Zoe says, frowning at me. "Don't make me ride the subway when this nice man is offering to drive us."

I glance at Linc. He's grinning because Zoe called him a nice man.

She's also wearing a Linebackers t-shirt, signed by the band. Linc arranged for each of the girls to get one.

"Please let me take you home," Linc says, his eyes still not leaving mine. "Otherwise I'll have to go party with the band."

"The band wants you to party with them?" Zoe asks, her mouth dropping open. "Like one of those all night debauched things?" She leans closer, as though she's expecting more information.

"Yes. And I don't want to." Linc's talking directly to Zoe now, and she's smiling up at him. Damn, the old Salinger charm works perfectly on thirteen-year-olds, too. "But I want to go to bed with a cup of cocoa and a good book. So please do me a favor and let me drive you both home."

Zoe looks torn. Knowing somebody who parties with the band is extra kudos. But she also has that selfish gene that most teenagers do.

"I mean, you do look tired," she concedes.

"I'm exhausted." He nods, his expression totally serious.

"And you got us the tickets, so I should probably do you the favor." She's still teetering between her two desires. I'm trying not to smile.

He shakes his head. "No, that's not how it works. The tickets were a gift. You said thank you. You don't owe me anything else."

Zoe blinks. "I don't?"

"No. And do me a favor. When you're older, if a guy takes you to dinner or gives you a gift, remember you don't owe him anything either."

Oh. My. God. Salinger is giving dating lessons to my thirteen year old. I don't know whether to laugh or cry.

The thing is, I like that he's making the distinction. How many times when I was younger did I go out for dinner with a guy and feel bad for not putting out after?

"I'd always pay half," Zoe says and Linc smiles and nods.

"That's very wise."

"Where's your car again?" I ask him, and his eyes crinkle, like he knows he's won.

"Over there." He points at a sleek black Audi. Zoe runs over to it and we follow behind.

"Just so you know, I'm absolutely expecting you to put out since I got the tickets," Linc murmurs in my ear.

I start to laugh. "We're not even dating."

"Yeah, well. We'll be talking about that very soon."

I turn to look at him. "Zoe's watching," I remind him. And yes, I let him kiss me in the auditorium. It felt good. Too good.

But here, in front of her, I need to be the mom again.

"I know. I'm keeping it completely PG." He looks over at Zoe. "You can pull the handle. It'll unlock automatically."

She does as he says and sure enough the door opens. "Cool," she says.

"Talking about putting out isn't PG," I tell him in a low voice.

"The talking is. The doing isn't. And the things I fucking want to do to you, Carmichael. It'll make Exuma look like a Disney movie."

I start to laugh again. It's a mixture from the high of the concert and the way he's so persistent.

It's nice. I like feeling wanted.

And I'm stupidly attracted to this man even if I don't want to be.

"You're driving us home and then you're leaving," I tell him. "That's it, right? You know you can't come in for coffee."

"I wouldn't dream of it," he says, looking absurdly pleased with himself. "I just want to make sure you both get home safely."

Oh. He's gone from being dirty to sweet in one easy move.

The Linc Salinger effect gets everybody eventually. Including me.

———

LINC

. . .

"What the fuck happened to you last night?" Ryker asks me. It's late morning and we're eating brunch in his hotel room. He looks exhausted, but the band has another show tonight, so he can't sleep off the hangover he managed to cause himself.

"I needed to get Tessa and her daughter home," I tell him, taking a bite of a pastry. My stomach growls with appreciation.

"The chick from last night. Did she like my song?" He gives me a sly look, and I know he's trolling me.

"She kept her panties on, if that's what you're asking," I say dryly. I'm not worried about him. For starters, Ryker can't hold a relationship down for two seconds.

"For you too?" Ryker asks, grinning. "Oh man, you've lost your touch."

"I don't have a touch," I say, rolling my eyes. Because that's the problem that Tessa has with me. She thinks I'm not serious. That I'm drama.

I need to clean up my reputation.

It's not a completely unfair reputation either.

"How do you know her anyway?" Ryker asks. Sondra comes in with a pile of photographs for him to sign. He takes the pen and squiggles across each one, while still looking at me.

"We work together."

"Hoo boy. That'll be a mess when you end things." Ryker lifts a brow. "This is why I don't get the whole corporate culture, non-fraternization thing. Just join a band. Everybody sleeps with everybody then we all move on to the next one like we're on a merry go round."

"There's no non-fraternization clause at my work." Because yes, I've checked. Mostly because I know how much Tessa needs this job. I'm not going to do anything that puts her livelihood in danger.

"Yeah, but you know why there should be, right?" Ryker smirks. "You've seen *Mad Men*. All that fucking drama when it goes wrong. Which it always does."

Drama. There's that word again.

The one thing that Tessa doesn't want is drama.

I finish my coffee and check my watch. Shit, it's later than I thought. "I've gotta go," I say, standing.

"What's the rush, my man?"

"Got a final fitting for my groomsman suit," I tell him. "My brother's getting married."

"Which one?"

Once again, I'm surprised that Ryker remembers this stuff. We spent a weekend together filming almost two years ago. And yeah, we get together for a drink whenever he's in New York, but the man must have an encyclopedic brain.

"Holden. The doctor."

"Jesus. They're all getting shot down one by one. What is this, the third wedding in recent years?"

"Fourth."

Ryker lets out a low whistle. "Aren't you the fifth brother?"

Wikipedia needs to use this man's mind as a server. How does he keep that much information in his brain when at least half of it has to be pickled by alcohol. "Yeah, that's right."

"So it's your turn next then." He starts to laugh. "Can you imagine it? Linc Salinger, settling down and saying I do."

But I'm not laughing. Because I hate that even Ryker thinks I have a reputation. If he thinks that, what chance do I stand with Carmichael?

"Gotta go," I say. "See you later."

"Not if I see you first." Ryker stands and gives me a hug. "And by the way, Salinger. Your girl is beautiful. Now go sort your fucking life out."

———

"I need you to fly to London tomorrow," Roman tells me as we take the elevator up to his office. I've just come back from the suit fitting. At first, Holden tried to coordinate it so we'd all be at the tailors at the same time, but in the end we each made our own appointments.

Which is good. Because I still haven't quite gotten over the bachelor party. I need another week or two before I meet up with my brothers again.

"Tomorrow?" I frown. "Why?"

"Because a client is pissed." He looks at me with a 'why else?' expression. "I've asked my PA to book your flights. Should only take a couple of days. You can check in with Celine in Paris on your way back." He grins at me. "You can spend the weekend there. Enjoy the city in spring."

I've been to Paris about twenty times in the past two years. I love the place, but the thought of going there now makes my stomach twist.

The elevator pings and the doors open. Roman steps out and I follow him.

"Let me see if I can talk to them by video," I say, trying to smooth the sting of my words. "Save the cost of a flight and the environment all at the same time."

"If I wanted to do it by Zoom I'd do it myself," Roman tells me. His voice is even but I can tell he's annoyed.

I'm his troubleshooter. Always up in the air. Linc the traveler.

But I want to stay right here for a while.

"I have an appointment," I tell him. "I can't change it."

"Who with?" he asks, frowning. We've made it to the offices. The desks are only half full because there's a big presentation going on in the boardroom. But when I glance over at the corner office I see Tessa there, and my throat tightens.

She's leaning over her laptop, her hair pulled back into a bun, revealing the contours of her face. She's wearing a white silk blouse that I can almost feel between my fingers. I imagine pulling at it until the buttons pop open and her luscious body is revealed.

If I ran this company I'd stride into her office and fuck her over the desk until we were both breathless and sated.

"Salinger?" Roman prompts. "What's the appointment?"

"Just a check up with the doctor," I lie, aware that I'm really bad at it. "And it's my brother's wedding the following weekend. I've booked PTO for that." Because I know that Roman's next suggestion will be for me to go next week instead.

Roman looks frustrated. "But I need you in the air, Linc. You're the secret weapon here. I need to have somebody I can rely on to go anywhere at a moment's notice."

I look over at Tessa's office again. She's stopped typing and is looking at her phone.

She's so damn beautiful it makes my heart hurt.

And then she turns and catches me and Roman standing there in the hallway. She gives me the sweetest of fucking smiles.

"After the wedding," I tell him. "I'll be back on my 'A' game. I promise."

"Good." Roman nods. "Now go see if you can set up that damn video call."

———

TESSA

I watch as Roman finishes talking to Linc about something. I can't tell what it is, but Roman's frowning which is never good. Linc stands there for a moment, then runs his hand through his hair and turns to look at me again.

Our gazes connect and it makes me breathless.

And then he starts walking toward me. Somebody in the main office calls out his name and he nods, but his steps don't falter as he walks into my office and closes the door behind him.

"What are you doing this weekend?" he asks me.

I look up at him, surprised. "Hi," I say, smiling.

"Hi. This weekend?"

"We're refinishing the living room floor." The electricians have promised me they'll be done with the wiring by Friday. Which means we can finally sand and varnish the floor. The hole-free floor.

I'm so excited I could burst.

"Who's we?" he asks, looking wary.

"Zoe and me," I say. "Though she may be more of a hindrance than a help."

"What time are you starting?"

Ooh, he's very abrupt today. "Did you wake up on the wrong side of the bed?" I ask him. "Was it the concert? Did you have ringing in your ears last night?"

"Something like that," he mutters and I have to bite down my smile.

"Thank you for the ride home," I tell him. "Zoe didn't stop talking about you this morning. She wanted to know everything about you. I think she likes you as much as she likes Ryker."

"Yeah, well he liked you."

"How do you know?" I tip my head to the side.

"Because I had brunch with him. He was asking about you." He looks grumpy and I hate that I like that. "He wanted to know if you kept your panties on."

I start to laugh and that makes Linc scowl. "What did you tell him?"

"That the only person you'll be throwing your panties at is

me." He steps closer to my desk. "So what time do you want me?"

"I'm sorry?" I blink. "Where?"

"At your house on Saturday. I'm coming to help you refinish the floors." He crosses his arms over his chest, as though he's waiting for me to protest. He looks like he wants me to. As though he's a soldier ready for battle.

And I'm the person he's trying to fight. Or fight for. I can't tell which.

"Do you know how to use a sander?" I ask him.

He shoots me a withering look. "Of course I know how to use a fucking sander. And how to varnish. I built my own cabin when I was eighteen."

I blink. I didn't think this man had the ability to surprise me any more. But there it is.

"You did? Where?"

"At my father's estate."

"Your father has an estate?" I repeat, shocked. "Like not just some land but an estate?"

He shrugs. "We're getting off the subject. What time are you starting on Saturday?"

"I won't be able to drag Zoe out of bed until ten. But I'll be getting everything ready before that."

"Great. I'll be there at nine. I'll bring breakfast."

I run the tip of my tongue over my dry lips, looking at him. "Why?" I ask.

"Why what? Why nine? I can make it earlier. Just give me a time and I'll be there."

"Why would you come over and sand my floor?" I ask. "You know nothing can happen."

"Then or ever?"

His question feels like a little warning shot in my chest.

"Before you answer, know this. I'll be there on Saturday no matter your answer. I want to help, but more importantly I want to spend time with you. Drama free, boring fucking time."

My lips curl into a smile.

"I'll make it so damn dull you'll have problems keeping your eyes open," he promises, his eyes warm.

"Just Saturday," I whisper. "Nothing's going to happen then."

"And ever?" he asks, his eyes not leaving mine.

"Let's just see how bored you can make me."

CHAPTER
TWENTY-ONE

TESSA

Just as promised, Linc knocks on my door at exactly nine on Saturday morning. His promptness makes me smile.

I'm wearing a ratty old pair of jeans and a black band t-shirt that keeps sliding off my shoulder, because dressing pretty just to renovate my floor seems stupid. Still, I check my reflection in the hall mirror as I pass it. My hair is up, my face scrubbed clean, because if I put on make up Zoe is going to notice.

And I don't want her to think Linc visiting is anything out of the ordinary.

When I open the door my breath catches in my throat. The smell of his shower gel makes me think of Exuma and how the bathroom would smell after he used it. But he's not dressed for Exuma. He's dressed for work. Manual, dirty work.

Torn jeans. Gray Henley. Unshaven face with just the right amount of beard. I like it a little too much.

"Good morning," I say, as he lifts up the brown bag and

tray of styrofoam cups he's holding. The smell of coffee makes my stomach growl with appreciation. I try to peer into the bag to see what food he brought.

"You're so greedy," he complains, pulling the bag away from me as he steps inside. "Nice place."

He only saw it from the outside when he dropped us off after the concert. And the exterior is pretty decent.

"Thanks. Oh, mind that hole."

I try not to giggle as he almost falls into it. "I thought you said there weren't any more holes," he mutters.

"In the living room," I say. "But the plumbers had to go down into the pipes in the hall yesterday." Now that the electric is done, the plumbers are getting ready to help me change the bathroom around. Luckily, there are no pipes beneath the living room, so I get to make it into my haven without more delay.

"Where's Zoe?" Linc asks as we walk into the kitchen. He puts the bag and tray down on the tiny table in the center.

"Give me coffee and I'll tell you," I say. "I can't think straight without one."

"You haven't made coffee yet?" he asks. "That's a mistake. Even I know you're a grouch without caffeine."

"I'm not a grouch." I pout. His eyes catch mine and there's a darkness there I feel pulse through me.

"Yes you are."

Okay, so I am.

He pulls the four cups from the tray. "I didn't know if Zoe drank coffee or would want hot chocolate, so I bought both."

"Did somebody say my name?" Zoe asks, her voice groggy as she pads into the kitchen. She's still wearing her pajamas and strands of her hair are plastered to her face from where she's been sleeping. "Oh, hi Linc."

She doesn't blink an eyelid at him being here. Like it's just another normal day.

"Morning, kiddo. Hot chocolate or coffee?" he asks her.

STRICTLY THE WORST 193

"Both. I like mocha."

For a moment I wonder if I'm in a parallel universe. One where it's completely normal for a handsome guy to walk into our place on a Saturday morning bringing food for Zoe and me.

It's amazing how easily she's accepting this. Whatever this is.

I wish it was as easy for me.

He hands her both cups and she takes a sip out of one then the other, mixing the liquid in her mouth like a damn washer.

"Put them into a cup," I tell her.

"God." Zoe rolls her eyes, but gets a mug out of the cupboard and pours half of each into it. "You need to take a chill pill, Mom."

Linc starts to laugh and I send him a narrow-eyed look which only makes him laugh more.

"Go get dressed," I tell her. "We start work in half an hour."

"What food do you have?" Zoe asks Linc, completely ignoring me.

Linc glances my way. "Pastries. But you probably need to do what your mom says."

Thank you. I send him a smile.

"Well that's sad. I was hoping for more from you," Zoe says to him.

He frowns. "Like what?"

"I thought we could gang up on Mom. Tease her. Annoy her."

He shrugs. "I can do that."

"No you can't." I purse my lips. "I thought you were on my side."

"I'm easy," he tells me, smiling. "I can be a double agent if needed."

"See, today's gonna be fun." Zoe gives him a grin.

"Go get dressed," I tell her again. This time I add in a growl.

She saunters back to her room whistling and I look at Linc.

"Drink your coffee," he says soothingly. "Everything's going to be okay."

I take a long mouthful, swallowing it down.

"You still look grumpy," he observes. "Here, take this." He pulls a croissant out of the bag and tears a piece off, sliding it between my lips. I take it into my mouth, and let out a groan. I'm hungrier than I thought.

"Mom?" Zoe shouts out from her bedroom. My head is already throbbing and it's hardly nine o'clock.

"Yes?"

"I don't have to shower, do I? Since I'll be doing manual work."

Ideally she'd shower before and after, but I've learned to pick my battles. "No, that's fine."

Linc smirks like he's enjoying himself listening to the two of us.

I take another sip of coffee. This is the strangest Saturday morning I've had in a while. I'm just recovering my Zen when Zoe calls out again.

"Hey Mom?"

"Does she always shout like that?" Linc asks. He looks impressed.

I shrug. "Yes honey?"

"Maisie and Alice are going to the movies this afternoon. Can I go?"

I wince at the volume of her shout. "No. The floor is gonna take all day."

"But they're going to see the latest Anime," she hollers. "We always see them together."

"You're breaking her heart," Linc murmurs.

"You're not helping," I tell him. Then I take a deep breath.

"Can you come out here to talk so we can stop shouting, please?"

There's a huff and she reappears, still in her pajamas, still clutching her mug. "Please can I go?" she asks. "Linc is here. It won't take as long as we thought it would."

I let out a long breath. "Okay. But we have to work super hard this morning."

"Thank you!" She jumps up, her makeshift-mocha spilling over the rim of her mug. "I'm gonna make that floor shine before I go."

She runs back into her room and Linc runs his palm down my back. "Interesting," he murmurs.

"What's interesting?" I turn to look at him.

"If Zoe's going out this afternoon that means when she leaves we'll be all alone without a chaperone. It'll officially count as our first date."

————

LINC

Carmichael can sand floors like a fucking demon. She's put me on finishing duty, polishing the wood with a higher grade sander, but she's in charge of the push-along beast, biting her lip as she maneuvers it around the room.

Zoe, taking full advantage of the fact that I'm the second laborer and have effectively taken her job, spends half her time on her phone, and the other half asking me questions about Ryker.

"When did you meet him?" she asks.

"A couple of years ago in London. They were recording some music for an advertisement." They also got so drunk that night that I ended up bailing them out of the local police station. But I don't tell Zoe that.

I'm on my knees on the floor. Carmichael and Zoe are still standing up, making me feel like I'm begging them for something.

"Does he have a girlfriend?" Zoe asks, stuffing the last of the croissants into her mouth.

"Yes. Several," I say dryly. Carmichael shoots me a look.

"PG," I mouth and she smiles.

And fuck I like her smile. Way too much. I like being here. I haven't gotten my hands dirty renovating anything in more than ten years. But there's something satisfying about it. Fun, too, when you're doing it with people you like.

"Does he have a big house?" Zoe asks, licking her finger and putting it into the bag to capture the flakes of croissant at the bottom.

"Not that I know of," I say. "He bought his mom a house in Wisconsin."

Tessa lets out a sigh. "That's sweet."

"I don't think Ryker can be described as sweet," I say, lifting a brow. Her eyes meet mine and I'm remembering the panties.

Fuck, I want Carmichael's panties. I find myself wondering what kind she's wearing today.

And then her daughter speaks again and I remember where I am.

"So does he live with his mom?" Zoe asks. "When he's not touring, I mean."

I cough out a laugh. "Jesus, no. Just flits around from hotel to hotel I think. Maybe the band rents an Airbnb sometimes."

"That's sad that he doesn't have anywhere permanent." She sounds genuinely sorry for the guy. I make a mental note to tell Ryker. This kid is killing me.

"Linc flits from hotel to hotel, too," Tessa tells Zoe.

"Do you?" Zoe tips her head to the side. "Why? Don't you have a home?"

"I have an apartment," I tell her. "But I have to travel a lot."

"Like when you and Mom went to Exuma?" she asks.

"Yeah. Usually not quite as exotic as that. Mostly Europe."

"Where in Europe? I've always wanted to go." Zoe's eyes widen.

Carmichael clears her throat and I realize I've stopped sanding. I wink and start again.

"So where have you been?" Zoe asks, following me as I move to the next area that needs sanding.

"Zo, can you at least pretend to work?" Tessa says. "Poor Linc is picking up all the slack here."

"He's doing good. I'm supervising him," Zoe says and I have to cough to hide my laugh. Carmichael's kid is clever. She has balls.

"Thanks," I say dryly. "Your approval is appreciated."

Zoe grins at me. "So, have you been to London?"

I spend the next thirty minutes trying to juggle sanding with a grade A interrogation from Carmichael's kid. Tessa sends over a few looks but I just shrug.

It's fine. Zoe's chatty, that's all. I can work with chatty. It's silence I don't like.

We break for lunch. I order some takeout to be delivered, just bagels because we don't have a lot of time, and there's still a lot of floor to cover. Tessa wants the sanding finished by tonight, then she'll wash everything down and varnish tomorrow.

"That bagel was good," Zoe says, wiping her mouth with the back of her hand. "You can come over any time."

"Thanks," I say dryly. "Any time you want to supervise, just shout."

Zoe jumps up. "And now I have to shower and get ready for the movie. Keep working hard, guys."

She runs to the bathroom and Tessa looks at me. "Have we put you off yet?"

"Nope." I bite off a mouthful of bagel. "Am I boring you yet?"

"No." There's a smile playing on her lips. "I think you're gonna have to try harder."

"I can go hard. Really hard. I'll bore the fucking tits off you."

Tessa's eyes widen. "Linc! Zoe can hear."

But then the shower turns on.

"No she can't. So how am I doing?" I ask her. "Am I domesticated enough yet?"

She looks at me carefully. "You've been a godsend. But you must be bored to death."

"I like boring," I tell her. "I love it."

And it's the truth. I can't remember the last time I had such a good time. Fully clothed, at least. Truth is, I wasn't looking forward to this. I was resigned to it, more than anything.

A chance to prove to this woman that I can be the kind of man who deserves her.

I can remember when my brother Myles started dating his now wife. He told me that his favorite way of spending time was watching a movie with her. I'd laughed at him. Probably called him boring.

But there's nothing I want more than to sit with her snuggled up against me watching a movie. I'm sick of being on a fucking plane. I'm tired of not having someone to come home to.

I want to come home knowing she's waiting for me.

Those days in Exuma spoiled everything else for me. And today has just confirmed it.

I'm ready to settle down.

"What are you thinking?" Tessa asks, her voice soft as Zoe starts to sing in the shower.

"I was wondering how long an anime movie lasts," I tell

her. "And whether you want me to bore you from behind or in the missionary position."

I'm kidding, but the way her mouth drops open is worth it.

"MOM!" Zoe's scream cuts through the small house.

Her head snaps up at the same time as I shoot to my feet, Zoe's scream sending a rush of panic through me.

We both rush to the bathroom, but I get there first.

"I'm here, honey," Tessa shouts, pushing me aside. "She might be naked," she says to me.

Oh shit. Yeah. I turn my head as the door opens and Zoe walks out. From the corner of my eye I see she's wearing a towel.

She's also holding one of the faucets. The cold one I think.

"It snapped off," she says breathlessly. "There's water everywhere."

CHAPTER
TWENTY-TWO

TESSA

Water is flowing out of the pipe where the faucet once was, shooting up like a geyser then tumbling down onto the bathroom floor. "Shit." I take the broken faucet from Zoe and try to cover up the broken pipe with it, but then the water turns into a spray that hits my face and my chest, and I'm spluttering as I step away.

"Where's your water shut off?" Linc shouts, following me inside the bathroom.

"In the kitchen."

He takes the faucet from me. "Go turn it off. I'll try to catch the water." He wrenches open the hallway closet, grabbing the mop bucket, and tries to catch the water as it flows out of the pipes. Only a little lands in the bucket, most of it lands on him.

He looks like he's dancing in the rain, and I'm trying not to laugh.

"Turn the water off, Carmichael," he shouts, narrowing his eyes at my smile. I nod and run to the kitchen.

"I'm just going to get dressed," Zoe shouts. "I need to leave in a minute."

Of course she does. It's the teenage playbook – make the mess and run. I'm pretty sure I did the same when I was a kid.

Dropping to my knees I swipe away the cleaning bottles beneath the sink, reaching in to turn the valve. Water is dripping from my face and when I look down my t-shirt is glued to my skin. I grab a clean cloth and wipe myself, but it does nothing.

"It's off," I shout to Linc.

When I get back to the bathroom he's leaning over the tub, the bucket still in his hands. His wet t-shirt is clinging to his chest, revealing the lines of his muscles. I try – and fail – not to stare.

Taking a deep breath I walk over to him. "How is it looking?" I ask him.

"Like we need to call a plumber."

It's funny, but just one little word change and I immediately feel safe. Not 'you need to call a plumber' but 'we'.

"The new bathroom install starts on Monday," I say. "There's no point in calling anybody out before then." I'm not paying for an emergency plumber to replace a faucet only for it to be replaced again next week.

"You can't be without water until Monday," Linc says, frowning. "Let me call somebody. Just to hold you over."

"No, it's fine, honestly. We've managed worse than this." And thank god Zoe is a trooper. Even if she's also the instigator of this particular mess.

"I need to go," she says, walking out of her room. She's fully dressed. And dry. She takes a look at us both. "Unless you need me to stay and help?"

Linc and I share a glance.

"No, you go," I tell her. "Have a good time."

"I'm sorry, Mom." Her eyes meet mine and I can see that she really is.

"Not your fault, kiddo. The whole bathroom should have been condemned years ago. I'm surprised it didn't happen before now."

She nods, still looking sheepish. "I'd hug you but…"

I look down at my soaked body. "Yeah, best to avoid that. What time will you be home?"

"About eight? Maisie's mom is taking us for dinner after the movie."

"Perfect. I'll see you then. Keep an eye on your phone for updates."

She grins at me and then leaves, slamming the front door closed behind her. I take a deep breath and start to shiver.

Damn, it's cold in here.

"You better go change," Linc says. "Before I get distracted by your nipples."

I look down, and sure enough, they're pushing against my wet t-shirt. And then I look back up at him.

"What about you? You should go home. Get changed. Before you catch a chill."

"And leave you to have all the fun sanding? No way." He winks. "Don't you have some clothes I can borrow?"

"I'm half your size," I say. But he follows me to the bedroom anyway. I open the door and step inside, frowning because now he's going to know I sleep on a mattress on the floor.

He's standing in the doorway when I look over at him, staring at my bed. It's impossible not to feel embarrassed.

"It's a work in progress," I tell him. "Not exactly five star."

"I wasn't thinking that," his voice is so soft it sends a shiver down my spine.

Grabbing two towels from a drawer, I throw one over at him. He catches it easily, using it to wipe his face and hair.

"What were you thinking then? I ask, pressing the towel

against my face. When I pull it away he's peeling off his wet t-shirt. I swallow hard as the hem rises, revealing the hard ridges of his stomach, the defined planes of his pectorals.

My nipples press harder against my t-shirt. Linc pulls the wet fabric over his head and then looks at me, his hair askew.

Our eyes lock.

Without saying a word, he walks over to me, taking the towel from my hands and rubbing it in my hair. He uses just the right amount of pressure, enough to soak up the water dripping from it.

"Take your top off," he tells me.

Alarmed, I catch his eye.

"Just so I can dry you off."

I nod and do as I'm told, peeling the wet t-shirt from my body and throwing it on the floor. Linc's gaze takes me in, his eyes dipping to my wet bra and my pebbled nipples.

He wraps the towel around me, drying my torso. Then his hands wrap around my back and unfasten my bra.

It doesn't feel wrong. It doesn't even feel particularly sexual. It just feels like I'm being taken care of.

I can't remember the last time that happened.

Linc drops to his knees. "Jeans next." He's close enough for me to feel the heat of his breath on my stomach. I nod and unfasten the buttons with shaky fingers, even though they're barely wet. And then he takes over, peeling the denim from my legs.

"Step out," he murmurs and I do.

"The socks can go too, Carmichael."

I hold my feet up for him to take each one off.

"And the panties?" I whisper. Because that's all I have left on.

"That depends." There's a hint of a smile on his face. He looks like a little kid in a toyshop as he takes me in.

This man makes me feel wanted. Special.

"Depends on what?" I ask him.

"Depends on if I'm the kind of guy you'd take your panties off for."

I reach down to cup his face, feeling the roughness of his jaw against my palms. My heart is thudding against my chest. This man is just so damn attractive.

"What if you take them off," I ask him, ignoring the way my heart is racing.

I can feel his smile against my hands. Taking them from his face he stands up, though he doesn't let my hands go. Instead he pulls me closer to him so there are only inches between us. He's wearing a pair of wet jeans and I'm wearing... well almost nothing.

"I've never seen anything more beautiful," he tells me. There's a truth to his voice that hits me right in the heart. "Do you know how long I've waited for this?"

"It's only been a few weeks since we left Exuma," I tell him.

"Exactly. A fucking millennium."

Our eyes lock. And part of me knows I need to be careful. It would be so easy to fall for this man. He makes me laugh, which is something I haven't done in a very long time. He helps me with my messy, falling apart house. The man even knows how to talk to my lovely, but sometimes stroppy teenage daughter.

"You okay?" he asks.

Oh, and he does that too. Checks in with me. Makes sure I'm ready.

I like that more than anything.

"I am," I breathe.

He puts his hand beneath my chin, tipping my head up until my lips are almost touching his.

"Just so I know," he murmurs. "How boring do you want this to be?"

I start to shake with laughter as he kisses me, his lips soft against mine. He runs his palm down my back, into the dip of it as his tongue slides inside my mouth. Tasting, giving, causing shivers to snake down my spine.

Before I can kiss him again he drops to his knees. "This is getting to be a habit," he mutters.

"I like you down there."

There's a wicked glint in his eye. "I know that, Carmichael. Now let's get these off." He tugs at my panties, sliding them down my hips and legs, then helping me step out of them.

"Christ you're wet." He grins and throws them to the floor, then lifts me gently onto the mattress. "Do you really sleep on the floor every night?" he asks, frowning.

"Mmm."

"Have you touched yourself in here since you've been back from Exuma?" He tips his head to the side, waiting for my answer.

"Maybe…" I feel suddenly coy. Which is stupid because this man has already been inside of me. He's made me come more times than I can remember.

"Were you thinking about me?"

My lips part. "Sometimes."

"I thought about you every time," he tells me. "Every single damn time I touched myself. Which was a fucking lot."

He pops the button of his jeans, sliding the zipper down, before forcing the wet denim to the floor. I can see the thick ridge of him pushing against his shorts. I'd forgotten how hard he could get.

No I hadn't. But I tried.

"Show me," I whisper.

"How I touched myself?" he asks, his eyes catching mine.

I nod. He pulls his shorts down and I swallow hard. His cock looks impressively thick. He palms it, moving his hand up and down. Pre-cum glistens from the tip.

"Want to know what I thought about?" he asks, his voice gritty as he moves his hand up and down.

"Tell me."

"You. Sucking me. Looking up at me with those pretty brown eyes with your lips curled around my cock. Feeling the flutter of your tongue. Seeing your eyes water as you gag on me." He's found his rhythm. His breath pants to the beat of his hand. "Fucking your face with my fingers curled into your hair." He grunts. I can't take my eyes off him. Yes, I've touched myself thinking about him, but it's been nothing compared to this.

My imagination doesn't come close to the reality. I sit up and crawl across the mattress to him.

"I'd fuck your mouth hard," he tells me. "I wouldn't be gentle."

"I wouldn't want you to be."

The corner of his lip curls. His fist is tighter now. His cock harder. He's fucking his palm like I want him to fuck my mouth.

"And when I come in your mouth, you'd swallow it all down," he tells me. "Like the good girl you are."

"Yes I would." I reach for him. "Let me taste you."

He keeps hold of his cock, running the tip along the seam of my mouth. I lick without hesitation, tasting the salty potency of him. He slides against me again, and I open my mouth, taking in the plushness of his head. Fluttering my tongue against him like he described.

"Christ, Carmichael," he moans. "Your mouth is heaven." He pushes in further. "Look up at me." So I do. Just like his fantasy. I give him the most innocent look I can manage with his dick in my mouth.

"Such a good girl. I'm going to fuck your mouth now."

And I want him to. I don't want him to be gentle or kind or caring. I know he can be that. He's showed it today and for the last week. But right now I need him dirty. So I nod and he thrusts his hips, making my eyes water as the tip of him skims the back of my throat.

"Breathe," he murmurs, pulling back. And I do. His eyes catch mine and I know what he's asking. Is this okay? Can he do it again?

I nod and he thrusts.

"Jesus fucking Christ, I'm not going to last." His fingers tangle in my hair, the pads pressing against my scalp. I reach around him, my own palms against his ass, encouraging his movement, loving the sound of his groans. The taste of him coats my tongue.

"Two seconds, Carmichael," he tells me. "Your choice."

They're like magic words. Because all of this is my choice. Having him here. Having him in my mouth. Letting him explode inside me.

Everything is up to me. And I want it all.

I flutter my tongue against him again and he lets out a low grunt, before he pumps into my mouth, his seed spilling on my tongue. His body is still, the only part of him moving the part between my lips. And when he stops coming he drops to his knees, cupping my face as I swallow him down.

"Fuck. Me," he mutters.

"A bit late now," I say, and he rolls his eyes.

"That was the most..." he screws his face up. "Boring blow job I've ever had."

I start to laugh and he kisses me, even though my mouth must still taste of him. Then he lifts me onto the bed and wraps me in his arms.

"I've missed you," he murmurs, stroking my hair. My face is resting on his chest. "Want to fly back to Exuma with me and escape from all this?"

"Do they have working bathrooms?" I ask.

"Yep. And marble floors." His hand slides between my legs. "Christ, you really are wet."

"That's my tears from choking on you."

He lifts his head to kiss me again, his finger slowly

touching me. He finds the part of me that needs him most, circling against it.

"Is this how you touch yourself?" he asks me, brushing his lips against my neck.

"No, I usually use a twelve inch dildo."

He laughs against my throat. "Move my hand. Show me what you like."

It's funny how intimate his request is. It feels more revealing than having him inside of me. And yet I take his hand, covering his finger with mine, pressing him against me. The roughness of his pad makes my breath catch.

He slides down, capturing my nipple between his lips. His tongue flutters over me, the way I fluttered over him.

"I've missed these, too," he mutters, moving his mouth to my other breast.

"They missed you."

"Push my finger inside you," he tells me.

So I do. He adds a second, flicking his thumb against my clit. My breath catches as he moves in the slowest of rhythms, his mouth dragging against my nipple.

Then he kisses his way down my abdomen, before pulling his hand away from mine and burying himself between my thighs, dipping his head to run his tongue languidly along my seam.

"Jesus, you taste good."

"Seriously?" I ask. "Or is that just what men...oh... say?"

His tongue flutters against my clit as he looks up at me. Oh, now I know why he likes me looking at him when he's in my mouth so much. The connection between us hits me in the chest.

"Seriously," he tells me.

Before I can respond he's sliding his fingers back inside of me, then he sucks at my clit with the perfect amount of pressure. My eyes roll as he curls his fingers, like he's beckoning me to come.

And I can feel it. The coiling. The pleasure he's creating.

His tongue is getting faster now. He pushes in a third finger and my eyes widen. It feels so full. Maybe too full. But then he twists them and it's everything.

"Linc," I gasp. "I'm going to come."

"Good. Give it to me." He twists them again, and I convulse, my back arching up as pleasure explodes inside me. My thighs tighten around his face, as he continues to lick me into oblivion. And his fingers, those teasing, beautiful fingers, he twists them inside as he slowly brings me down from my high.

When he lifts his face up I can see his jaw is glistening. He kisses my lips, a smile curling them as he does.

"That was…" I let out a sigh. "Definitely not boring."

"Good. Because I intend on not boring you a lot more."

CHAPTER
TWENTY-THREE

TESSA

Somehow we manage to drag ourselves out of bed and finish the sanding. Every few minutes Linc stops what he's doing to take his mask off and kiss me, and I find myself melting into his arms.

He takes over the big sander when my arms start to ache, and tells me to sit down and watch him be manly. By seven, the floor is finished. I can't clean it up because we have no water, but I'm still happy with what we've achieved.

In fact, I can't stop smiling.

"Go pack a bag for you and Zoe," Linc says when we walk out of the living room.

"I'm not moving into a hotel because we have no water," I tell him. "It's fine, I'll ask the neighbors if I can use their bathroom for a couple of days." They already offered to help while the bathroom is being updated. I'm pretty certain they won't mind me extending it a few days earlier. "And anyway, Zoe'll be at her dad's after tomorrow."

"You're not staying here without water," he says again. "Not when I have an apartment big enough for all of us."

"Are you asking me to move in with you?" I ask, fluttering my eyelashes at him. "That blow job must have been better than I thought."

"It was perfect." He kisses me again, smiling at the memory. "But no, not yet. I'm just offering you somewhere with water for a couple of nights."

I tip my head to look at him, the 'not yet' echoing in my ears. "And where exactly will we sleep?"

"My apartment has three rooms," he tells me. "Enough for all of us."

I press my lips together. It's a kind offer. One I would jump at if it was Angela making it. And if I called her now, she probably would offer. "I was thinking of asking Jared if Zoe could go over there tonight," I tell Linc.

"And miss out on your Sunday with her?"

Oh this man gets me. My heart does a little leap. "He'll throw a fit if he finds out I kept her here with no water."

"What's it got to do with him?" he asks.

"He's her dad," I say. "He does get to have an opinion."

"Hmm." Linc doesn't look impressed. "Well either way you're staying at mine. Until the bathroom is done. Think of it as Exuma part two. But without the pigs."

"I loved the pigs," I say smiling.

We argue good naturedly for another five minutes, and then he chases me into my room where I pack my bags. I message Zoe that we'll meet her at the pizza place where Maisie's mom has taken them. Luckily, she's already packed her bag for her dad's – and she has a lot of stuff that stays there – so she tells me the few things to add to it, and then Linc is taking her bag and mine and carrying them to his car.

"Are you sure about this?" I ask him. Because I'm not.

"Deadly. It's either this or I drive over every hour to supply you with a bucket of water."

"How would you stop it from spilling in your car?" I ask as he pops the trunk open and loads our bags in.

"I wouldn't. That's how much I want to keep you hydrated. Now get in the car and let's get Zoe.

The pizza place is jammed when we arrive. Linc stops at the counter to pick up the order he had me place online as we drove because in his words, he's 'fucking starving'. And I walk over to where Zoe is sitting. She grins at me as I say hi to Maisie's mom.

"Where is he?" Zoe asks me.

"Just picking up some pizza for us."

Actually he's already walking over, carrying two giant boxes. "Hey ladies."

I introduce him to Maisie's mom, who blushes profusely as he leans down to kiss her cheek.

"Are you ready?" he asks. "I can wait in the car if you're not."

I know he wants to eat some pizza. I remember from Exuma that the man loves his food, plus he's been very active all afternoon.

In every way.

"I'm good," Zoe says jumping up and hugging her friends. I try to pay for her dinner but Maisie's mom refuses. "Already got it," Linc murmurs to me as we leave.

"The tab?"

"Yeah. And the tip. All good."

"I thought you told Zoe to never let a man buy her dinner," I say, trying not to smile because is this man for real?

"I wasn't buying her dinner. I was buying her and her friends dinner. And Maisie's mom."

"Are you expecting Maisie's mom to put out?" I ask, feigning horror. "Because she's a married woman."

He hands me the pizza boxes and opens the door for Zoe, who's too busy checking the messages on her phone to listen to us, and then for me.

"Smooth," I say.

"I like to think so. And no, I wasn't planning on calling in favors with Maisie's mom."

Our eyes catch.

"Zoe's mom though," he murmurs in my ear. "She's definitely my type. I'd like to try my luck with her."

———

"Holy shit," Zoe whispers as we walk into Linc's apartment.

I turn to give her a mom-level stare, even though my reaction was just as shocked, although silent. "Excuse me?" I say, unable to really take it all in with my arms full of our pizza.

"Sorry," she says. "But this place is huge. You could fit our whole house into this room."

Yes you could, and we're only in the hallway. Linc closes the door behind us and carries our bags in. "Want the tour?" he asks Zoe.

"Absolutely I do." She claps her hands together. "Do you have a swimming pool?"

"No. And I wouldn't let you near it if I did. You and water aren't a good combination." His voice is teasing. She hasn't stopped smiling since we picked her up from the pizza place.

"Tell me you at least have a hot tub."

"I have a spa bath."

"Seriously?" Her mouth opens.

"Yes, and lucky for you it has no faucets. Just buttons."

She sighs. "We need to get a spa bath."

"A working tub would be nice," I say.

Linc puts our bags down on the floor as we step into the living area. There's a huge L-shaped leather sofa dominating one side of the room, along with the biggest television I've ever seen. The sofa faces the window that gives a floor-to-ceiling view of Manhattan.

"I think I've died and gone to heaven," Zoe says, running

her finger along the back of the sofa. "Can I watch movies in here?"

"If you'd like."

"You're going to your dad's tomorrow evening," I remind her.

She wrinkles her nose. "Can't I stay here?"

"No, you can't." Because Jared would probably kill me.

"The kitchen is right there," Linc says, inclining his head toward a sleek, perfectly proportioned kitchen. He takes the pizza boxes from me and puts them on the white marble countertop. Then he opens the top and takes out a slice.

He already ate two in the car. The man's an eating machine.

"Guest bedroom number one at the end," he says, swallowing a mouthful of pizza. "You can have that one, Zo."

She doesn't need to be told twice. She practically runs across the room to it, pushing the door open.

Through the doorway I watch as she throws herself on the bed.

"Sorry about that," I say.

Linc smiles at me. "Honestly, I like her enthusiasm. She's the first person I've brought here who's thrown themselves on the bed."

And just like that I'm thinking about all the women he must have brought into his apartment. Beautiful ones. Not ones with teenage daughters and a bathroom that's falling apart.

When I glance over at him, his eyes are trained on my face.

"Whatever you're thinking," he says. "It's probably not true."

"Am I that easy to read?" I ask him.

"Sometimes." He finishes off the slice of pizza and wipes his mouth with a napkin. "You sure you don't want some?"

"In a while." I'm not hungry now.

"Where's mom going to sleep?" Zoe asks, running out of the bedroom. "With me?" Her cheeks are tinged with pink. She looks so excited it's not funny.

"There's another guest room on the mezzanine," Linc tells her. "Just up those stairs."

I look over. They're made of wood so highly polished you can see the ceiling reflected in them. The banister is made of glass. The three of us walk up them – well, two of us walk and Zoe runs. I try to ignore the guilty feeling that I've made her live in a house with holes in the floor for months, because she's just so excited here.

"Here," Linc murmurs, as we reach a thick wooden door with a brushed chrome handle. Zoe opens it and there's a huge bed inside, made up with the kind of crisp white bed linen that makes you want to roll in the sheets. The floor is polished wood and on one wall there's a line of mirrored doors, while the other is a floor to ceiling window over-looking the city.

"I'm thinking of renovating," Linc says. "I hear mattresses on the floor are all the rage now."

I widen my eyes at him, because if Zoe puts two and two together she'll know he's been in my bedroom. He just grins at me, sending a shiver down my back.

"If this is the guest bedroom, yours must be huge," Zoe says.

Before Linc can say anything I shoot him a look.

"You can go see." He shrugs. "It's the next door over."

Zoe's speedy tour of Linc's apartment continues with her rushing to his room.

"There better not be any sex toys in there," I tell him.

"It's okay, the housekeeper makes sure to hide them all." He puts his hand lightly on my back as we follow Zoe to Linc's bedroom. "Notice something?" he asks.

I look up at him quizzically. "No, what?"

"There are no holes in my floor. And the boards don't creak."

"And?"

He gives me a grin. "And if somebody was to tiptoe along here in the middle of the night, hypothetically, the person sleeping in the guest room downstairs would never know."

"Holy shit, Mom, you should see the view in here," Zoe calls out.

"I'm blaming you for her bad language," I tell him, lifting a brow as we walk inside Linc's bedroom.

My mouth drops open. It's beautiful. Like downstairs, the whole wall is glass, with gauzy curtains on either side framing the perfect view. How did he afford this? Not on a PR director's salary.

"It's like having the biggest PC monitor in the world," Zoe says, pressing her nose against the glass. Linc doesn't seem bothered that her breath is misting the surface so I try not to be bothered either. "I bet you can see everything from here. A real life *Grand Theft Auto*."

"You play?" Linc asks.

"She does not," I say. "It's too violent."

The corner of his lip quirks.

"Can I see your tub?" Zoe asks.

Sure." Linc inclines his head at the door and she rushes inside.

"I'm sorry," I say softly. "She just hasn't been anywhere like this before."

"I'm kind of enjoying it," he tells me, his hand still pressed against my lower back. "It's nice seeing it through her eyes."

"Can I take a bath?" Zoe shouts.

"No!" My cheeks start to heat up. "Zoe, go downstairs and take your things to your room, please."

Linc is looking at me, his eyes crinkled.

"What?"

"The expression on your face. It reminds me of my mom. Do they teach that to you somewhere?"

"Yep. They take us aside as soon as we give birth," I tell him. "We get the facial expression lessons, the tone of voice lessons, and the how to instill guilt with a single eyebrow raise as a bonus."

His smile widens. "I knew it." He slides his hand to my waist, his fingers trailing my hips as he pulls me closer. "How long did you say your bathroom was going to take?" he murmurs.

"I didn't. Because I'm not staying here for the whole renovation. I'm really grateful you're helping." He has no idea how grateful. "But I can't stay here all week."

His lips brush mine. I tense.

"What's the matter?" he asks. "You've gone all stiff on me."

"Zoe's downstairs."

"And we can hear her talking on her phone," he replies, leaning down to kiss the sensitive skin beneath my ear. "So what's really getting you?"

I let out a breath. "You saw my place," I say, my chest tightening. "It's very different to this."

He frowns, as though he doesn't understand. "I love your place. And what you're doing to it. It's fucking amazing that in a few months you'll be able to sit back and know that everything you look at has been renovated by you. This place isn't even mine. It belongs to our family trust. I'm the third brother to live in it and none of us have left a mark."

"Ask Zoe which one she'd prefer to live in," I say dryly.

"With you. She'd prefer to live wherever you are. That kid loves you to death. I can see it in her eyes. And when I was a kid, I was the same way about my mom." He blinks, as though a memory has caught him. "She had the small house, my dad had all the real estate you can think of. And it was her I wanted to be with every time."

I try to imagine Linc as a kid. "Were you cute when you were little?" I ask him.

"I was a little asshole." He huffs out a laugh. "But anyway, we're not talking about me when I was little. We're talking about us."

"Are we?"

"Aren't we?" he asks.

I don't know. I close my eyes for a moment to center myself. Today has been... a thing. From the renovations to the bathroom fiasco to sexy times with Linc in my bedroom to this.

It's like a whirlwind. So much for no drama. Except this time, the drama's all mine.

"Why do you want me?" I ask him. It's an honest question. I don't understand why this man – who has all the money and women he could want – is pursuing me. A single mom with a dilapidated home.

"Because you're the one who keeps me awake at night," he says simply. "I can't stop thinking about you and that's never happened to me before."

He lets go of my waist and walks out onto the mezzanine floor, leaning over the rail to shout at Zoe.

"Hey Zo, wanna get some more pizza and watch me play *Grand Theft Auto*?"

"Hell yeah!"

I take a deep breath. This is going to be a long night.

CHAPTER
TWENTY-FOUR

LINC

"Oh my God, I can't believe you're so bad at this," Zoe says, laughing as she wins again. Much to her disappointment I didn't load up GTA, though I'm still kind of chuckling at the way it sent Tessa over the top.

Instead, we've spent the night eating pizza and playing *Super Mario Kart*, while Tessa does some work at the kitchen counter, because she's a Miss Goody Two Shoes and we're the wayward kids having a Saturday night blast.

"It's almost ten," Tessa calls out, peering over the top of her laptop screen. "Time to get ready for bed."

"I'm usually allowed to stay up until twelve," I tell her and Zoe snorts out a laugh.

Tessa's eyes catch mine and I give her the dirtiest sex look I can muster. Because I have plans for midnight. Plans that involve being firmly inside Carmichael. Quietly, of course.

"Can't I stay up for a while longer?" Zoe asks. "Linc is just getting good at this."

"Thank you for your encouragement," I tell her, deadpan.

"No. You have homework to do in the morning and then you're going to your dad's," Tessa reminds her. "And I have to go home and get things ready for the contractor on Monday."

Zoe mutters something under her breath, then hands the controller to me.

"Conceding defeat?" I ask her, low enough so Carmichael can't hear.

"You gotta learn to pick your battles," Zoe tells me, sounding so much like her mom it makes me want to laugh.

"True that."

She and Tessa disappear for a while. I assume they're having a chat as Zoe gets ready for bed, so I turn off the console and reply to some emails that have been filling my inbox all week. I check my schedule for next week. Roman's requested a meeting. I accept it, knowing that he's still pissed with me for not traveling.

But fuck, I'm glad I didn't. If I had I wouldn't have gone over to Carmichael's place today. And she wouldn't have given me the best blow job in living history.

And she wouldn't be sleeping in the room next to mine tonight.

It's weird having people stay in the apartment. I know that Tessa thinks I have a conveyer belt of women coming in and out of here purely for my carnal pleasure, but it's not true.

"Just getting a glass of water," Zoe says. She's in her pajamas. I smile because they are black patterned pants and a white top with the slogan – Eat, Sleep, Anime, Repeat.

"Use the dispenser on the refrigerator, the water's filtered."

"On it." She grabs a glass and fills it up. Then she puts it on the counter and walks over to me. "Thank you for letting us stay."

Before I can say anything she leans down to kiss my cheek. She smells of soap and fabric softener.

And for some reason, that little gesture makes my throat tighten.

"It's a pleasure, kid. Have a good sleep."

"Can we do something in the morning before I have to leave?" she asks.

"Sure." I'm stupidly pleased that she wants to spend more time with me. I don't think I've ever interacted with a thirteen-year-old before. At least, not since I was a teenager myself. Some of my brothers have kids but they're younger. "We could go out for breakfast maybe. There's this diner that has the biggest pancakes you've ever seen."

"Chocolate chip?" she asks.

"Absolutely."

She holds her hand up for a high five. And when our palms slap I start to wonder if her high five was for her or for me.

Five minutes later, Tessa appears back in the living room. I look up from my laptop, smiling when I see she's in her pajamas too. But these ones are silk. Long pants and a camisole top.

"I can see your nipples, Carmichael," I say, my voice low.

"That's because you're a perv." She shoots a glance to her left to make sure Zoe's door is shut.

"Want a glass of wine?" I ask, handing her the remote. "Let's watch a movie or something."

"You want to watch a movie?" She sounds skeptical. "Isn't that a little… boring?"

"I thought we'd established that I like boring." I head to the kitchen and grab two glasses, filling them with some crisp cold Pouilly Fume I bought on my last trip to Paris. "It's you I worry about."

"Me?" She glances at me over her shoulder as I walk back to the table.

"Yeah. I know you're not used to this kind of lifestyle. That you're all about the hot guys and sex parties. But I thought maybe you could try my world for one night."

"Give me the wine, Salinger," she says, shaking her head. I pass her the glass and she takes a long sip. "That's good. Where's it from?"

"I can't remember," I lie, because I don't want to mention Paris. I don't want to mention anything that could pierce this little bubble we've got going on tonight.

Carmichael, me, and her kid. The three of us staying home on a Saturday night.

Thank god my brothers can't see me. They'd laugh their asses off if they could.

———

TESSA

"Bedtime," Linc says when the movie ends, holding the remote up to turn off his stupidly big television. I grab our empty glasses and carry them into the kitchen, loading them into the dishwasher.

We only drank two glasses of wine in the end. And then I kind of fell asleep for most of the movie. I remember startling awake when a shooting scene came on, only to find my cheek propped against Linc's shoulder, his arm around my waist.

It felt… safe.

Which if I think about for too long, makes me feel unsafe. I've spent the last two years rebuilding mine and Zoe's life. I don't want to rely on anybody else to make me feel safe.

I want to do it alone.

"I'm gonna take a shower," Linc tells me as we walk up the stairs. "Care to join me?"

"I can't." I look at Zoe's door. And then it opens. One side of Zoe's face is creased from where she's been lying on it. I can tell she's been asleep from the thickness of her voice. "Mom?"

"Yes honey?" I take the few steps back down.

"I think I forgot my gym bag. And we have track on Monday."

Linc sniggers.

"Are you sure?" I ask.

"Yep. Sorry. Can we pick it up tomorrow on the way to Dad's?"

"Of course." She could have asked me that tomorrow, but I assume she's woken up disoriented. Maybe not as excited about sleeping in a strange apartment as she made out. "Everything else okay?"

"I'm gonna head up." Linc walks up the rest of the stairs and along the Mezzanine, disappearing through his bedroom door.

"Can you talk me back to sleep?" Zoe asks.

It was something I used to do when Jared first moved out. Despite my best attempts to make everything smooth for her, she suffered from anxiety. Her therapist explained it was natural for her to be afraid. The rug of security had been taken from under her. She'd never thought her dad would leave, and now she was questioning everything.

Time and her growing older has helped. But I'm guessing tonight has gotten her a little edgy.

"Sure." I follow her into her room. She climbs into the large queen sized bed and I lay next to her. "What shall we talk about?"

"Is Linc your boyfriend?" she asks as she rests her head on my shoulder.

My stomach tightens. I wasn't expecting to have this conversation quite so soon. "He's my friend," I tell her. "I wouldn't call him my boyfriend."

"But you like him?"

Damn thirteen-year-olds and their perceptive ways. "I do like him, but he's just a friend. Kind of like when there's a new girl at school and you think she's great but you need to take your time before she's part of the circle." It's the best analogy I can think of, but it's not exactly great.

"I like him," she says. Her voice is sleepy now. "He's funny."

"Yeah, he is."

"And he's kind. He bought everybody's pizza, did you know that? Maisie messaged me to say her mom went to pay our check and Linc had already paid it."

"He's a gentleman." Okay, maybe that's going too far. I find my lips curling. I'm going to tell him I said that.

"I'm okay with him, if you want to date him," she says, her eyes closed now. "As long as you don't do all that kissing stuff in front of me."

"I don't know where this friendship is going," I tell her honestly. "All I can tell you is that you'll always be my priority. That I'll always be here for you."

"Like the Gilmore girls."

"Exactly." I lean down to kiss her cheek and all of a sudden I'm remembering the day we brought her home from the hospital. She was sleeping in her car seat and I remember Jared putting her down and asking me, "So what do we do now?"

I'd laughed and replied, "I guess it's our job to get her to adulthood without doing anything stupid."

Is wanting to be with Linc stupid? I'm not sure, but what I do know is that if everything ends then I'll be okay. I have to be.

I'm not going to let Zoe see her mom go through pain again.

———

There's a light rap of knuckles on my door as I step out from the shower. Then Linc opens the door, his eyes darkening as he takes in the towel wrapped around my damp body.

"Everything okay?" he asks me. "Zoe all right?"

I nod. "She's just… a little discombobulated." I take a deep breath. "She wanted to know if you and I are…" I trail off. Saying she asked if he was my boyfriend sounds wrong. Like I'm asking for myself. "Anyway, I told her we were friends. I think it calmed her."

"Friends," he says, his voice low. He slides the lock on my door closed. "Do you swallow all your friends' cum?"

I open my mouth to answer and close it again.

"Do you grind your pussy against all of their mouths?" he asks, stepping toward me.

My cheeks pink up at the memory. "No."

"Then in what possible fucking way are we friends?"

"I want to be your friend," I tell him honestly. "I like you. You make me smile. That hasn't happened in a long time."

He gently pulls the towel from my body, leaving me naked. His gaze travels down my body, a low breath escaping his lips. Then he takes my nipple between his fingers, twisting it. I let out a gasp.

"Do friends do this to each other?" he asks.

"No," I breathe as he pinches it hard. I'm somewhere between pleasure and pain.

"Good. I'm glad we're clear. If you want to call it friends, then do it. But we're exclusive friends. Friends who fuck like rabbits and don't let anybody else touch them."

Oh, he's being possessive. "You're the first man to touch me in years," I remind him.

His jaw twitches. "And you're the only woman that gets to touch me." He leans forward, the softness of his lips a contrast to the hardness of his voice. "Now I'm going to fuck you, then we're going to talk. Because I can't get my damn thoughts straight with you naked in front of me."

"Yes please. But you can't stay…"

"I know that. I wasn't going to." He pulls me against him until I feel the thick ridge of him pressing into my stomach. He pushes my hair from my face, his lips claiming mine. He tastes of toothpaste, his tongue lazily stroking mine as he slides his hand between my legs, checking if I'm ready for him.

And I am. So ready. He groans as he slides his finger into me, and I tighten around him.

"You're gonna kill me, Carmichael."

"Are you always going to call me that?" He slides his thumb against my clit and my words end in a gasp.

"Probably." His lips smile against mine. Then he slides his palms along the back of my thighs and lifts me onto the bed, letting me go so I'm splayed out naked before him.

The way he looks at me makes my breath catch. His eyes roam over my body, his chest falling and rising. "Do you know how many times I've imagined you on this bed?"

"Before or after Exuma?" I ask him, curious.

"After. Before I just wanted to ring your neck."

I start to laugh and he's grinning, too, as he pulls down his shorts and walks toward me. His erection is impressive, bobbing as his legs hit the end of the bed. He's brought a condom with him. He rips the packet and rolls it on.

"I'm not into choking," I tell him.

"Not yet," he murmurs, stroking himself. "Give us time."

I think he's joking. At least I hope he is. But I don't get a chance to think about it anymore, because he's claiming my mouth again, lifting my thigh to hook it around his waist as he pushes inside of me.

I let out a ragged breath.

"You with me?" he asks.

"Yes," I tell him.

He leans on his elbows as he rocks his hips, his movements lazy as his eyes catch mine. It's like he can't stop looking at me. I'm not sure I can look away either. My breath catches as he finds the right spot to grind against.

I swear stars start to sparkle in front of my eyes.

"Look at me," he tells me. "Don't look away."

His hand cups my face as he finds his rhythm. I move against him, loving the way he sends sparks right down to my toes every time he rocks into me. And I don't move my gaze. It stays fixed on him.

It feels more intimate than having sex. I can't remember the last time I stared at somebody for this long.

He pushes up to his hands, his palms flat on the mattress, and this time he hits a sensitive spot deep inside me. My eyes widen and I want to shut them but he shakes his head.

"Don't stop," I tell him.

"Wasn't planning on it."

His hips undulate as he moves inside my body. Still so slow. Still so sure. And my chest tightens because I can't remember ever feeling this alive. This wanted.

"Are you close?" he rasps.

"So close."

"Touch yourself," he tells me.

So I do, because right now I'd do anything for this man. I slide my hand between us, finding my swollen center. I place the pad of my finger on it, slowly rotating to the tempo of his body.

"You're beautiful," he whispers.

"So are you."

"Don't ignore my calls again," he tells me.

I smile because he has me exactly where he wants me. And maybe I have him where I want him too. Inside me. Over me. Everywhere.

"Need you to come now," he tells me. "Before I fuck everything up."

I start to laugh, and it sets off a chain reaction. The move- ment makes my body tighten around him and he stills for a minute, the tip of him hitting the exact right spot. My finger rubs my clit lightly, and I'm gasping because I'm right on the edge.

"Tessa… fuck…"

He starts to surge inside of me and I tumble over the edge with him, my fingers raking his back as I call out his name. He drops back to his elbows, putting his palm over my mouth to quieten me, his growl low and long as his orgasm reaches its peak.

And once we've both come back to reality he lets go of my mouth. His eyes are still on me.

"That could get weird if you do that at work," I tell him, imagining him following my every move around the boardroom.

"Make love to you in the office? Yeah, that would be weird." He smiles.

I try not to notice that he didn't call it fucking this time. And my heart does a weird little dance.

Because it didn't feel like fucking. It felt like something else. Something more. And I've no idea how to feel about that.

CHAPTER
TWENTY-FIVE

TESSA

"Mom?" The voice breaks through the thick veil of my dreams. I sit up and blink, seeing Zoe's face in extreme close up, her brows knitted.

I sit straight up, alarm rushing through me. "What is it?" I ask. "Is something wrong?" It takes me a minute to realize I'm in a different bed. In a different home.

And for a second panic rushes through me because the last thing I remember was Linc holding me against his chest as my eyes began to get heavy.

But he's not here. I let out a long sigh of relief. Clever, clever man. He must have gone to his bed after I fell asleep.

"Can't you hear that?" she asks.

"Hear what?"

"Linc. There's noise coming from his room." She looks worried. "Like shouting and stuff. Is there somebody with him?"

"No. Could he be on the phone?" I ask her.

She looks at the clock next to my bed. It's displaying 3 am.

Then he shouts out again. "No!"

The noise echoes through the wall next to my bed. It's plaintiff and scary. Zoe's eyes catch mine.

My heart plummets into my stomach. The nightmare. The one I never got to the bottom of in Exuma. Because I'm pretty sure he's not talking to anybody in the middle of the night.

"Go back to bed," I tell her. "I'll deal with it."

"Is he hurt?" she asks.

He calls out again and I climb out of bed. "No, but I think he's having a nightmare. He'll be fine. Go back to bed, sweetheart."

"What if he hurts you? I've heard of men killing their wives while they're asleep."

Oh Zoe and her imagination. "He won't hurt me," I promise. "But it's late and you need your sleep."

She hugs me before she finally does as I ask, padding back down the stairs to her bedroom.

I pull on a robe and walk to Linc's room, tapping on the door even though he won't hear me.

And then I push it open.

He's laying on the bed, curled up like he had been on the sofa bed in Exuma. He's naked, his body curled up in the fetal position, his arms wrapped around his chest like he's trying to protect himself. He's stopped shouting. Now, he's groaning, loud and gutturally.

Softly closing the door behind me, I walk over to his bed. The sheets have been kicked into a rumpled mess at the base of the mattress. One of the pillows is on the floor. I pick it up and put it beside him, then I reach out to touch his hair.

"It's okay," I soothe. "It's just a dream."

His throat rumbles as he lets out a whimper. It cuts right through me. The sound is such a contrast to this strong, virile, funny man.

It hurts me to know he's hurting.

And then his eyes fly open. He's staring right at me, but not seeing me. "Mom?"

I let out a lungful of air. "It's Tessa," I tell him. "You were having a nightmare."

His brow is damp with sweat as I touch it. His whole body is glowing in the moonlight. He presses his lips together, then looks around his bedroom, as though he's trying to work out where he is and what's going on.

He sits up, his shoulder muscles rippling, then his gaze lands on me. "Did I wake you?" he asks me.

"You woke Zoe."

"Shit." He squeezes his eyes shut. "I'm sorry."

"It's okay," I tell him. "She's gone back to bed. And I should probably go back to bed too. Will you be all right?"

He reaches for me, pulls me against him. His body is over-heated but I let him hold me. Maybe we both need it. And that's how we stay for at least five minutes. Not talking, just holding. Linc pressing his face against my hair.

It's only when I get back into bed that I realize he never answered my question. Will he be all right?

I hope so.

————

We're sitting on the roof terrace of his apartment building the following evening. The moon is almost full and the night sky is unblemished by clouds. We're all alone up here. According to Linc, half of the apartments in this place are empty. Owned by investors looking to diversify their portfolio.

They're missing out because it's beautiful up here. I'd rather be snuggled up to this gorgeous man and staring at the heavens than counting the money in my index funds.

Not that I have one. So it's a good thing we have this.

I dropped Zoe off at her dad's about three hours ago. We stopped off at home first, so she could grab her gym clothes and I could make sure everything is ready for tomorrow's bathroom demo. The water is still off and the contractor has agreed to keep me updated, but he thinks I should have a working toilet and shower by Thursday, ready to move back in.

Jared hadn't been there when we got there. There was only Melissa, looking stressed and upset because she couldn't get ahold of him.

It was strange watching her pace on the phone, because once upon a time that was me. I was the one waiting and wondering, I guess while he was in bed with her.

The weird thing was that I didn't get any satisfaction from seeing her so agitated. I just felt sad for her, because some people never change. It was like the final tiny thread linking me to my old life, my old relationship, had dropped away.

Thanks to this man sitting next to me.

I'd offered to take Zoe back home with me, but Melissa insisted she stay. I suspect she's still in that zone of trying to prove she's a good partner. And since Zoe's schedule was all planned out for her being at Jared's for school tomorrow, I agreed.

An hour later, Zoe sent me an update to tell me that her dad was home.

She found it funny but I'm not sure I ever could.

"What are you thinking about?" Linc asks softly, his arm around me as we sip at our glasses of wine.

"That I shouldn't be drinking good wine when I have to get up for work tomorrow."

"So stay in bed all day with me. We'll video call Roman and tell him we're playing hookey for love."

The thought of Roman's face if he heard that makes me giggle. "I can't. I've got meetings."

"Yeah, me too. But we have tomorrow night."

"Are you sure you're okay with me staying here until Wednesday?"

"Of course I am." He brushes my jaw with his lips. "If I had my way you'd be here until your whole home was ready for human habitation."

"We've managed up until now," I point out.

"Yeah, but you didn't have me then."

I tilt my head up and look at him.

He sighs. "Go on then."

"Are you a mind reader now?" I ask him.

Linc lifts a brow. "I'm a Tessa Carmichael reader. And I know you want to ask me about last night. It was just a nightmare. I get them occasionally. I'm blaming Zoe for making me play video games all night."

He's making light of it. I thought he would. He's a man who doesn't like to show the chink in his armor. He plasters all the cracks with humor, hoping nobody will see underneath.

But I'm like a dog with a bone when I latch onto something.

"You had a nightmare when we were in Exuma too."

His expression betrays his surprise. "Did I?"

"Yes. The first night. You were sweating buckets on the sofa bed."

Linc swallows, his Adam's apple undulating in his throat. His profile is illuminated by the moonlight. "I get them sometimes."

"How often?" I ask him, curious.

"A few times a year," he says, staring into the distance. "I guess more often recently."

"Twice in a few weeks," I agree. "Is it the same nightmare or something different?"

His lips part as he exhales softly. "The same one."

When his eyes catch mine I'm reminded of the way he stared at me last night. It feels like we're looking into each others' souls. "I'm sorry I woke you. And Zoe. I wasn't sure whether to talk to her about it or not."

I give him a half smile. "Funny thing about teenagers, they're more observant than you'd think, but they care less than you'd think too. If it doesn't revolve around her, she'll probably file it under 'things that aren't that important'."

"I get nightmares about my mom," he says. The sudden admission takes me by surprise.

"What about her?"

He's looking at me again. Like he's searching my face for answers. "This can't go any further. Nobody knows. Except me and her."

I nod, because I'm not planning on telling anybody. "You can trust me," I tell him.

"When I was twelve I found her unconscious on her bed. She'd taken a lot of pills. She was unresponsive."

I gasp audibly. "You were twelve?" I ask. My stomach tightens. He was younger than Zoe is now. "What happened?"

"I'd watched enough television to know I needed to make her throw up. I was a big kid, even then." He runs his tongue along his lip, deep in thought. "I was hyperventilating. Pleading with her not to die. My dad had just left us and I was so fucking scared that we were going to lose her, too."

"Your brothers were there?"

He shakes his head. "Just me. Brooks was at a friend's house. I was supposed to be there, too, but I came home to pick something up. And that's how I found her."

I blink. In some of the very darkest moments in my divorce, I remember wanting it all to end. But I couldn't have done it. I knew Zoe needed me. That's the only thing that kept me going.

"She must have been in a very dark place."

"Yeah. I guess she was." He reaches for my hand, sliding his fingers between mine. I squeeze it back, because I need him to know how much I care.

"What happened next?" I ask. He's talked about her so I

know she's alive. I also know his family is complicated. But I really need to know what happened to that boy who was scared he was about to lose everything.

"I called the paramedics," he says. "They came pretty quick." He squeezes my hand again. "The rest of it, I can't really remember. Like I've blanked it out. But I think they pumped out her stomach and then she went into some outpatient therapy. All I can remember is her apologizing to me, promising me she wouldn't do it again. Begging me not to tell anybody because she didn't want our dad to take me and Brooks away from her."

"Didn't the police alert him?" I ask.

"I guess not. Maybe things were different then. All I know is she kept her promise. Things got better. A lot better."

"But you still dream about it."

"I dream about the what ifs," he says. "What if I hadn't gone home? We were at a sleepover. We weren't supposed to be home until the next morning." He looks at me carefully. "I know it wasn't my fault. But I guess sometimes in the darkness of night..." he trails off.

"The little boy you once were comes out."

"Something like that." He runs the pad of his thumb over my palm. "So now you know my deepest darkest secret."

"It's not your secret," I tell him. "It's hers. Have you told her about the nightmares?"

He frowns. "No. And I'm not going to. As far as she knows I've forgotten it, and I want it to stay that way."

"Why?" I ask him. "Are you afraid she'll try again?"

Linc blinks, staring into the inky sky. "She won't do it again. She's happy now. She has been for the longest time." He turns his head to look at me. "You're the first person I've spoken to about this since I was twelve."

"You should talk to your mom," I tell him. "I'd want Zoe to talk to me. Or if you can't talk to her, maybe a therapist could help."

"I'm talking to you," he says gruffly.

Yes he is, and my heart is tight with gratitude that he trusts me enough with this. Before I can tell him so, he's circling my waist with his hands, lifting me onto him so I'm straddling his legs, our faces a breath away from each other.

"But if you really want, you can give me some physical therapy," he says, brushing his lips against my jaw, my cheek, my lips.

"Here?" I ask, looking around.

"Here," he agrees, sliding his hands beneath my top.

And I kiss him back, because I think we both need this.

CHAPTER
TWENTY-SIX

LINC

I'm picturing you naked, riding me, your hair flowing down your back, your skin all fucking shiny. The way it was this morning. – Linc.

I send the message, smirking when she pulls out her phone to read it, her eyes wide before she quickly turns the screen off and pretends to listen to Roman as he goes through our quarterly reports.

He's still pissed with me. And I'm absolutely okay with that. Yes, I'll fly to London next week, and then on to Paris and Rome like he's asked me. But after that, I need to find some kind of equilibrium in my life. If I have a shot at a relationship with Tessa, I'm not going to mess it up. She doesn't need another person in her life who'll flit in and out on his own schedule.

She deserves my full attention.

The last few days with her in my apartment have been the

best of my life. That's no exaggeration. Waking up to this woman in my bed, eating breakfast with her, talking shit about our day.

It's been perfect. And yeah, we've kind of jumped the gun by having her move in. And I'm absolutely okay with the fact she'll be going back to her own home with Zoe once they have a bathroom.

She needs to put her kid first. I like that. Heck, I love that she does. But the weeks when Zoe's with her dad, I'm determined to be here to spend time with Tessa. I can't do that if I'm flying all over the damn world.

"What do you think, Linc?" Roman asks.

I glance at Tessa. She's trying not to smile.

"Ah, maybe…" I say, trying to give myself time as I move my phone beneath the table and tap out a message.

Give me a clue. What am I supposed to be thinking about? – Linc

It's a good thing I've got nimble fingers.

Roman wants to open a Paris office. – Tessa

I pull my lip between my teeth, taking in her words. "Yeah," I say, "We have enough work there to justify it. I guess having some full time Hampshire staff in Europe would be a good thing. It'll help to have more French speaking employees." Right now, I'm the only one. Which means that the majority of the client-facing work falls to me. There's no way I'm going to disrespect our clients by not speaking their language.

Roman smiles. "Exactly. You and I can talk more about

this later, but I see it as a growth opportunity. You've built excellent relationships with our clients there. We're beginning to make our own name in the city. Plus, Paris is close to Rome and London. We have a lot of business there, too." He gives me a nod. "I've been thinking a lot about what you said regarding our environmental impact. This should ease that. So you'll fly over next week to start things off. Schedule a meeting with me before Friday and we can run over the budget and the project timeline." He looks around at the rest of the management team. "Good work, all of you," he says. "It's been a great quarter, with the Exuma project and now this."

Roman stands and goes to walk out, before realizing he's left his laptop on the table. He grabs it and smiles at me. For the first time since I told him I wasn't flying anywhere this week.

Looks like I'm back in his good books. That's one thing at least. My phone flashes as I stand up and roll my neck to get the kinks out of it.

The group chat with my brothers seems alive and well.

What time is everybody arriving at Misty Lakes on Friday? The wedding planner wants to know. – Holden

Misty Lakes is my father's estate. Where Holden and Blair's wedding is taking place this weekend. The rehearsal dinner is actually a cookout. A big one, but at least it's not a formal affair.

We'll be there in the afternoon. Just after lunch. – Myles

• • •

Ditto. – Liam

Probably a bit later for us. Maybe around 3pm? – Eli

Not sure. Need to talk to Linc. What time are we traveling down, bro? – Brooks

I have to work in the morning. Probably head out after lunch. Should get there by six pm if the traffic is kind. – Linc

Shit. I hate driving in rush hour. Can't you ignore work for one day? – Brooks

Who would have thought Linc would be the workaholic among us? – Eli

He's not a workaholic. He just wants to bone a woman at work. Bet you a thousand dollars that's why. – Liam

What woman? – Holden

Linc has a woman? Is it that French beauty that keeps tagging him on Instagram? – Eli

Why the hell are you stalking me on Insta? – Linc

. . .

I don't. But Mac does. We have a bet going. – Eli

What kind of bet? – Linc

All the wives do. They're running a lottery on when you'll settle down. Ava's got this year and she's absolutely excited about this woman. – Myles

She's not French. And it's none of your business. - Linc

Uhoh. Must be serious. Linc's never usually coy about women. – Eli

Can you all fuck off? Some of us have work to do. – Linc

Is she in New York? – Holden.

I let out a mouthful of air.

Yes. – Linc

That's it, I'm not answering any more questions. I start to feel guilty, because I did the same thing to Holden when he and Blair started dating. Gossip is always fun when you're not the one at the center of it.

· · ·

Bring her to the wedding. We've had a couple of cancellations so there's plenty of space. – Holden.

Okay, one more reply and I'm done.

I'm not bringing her to the damn wedding. You'll scare her off before we've even started. I'm turning my phone off now. Brooks, I'll pick you up at two on Friday. – Linc.

———

TESSA

"Come with me to my brother's wedding this weekend," Linc murmurs as we sit on his sofa watching a movie. He's sitting in the corner of the sofa, his legs stretched out, his feet resting on the coffee table. I'm curled up next to him, my head on his shoulder. He's absentmindedly playing with my hair.

"What?" I ask. "Don't be silly. I've never met him. He won't want me there. Anyway, I need to be here for Zoe."

"She doesn't come home until Sunday," he tells me. "I can have you back home by then."

He's been a little off all evening. He waited for me after work, then drove me to my place so I could check on the bathroom renovations, which are going great, thanks to the hard work of the contractors. It looks like everything but the tile floors will be done by the end of the weekend, and since I'm doing the tiling, their job will be done. They've promised to make sure the shower and toilet are usable by end of day Saturday, so Zoe and I will be able to move back in on Sunday.

He kisses my jaw. "I have to fly to France on Monday. I need more time with you before then."

I smile at him. "You'll be back though, right? I think we can survive a week apart."

There's a little twinge in my stomach. Because staying with him this week has been... perfect. They say you don't know somebody until you live with them, but Linc has been exactly how I thought he would be.

He's lived alone for a long time. He's self sufficient. He's over the top extravagant with money. And he likes having sex. A lot.

Truth be told, I'm going to miss this. I'd forgotten what it was like to have another adult to talk to in the evenings. Even when Jared was living with us, he wasn't really *there*. Looking back, I haven't had this kind of intimacy for a long time.

Linc takes my hand in his, using his finger to trace the lines on my palm. "I had a meeting with Roman this afternoon."

"To talk about the Paris office?" I ask him, trying not to smile at the memory of him looking so shocked when Roman said his name. It served him right for sending dirty messages to me when he should have been concentrating.

Not that I minded. Truth was, I was thinking about sex, too. Something I seem to be doing a lot recently.

Because sex with Linc Salinger is mind blowing. The kind of sex I didn't realize was possible. He's a generous lover. I've never seen him more intense than when he's coming inside of me.

"He's expecting me to run it." His voice is low. He's staring straight ahead.

"While you're setting it up?" I ask.

Linc shakes his head. "No, full time. He's offered me a partnership. Wants me to move to Paris permanently and be in charge of European operations. He wants somebody he can trust to run the business there."

My chest tightens. "So you'd live there?"

He lets out a long breath. "Yeah, I guess." He turns to look at me, deep furrows lining his forehead. "I told him I'd think about it, but I'm going to say no."

"To a partnership?" I ask, my voice lifting. "Why would you do that?" It's the pinnacle of our business. Nobody in their right mind would say no to a partnership. The chance to earn the big bucks. To be your own boss. Linc already brings in the clients. This is a chance to cash in on the profits he creates.

"Because it's in France," he says, frowning at me.

"And? You've been flying there for the last two years. It's not like you don't know the place." And now I'm thinking of his client. The beautiful one – Celine. And part of me wants to cry because the world is full of beautiful women, and Paris must have more than its fair share.

He's still looking at me. "But then I won't be able to spend time with you."

There's an intensity to his stare that makes my breath catch in my throat. "We can still see each other. Sometimes."

"How? I can't see you hopping on a red eye to Paris every couple of weeks."

"I could try," I say, my voice small. Because I think we both know it wouldn't be possible. Because of Zoe. I can't be in another country without her on a regular basis. Exuma was hard enough.

Linc shrugs. "It's okay. I've made my mind up. I'm going to say no."

Alarm rushes through me. "You can't say no because of me."

Those lines are back on his forehead again. "You want me to go?"

I try to breathe in but my chest feels tight. I don't feel prepared for this conversation. "I don't think it's about me, it's about you. If I wasn't here, would you go?"

"Yes."

That's what I thought. And in a weird way, it's almost a relief to hear.

"Then you have to go," I tell him. "It's too good an opportunity to ignore."

He shifts his position, pulling his feet from the table. I sit up as he turns to look at me.

"Do you want me to go?" he asks, his voice low.

"That's not what I'm saying." I blink, because he looks angry now.

"Then what *are* you saying, Tessa? Because I want to hear it."

It's the first time he's said my first name when he's angry and I hate it. I inhale a ragged breath. "I'm saying that if it was me, I'd take it." It's a lie, but I can't think properly. My brain is a mess.

"You'd leave me for a job opportunity?" His voice lifts. He's not just angry, he's furious. His eyes are trained on mine, his lips pressed together. I pinch the bridge of my nose to try to get my thoughts to work properly.

"It's not just a job opportunity," I whisper. "It's the chance of a lifetime. To be in charge of your own business. To earn the big bucks."

"I don't need the big bucks." He stands up, shaking his head. "But it's good to know where I stand with you." He picks our empty wine glasses up and stalks over to the kitchen, yanking the dishwasher open.

"I can do that," I tell him, jumping to my feet and walking over to the kitchen.

"It's fine," he says tightly. "I've got it." He slides the glasses inside then adds a tablet, switching the machine on to wash. "I'm heading upstairs. I need to pack for the wedding."

Oh god, I'd forgotten that we were talking about that before everything went to shit.

"Can't we talk about this?" I ask him.

He shakes his head. "I need to think. And I need to pack." He inclines his head at the paused screen of the movie we were watching. "You finish the show. I wasn't really watching anyway."

And then he stalks upstairs, leaving me standing open mouthed in his kitchen.

I've no idea what just happened, but I think I messed everything up.

———

LINC

I'm throwing clothes into my suitcase without a real plan for what I'm going to wear. My suit is in a garment bag – thank god I remembered to pick it up from the tailors. I've been known to forget about things like tuxes before. The rehearsal dinner tomorrow night will be casual – Holden and Blair are laid back people – and Sunday we're having a family brunch before everybody goes their separate ways.

Grabbing some socks, I throw them on top of my jeans, then jump out of my damn skin when I see Tessa standing in the doorway.

Her eyes are wide and red-rimmed, like she's upset.

"I'm sorry," she whispers, not moving. "I'm scared. Really, really scared."

Her words surprise me. "What are you scared of?" I ask her. I'm not sure I've ever met anybody stronger than this woman. I admire her in every way possible. I'm about a week away from falling in love with her.

Fuck it, I'm already in love with her. My brain just needs to catch up with my heart.

"So many things," she says softly. "But I'm mostly afraid

of being hurt again. Of falling for you. Of losing you. Of not being the independent woman I've learned to be. I'm scared that if I admit I don't want you to go to Paris then this thing between us is serious, and I'm not sure how to deal with that."

"This thing is serious, Tessa. Don't you know that already?" I walk over to her, reaching for her hand. It's so soft against my palm.

"I just... I wasn't ready for you." Her chest drops as she exhales. "I wasn't ready for anybody. It took a long time to heal my heart after my divorce. I don't know how to make myself vulnerable again."

She looks so scared I'm worried she might be sick. "Baby..." I pull her into my arms. "I'm not going to hurt you."

"You can't promise that." Her voice is soft as I stroke her hair. "Nobody can. And maybe it would be okay if it was just me. But there's Zoe to think about. She's been through so much."

"I get that," I tell her. "I really do. She's number one in your life. She should be."

Her eyes meet mine. "You deserve to be number one in somebody's life."

"I'll take second place if it means I get to be with you."

She lets out a soft sigh. "Why do you always have to say the sweetest things?"

"Because I mean them. I wouldn't want to be with somebody who didn't put their kid first. I've been that kid..."

Her face drops. "Oh Linc."

"It's okay." I press my lips against her brow. "But you never have to apologize for protecting Zoe. Hell, I want to protect Zoe. She's a good kid."

"She likes you," Tessa murmurs. "She asks about you every night when I call her. She wants to come here again and play Mario Kart with you."

My chest tightens. "You have no idea how much I'd like that."

"Really?" Tessa blinks.

"Really," I agree. "I like your kid. She's part of you. I want to be part of both your lives."

"I can't stand in the way of you and your promotion," she tells me. "It's too soon. What if you turn it down and we don't work out?"

I swallow hard, because the thought of things not working out with this woman slays me. I can't remember the last time I was this happy. I think never might be the answer.

"What if I take it and it ruins us?" I ask her.

"It won't." She cups my face, her eyes soft as they catch mine. "You told Roman you'd think about it. How long do you have?"

"I asked for a couple of weeks."

"Okay." She nods, looking serious. "So you fly to Paris next week and you think about it. Really think about it. And if that's what you want, to work there, then do it. For me."

"And leave you?"

"We can do long distance." The corner of her lip curls. "Think about the reunions."

"I'll rub my cock raw," I mutter and for the first time she laughs.

"Please?" she asks. "Tell me you'll consider it."

I let out a long breath. I don't want to. I want this concluded now. Because when you meet the person you've been searching for your whole life, you'd be a fucking fool to give that up.

"Okay," I say. But I'm not happy about it.

CHAPTER
TWENTY-SEVEN

TESSA

Just so you know. Weddings make me horny. You're missing out. – Linc x

I smile at his message. I get the feeling that he doesn't hear the word no very often. But there's just no way I was going to his brother's wedding when I've never met his family.

What exactly is it about watching a family member say 'I do' that fires your libido up? – Tessa x

I hit the send button then lift the cloth back up. Now that the water is back on I'm putting the finishing touches to the living room. Angela is here helping me, though she's been talking more than she's been cleaning up.

"So then Lisa told me she was on her period," Angela

continues. She's been trying to tell me this story for the last ten minutes but we keep getting interrupted. First by Zoe stopping home on her way to brunch with Jared and his parents, because she had to wear the skirt that she bought from some previously-loved clothes app the other day. Then by Linc who insisted on sending me a photograph of him in his tux.

And yes, he looks amazing. Even Angela looked a little flustered when I showed her.

"Are you even listening to me?" Angela asks.

I look at her, blinking. "You were telling me about Lisa's period."

"I told you that three times. And then I told you that Ryan told her that PMS is no excuse for the other three weeks out of four that she's a bitch and then she actually body tackled him to the ground."

"At work?" I murmur. "Wow."

"No, not at work. This was at a conference for work. And they're definitely fucking." Angela shakes her head. "Anyway, it's a boring story. I only started telling you it because you told me to stop asking you about Linc."

I bite down a smile. I did ask her that, mostly because she's had way too many questions I don't have the answers to.

Before I can say anything else, another message flashes on my phone. I go to look at it but Angela snatches my phone from me, grinning as she reads whatever Linc's decided to put as a reply to my question about weddings making him horny.

What makes me horny is the thought of you in a dress in my cabin, bent over my bed while I fuck you until you scream my name. – Linc x

• • •

Angela reads every word out loud. I roll my eyes at her. "Give me that," I say, grabbing it back from her.

And then somebody clears their throat.

My first thought is that it's Zoe. She only just left, so she's almost certainly forgotten something. And the poor kid definitely doesn't need to hear that about her mom. I turn to apologize to her, but instead Jared is standing in the doorway.

"Oops." Angela puts my phone on the mantlepiece above the fireplace.

"Zoe already left," I tell him, my voice thick. "Did she not come back to the car?"

"Yeah, she's waiting for me there." Jared's voice is slow. "Can I have a word, please?"

I glance over at Angela, who seems very interested in her nails. She's turning her hand this way and that, staring at it like she might find all the answers to the meaning of life in her cuticles.

"Now?" I ask, my voice lifting with alarm. "Aren't you going to be late to meet your parents?"

"It won't take long."

"Don't mind me," Angela says lightly. "I'll go make us another coffee."

"Not for me," Jared says.

"I wasn't offering you one." She rolls her eyes at him and leaves the room, her footsteps padding toward the kitchen.

"I see your friends are delightful as usual." Jared lifts a brow as he looks around the living room. "How long until the rest of this place is done?"

"A couple more months." I can already feel the annoyance rising in me. I know I shouldn't let him get to me, but somehow he always does.

"It's not good for Zoe to live like this."

My jaw tightens. "What can I do for you, Jared?"

He lets out a long breath, like being near me is actually painful for him. "Zoe said she stayed at another man's house with you last Saturday night. Isn't that something you should have consulted me about?"

"We stayed at a friend's house," I correct him. "In his spare room because we had a problem with the bathroom here. There was nothing to consult about."

"A friend from work?"

"That's right." I hate that I have to explain myself to him. Especially after he spent time in another woman's bed *while we were married*.

And truth be told, I'm lying. I didn't just stay in his guest room. Linc came in there with me. My cheeks pink up at the memory of what we did.

"Why didn't you call me?" Jared asks, looking totally serious.

"Why would I call you?" It's a genuine question.

"Because if my daughter needs a place to stay, I'd like to know. I could have spoken to Melissa. We could have let you stay in our spare room."

I can't help it, I start to laugh. "Seriously?" The thought of me staying with him and his new partner is unbelievable. He can't mean it.

"I'm completely serious, Tessa. I don't want you taking my daughter to strangers' houses."

"He isn't a stranger. I told you, he's a friend."

"A friend that you fuck?"

His words feel like a slap to my face. This is so like him. His standards aren't just double, they're cubed.

"That's none of your business," I tell him, hating the way my face is going red.

"Of course it's my business. Anybody who spends time around Zoe is my business. Who is this guy? How do I know he's suitable to have around my child?"

"I don't remember you worrying about that when you and Melissa were spending nights in hotel rooms all over town."

It's his turn to redden. "That's got nothing to do with this."

"So it's okay for you to have an affair, while we were married, but it's not okay for me to date somebody when I'm free?" The gall of this man. I hate the way he manages to rile me up every time.

"Everything okay here?" Angela asks, putting her head around the doorway. Her eyes search for mine, as though she's trying to see if I need help. I give her the slightest shake of my head.

"Can't we have a conversation without her getting involved?" Jared shoots Angela a dirty look.

"No, you can't. Not when you're being an asshole." Angela rolls her eyes at him. "And by the way, she's right and you know it. You don't have a leg to stand on. Not when you and Melissa were fucking like rabbits without a thought for Tessa, let alone Zoe."

"Angela…" I shoot her a pleading look. I know she means the best, but it's not helping.

"Maybe if I'd been fulfilled in my marriage I wouldn't have had to look elsewhere," Jared counters.

"Maybe if you didn't have such a tiny dick, you would've had better luck," Angela shoots back.

Ouch.

I'm half inclined to leave and let these two go at it. But the only person who matters in all of this is Zoe.

"Can you both be quiet?" I ask. "Jared, do not come into my house and start shouting. Angela, thank you for trying to stand up for me, but I've got this."

She lets out a growl but says nothing.

And this is why I love her.

"Honey?" I say to her. "Can you go make those coffees?"

"I guess." She glares at Jared. "But I'm around if you need me."

"I know you are." I smile at her. This girl always has my

back. As soon as she's stomped out of the room – *again* – I turn to look at Jared.

"What I do in my life has nothing to do with you," I say, my voice low.

He opens his mouth to respond, but I put up my hand.

"But I agree. What happens in Zoe's life is both of our concerns. She will always be my first priority." I look at him pointedly. "She always has been. So she won't be spending nights anywhere else unless there's an emergency. Which there was."

"Good."

Oh he's so smug. I hate it.

"But as for me," I tell him. "What I do in the privacy of my own time is up to me. So don't you ever come into my house and accuse me of the exact things you were doing, except when you were doing them, you were wrecking a marriage."

"That's not fair…"

But I'm not finished. I've spent years trying to keep the peace with this man. "I'll date whoever I want to date. And when I'm ready to introduce them to Zoe as my boyfriend, then I'll do so. But unlike you, I'll do you the courtesy of letting you know first."

He inhales sharply, his dark eyes on me.

"What if I don't like him?"

"I don't give a rat's ass," I tell him. "You don't have to like him. You just have to trust my judgment that I know he's a safe person to spend time with Zoe."

And the stupid thing is, I know Linc's safe. He's kind. He's funny. He genuinely likes my kid.

"I'd want to meet him."

"That's your prerogative," I say, keeping my head high. "Anything else you want to talk about? Or can I get back to cleaning up my floors now?"

"You know it won't last, right? Zoe said he has no kids. That he's younger than you. He's just using you, that's all.

Any single guy worth anything isn't gonna saddle himself with a single mom. Especially not one approaching forty."

I let out a long breath. "Fuck off, Jared."

He blinks as though I've just struck him. But seriously, who does he think he is?

"Who I see is my business," I say again. "Now don't you want to go and spend some time with our child?"

"Fine." He turns on his heel and walks out of the door. A moment later, Angela walks back in carrying two cups of coffee.

"Where's assface?" she asks.

"He's gone."

"Good riddance."

My phone lights up again with another message from Linc. This time Angela doesn't do anything to hide the fact that she's reading it over my shoulder.

I've organized for a car to pick you and Angela up at seven. Dinner will be served to you both at my place. If I can't have you in my bed at least I can have you safely in my apartment for the night. – Linc x.

"Ooh," Angela says. "That man is one smooth talker. Does he have any brothers?" she asks.

"You have no idea."

But this one is mine. And he's giving me all the sweet feels.

————

LINC

. . .

"Darling, come dance with me." My mom holds her hand out to me as the band strikes up another song. The rest of the family are on the dance floor already. Holden and Blair are in the center, the two of them swaying softly, as Holden whispers something in her ear. Blair smiles and I'm almost certain whatever he said to her was dirty.

Truth is, I don't feel much like dancing. Which is weird, because I've always loved to dance. But I'm feeling stupidly moody and I'm missing Tessa.

I stand and take my mom's hand and lead her over to the rest of the family. Myles and Ava are dancing and laughing. Liam and Sophie are staring into each other's eyes. Eli and Mackenzie are clinging to each other like they never want to let go.

Even Brooks is dancing with some pretty woman he was sitting next to at dinner.

It doesn't escape my attention that I'm the only brother who is alone tonight.

"You're very quiet tonight," Mom says. "Is everything okay?"

Immediately, my gut tightens.

"Everything is fine," I say, pasting on a smile. "Why wouldn't it be?"

She says nothing for a moment. From the corner of my eye I see my father and Julia, his wife, dancing. She's actually his fourth wife, though no one ever talks about his first wife. But the others are here. Linda was his second wife – she's the mother of Myles, Liam, Eli, and Holden and she's currently dancing with Francie, my little sister.

I used to hate how complicated our family was. I blamed my mom's attempt at leaving the world on that.

Now that I'm grown up I've realized that everybody's life is complicated. Just in different ways.

"I heard through the grapevine that you've been seeing

somebody," she says as the band segues into another song. It's a little faster, but nothing we can't handle.

"Yep."

She takes a deep breath. "And she's a single mother?"

Her eyes catch mine and I frown. "You say that like it's a bad thing."

There's a softness to her mouth as she gives me the smallest of smiles. "I didn't mean to sound like that. It's just..." she trails off. "I suppose I was surprised when Linda told me."

"Linda told you?" My older brothers' mom and my own are close. But I'm still surprised Linda knew about this.

"Apparently Ava let it slip," Mom says. "Not that anything can stay secret for long."

"Some things can," I point out and she winces. And yeah, we start avoiding that subject again.

"So tell me about this woman. What's her name?" Mom asks.

"Tessa Carmichael." I can't help but smile as I say her name.

"And you work with her?" There's still no expression on her face. I can't read her at all.

"Sort of. We both work for Roman. I didn't really get to know her until a a little over a month ago."

A look of relief catches Mom's face. "Oh, I thought it was more serious than that."

"It is," I say firmly. "I'm very serious about her."

She blows out a mouthful of air again. "How many children does she have?"

"One. Zoe. She's thirteen."

"She has a teenager?" Mom's voice rises. "How old is this woman?"

The way she's questioning makes me grit my teeth. Of all people, I didn't expect this kind of response from my mom.

"She's a couple of years older than me. And I'm surprised at you."

"What do you mean?" she asks, sounding genuinely confused.

"I mean you've been a single mom for a long time. I thought you'd be on her side."

"There are no sides, darling," she says smoothly. "And if there were, I'd always be on yours. I'm just concerned, that's all. You've gone from zero to a hundred with this woman. Do you really know her? Have you considered how difficult it will be if you become serious? I just feel like you're rushing this, that's all. She's a mom. You'll never be number one in her life."

"I wouldn't want to be," I tell her. "Kids should always come first."

She winces again. "I know I let you down. I just..." she sighs. "I don't want to see you repeating any patterns."

"What kind of patterns?" I'm getting annoyed with her.

"The kind where you try to save the single mom all over again."

"Jesus, Mom. I've no idea where you're getting all this pop psychology from, but I'm not trying to save anybody. Now can we change the subject, please?" I ask.

Her gaze catches mine. "I'm sorry. I just care..."

"I know you do." I give her a tight nod. "But now I need you to back off."

"Okay." She nods.

And now I feel like a douche for hurting her feelings. "When you meet her you'll understand," I tell her.

And then I lead us to the side of the dance floor, smoothly handing Mom over to Liam, who just happens to be standing there, watching his wife dance with our dad.

Turning my back on them all, I go stand at the bar. Even though I might not be feeling this wedding, I love my brother to the moon and back, and it's his day so he deserves to be celebrated.

———

By the time I can sneak away and call Tessa it's almost eight and the sun is starting to fade over the lake. More people are on the dance floor now. The band has finished playing and a DJ has taken over, much to the younger contingent's delight.

In the corner, my mom, Linda, and Julia are sitting together, gossiping. Francie and a couple of my nephews are sitting on their laps. My brothers are hanging out at the bar and their partners are dancing to Beyoncé.

And I'm standing on the edge of the pier, watching the reflection of the moon along the surface of the lake. My dad used to say that when the moon and sun could be seen at the same time, all your wishes could come true.

"Hi." Tessa's voice when she answers the phone makes my chest feel warm. "How was the wedding?"

"Good."

She starts to laugh. "Is that it? No description of the bride, no gushing over their vows? What kind of flowers did they have?"

"If you'd been here you'd know." Oh boy, that came out more pissy than I'd meant. "I'm sorry. I miss you."

There's a pause. "I miss you, too. Thank you for arranging dinner for Angela and me. She just left." Which means Tessa is still at my place, alone. I insisted, because her place still isn't habitable.

"It was a pleasure." It was the most fun I had today. "How's the clean up going?"

"Pretty good." Tessa let out a breath. "By the way, Jared came to see me today."

"Your ex?" I frown. "What did he want?"

"He found out that we stayed with you last weekend. He wasn't happy."

"Why did it matter to him?" I ask, feeling annoyed now. The thought of her talking to him makes my hands curl into fists. I've never met the guy but I dislike him intensely.

"He's Zoe's dad," Tessa reminds me.

"When it suits him. I hope you told him off." Or I will. Because I'm not letting that asshole come between us. Not when things are already complicated enough.

"I told him that if things get serious between us I'll let him know."

"What do you mean 'if'?" I ask her. A bird swoops down into the water, creating ripples across the surface. "We are serious, Tessa."

"It's only been a few weeks."

"We've known each other for years."

"We've disliked each other for years. And that's not what I meant. Please don't get mad at me. Dealing with Jared was bad enough."

"I'm sorry. I just don't like the guy." And I hate the idea of him being around her.

"Me either. But I have to co-parent with him. And sometimes that involves doing things I don't particularly like. For example, talking to him."

"I can talk to him for you. Just say the word."

She laughs and it feels like music coming through the phone. "I know you could. But I've got this." She lets out a sigh. "I wish I'd just come and hidden in your cabin. We could have spent tonight together."

Why the hell didn't I think of that? "Fuck. I should have gotten us a hotel room."

"Yeah, but I did need to get some cleaning done. The living room is almost finished."

"It is? Send me a photo," I instruct her. "And make sure you're naked in it."

She laughs again. "I've been looking at your picture all day. I've never seen a man fill a tux so perfectly."

"You should see me out of it."

"I wish I could."

I swallow hard, because if I thought I missed her before, now it's at another level.

"Linc? Myles is looking for you," Julia calls out from the shore. "Something about Holden and Blair's gift."

We've all gone in on their honeymoon together. Of all the places in the world, they chose Alaska. I guess they want to be alone. Myles plans to give it to them tonight.

"Okay," I say, nodding at my stepmom. "I gotta go. Call you later?"

"I'll probably be in bed by ten," Tessa says. "I'm exhausted."

I check my watch. "I'll call you in an hour then."

And I don't care what my mom thinks. I don't care what Jared thinks either.

I'm fucking obsessed with this woman. And I'm not letting anybody ruin that.

CHAPTER
TWENTY-EIGHT

TESSA

I'm woken by soft lips pressing against mine.

"Huh?" My eyes fly open to find Linc leaning over me. He's dressed in his tux, and his hair is disheveled. "Linc? What are you doing here?"

I'm laying in his bed, because he insisted I stay at his apartment tonight after Angela and I had dinner. He'd ordered three courses from a new restaurant in Manhattan and had it brought over with the car he sent for us.

Angela and I had pretty much spent the whole meal giggling about how sweet he is. Because nobody's ever done something like that for me. And when she left I spent an obscene amount of time in his huge tub, playing with every jet until the muscles in my back finally eased.

"I couldn't sleep without you," he says. "Decided to come home and get some shut eye."

I'm fully awake now. I take in the way his black tie is hanging around his neck, the top button of his white shirt unfastened. He's still wearing his dress pants but he doesn't have his suit jacket on anymore.

His shirt sleeves are rolled up, revealing tan skin and a Rolex. For a second I wonder if I'm having some kind of dream, because he looks too good to be true.

"You're supposed to be at your brother's wedding," I whisper, as he pulls his tie off and starts unbuttoning his shirt. And yes, I stare at him without embarrassment as he shrugs it off, then pulls his undershirt over his head.

Dear God, I think I might combust.

"I was. Things were winding down. I decided to hop on a copter and come see my girl."

"You took a helicopter?" My voice lifts an octave. "How much did that cost?"

"I hitched a ride with a friend of my dad's. He lives in Manhattan." He shrugs as though this is an every day occurrence.

Maybe it is. I'm trying not to think about that too much.

He unfastens his pants, sliding them down his hips. I can see the outline of his thigh muscles where they meet his shorts.

"Won't your family be worried?" I ask him. "Won't they notice that you're not there in the morning?"

"We have a brunch planned. At eleven. And I'll be back in time for that."

My eyes widen. "In Virginia?"

He smiles as he pulls off his shorts. "Yep. I don't suppose you want to join me?"

I start to laugh. "No."

"Spoilsport."

"Zoe will be home tomorrow afternoon," I remind him.

He turns around and gives me the perfect view of his peachy ass as he walks into the bathroom, leaving the door open. A moment later the shower turns on, and I'm reminded of our time in Exuma. When I knew he was naked just a room away from me.

When I didn't know how much I was going to fall for this man.

"Maybe I'll skip brunch," he shouts out over the noise of the shower.

"You can't skip brunch. It's your brother's wedding." I still can't believe he's here, standing beneath his shower like he hasn't just traveled hundreds of miles in a helicopter to spend the night with me.

"Will Jared come in when he drops off Zoe?" Linc asks when he's out of the shower. He has a white towel slung around his hips, and is using another to dry his face.

"He doesn't usually. He's always in too much of a hurry."

Linc's eyes catch mine. "I don't want him upsetting you again."

"Is that why you came back?" I ask him. "Because I was upset?"

He drops the towel he's holding, then walks toward me, his gaze intent. "No. I came back because I've spent the day surrounded by the people that I love and I was miserable. I love weddings. I love parties. Or I used to. But it all felt… less… without you. Like somebody had turned the color down on life. And when my dad's friend said he was leaving for New York all I could think about was the fact that you were here and I wasn't. And I'd either leave with him or walk all the way home, because I want to spend the night curled around you."

"Oh," I say, my chest tight. "That's beautiful."

"Thank you." He pulls the towel around his waist off, then lifts the covers and climbs into bed beside me. He kisses me softly again, in a way that sends my heart racing. "And if you didn't get the message, I'm serious about you. I know we have things to sort out, not least my fucking job, but I'm all in, Tessa, no matter what anybody says."

"Do you mean Jared?" I ask, because I know he's annoyed with him for what he said.

"Yeah, something like that."

"Because you should ignore him. I am." I cup his face. He's freshly shaven. I can smell the pine scent of his shower gel. "By the way, I really like you, too."

He gives me the sweetest of smiles. "Good." He pulls me against him, and I'm overwhelmed by this man. By the way my life has changed so much.

I'm really trying not to think about the complications. Jared and work and my mid-reno home. I just want to enjoy this feeling of being in his arms.

"Tell me about the wedding," I say, as he runs his finger down my spine. He's already hard.

"The bride wore white. The groom messed up his lines because he's an imbecile. My aunt Gemma got drunk like she always does and now I need you to shut up because I'm going to fuck you."

He says them against my lips. And I start to laugh again, as he reaches between us, his fingers oh-so-soft as they slide against me.

"Jesus, you're already wet."

"I just saw you in a tux. Then not in a tux," I whisper against him.

He rolls on top of me, replacing his fingers with the part of him I need the most, his lips gentle against mine as he slowly slides inside.

And when we both come, he's cupping my face with his gentle palms, his eyes never leaving mine.

"We're going to make this work," he says gruffly.

———

It's three weeks later, and Linc's face is on my screen. I'm in bed and he's in a suit, looking dangerously attractive as he scowls at the camera. It's early in the morning his time, and I can see pale shafts of sunlight shining through the window behind him. It's after midnight here, and I'm so sleepy my eyes are drooping.

He's been working incredibly hard at opening the European office. He's also managed to fly home twice, even though I know he needs to rest. The first time was when Zoe was at Jared's and we spent the whole weekend in his bed.

The second time she was home. We haven't told her about us being together yet, and it touched my heart how casual he kept things. He helped us with more renovations and I felt bad that he was working on my place after such a busy week and flight, but he swore it was relaxing for him.

Angela insisted on taking Zoe to dinner and a show later that night – Godmother's rights – so we could have a couple of hours alone.

"This time difference isn't going to work," Linc says, his brows knitting together. "How the hell are we supposed to have phone sex when either I'm at work or you are?"

I giggle, because he really does look like he needs some release. "Can't you just… you know…"

"What, Tessa? What should I do?"

"Touch yourself," I whisper. "Make friends with Mr. Right."

"Mr. Right?" He sounds almost disgusted.

"Your right hand," I clarify and his scowl deepens.

"Why would I want my right hand when the most gorgeous woman alive is wet and waiting for me?"

"I'm not wet."

"You would be if I was there," he tells me.

Yes, I probably would. I'm learning that sex is Linc's love language. It's how he expresses himself. I can't say I'm sad about that.

"And I can't fucking come home this weekend," he says. "That's what I called to tell you."

Oh. I take a deep breath because we knew this was possible. He's meeting with clients every working hour to try to hit the ground running with the European Office of Hampshire PR.

"That's okay. I'm seeing my other boyfriend this weekend anyway," I tell him.

He rolls his eyes at me, still not amused.

"You can call me early on Sunday morning your time," I tell him. Which will make it after midnight here. "I'll make sure I stay up late."

"For what?" There's a hint of interest in his eyes now.

"You know what for."

"So you can help Mr. Right along?"

I grin. "A threesome? So early in our relationship." I can still remember our talk about that. And I'm mostly okay that despite him being younger than me he's so much more experienced. In sex anyway.

"I'm not sharing you with anybody," he tells me. "And just so you know, when I fly home next, you need to take a few days off work because you won't be walking."

"Is that all you want me for? My body?" I tease.

His face turns suddenly serious. "No. I want you because you make me smile. Because I like talking to you. Because I can't sleep unless I'm wrapped around you. Did you know I only got three hours last night?"

"No wonder you're grumpy," I say smiling.

"Damn right."

I blow him a kiss and then I feel my eyes start to get heavy. "I need to get some sleep," I tell him. "I have a meeting at eight."

"Okay," he says softly. "But don't turn off the the video. I want to watch you."

"You pervert."

"Damn right I am. Sweet dreams, Carmichael."

———

"Mom, look!" Zoe runs into the kitchen. It's the following week and I'm cooking pasta in one pot and stirring pasta sauce in another and I'm just plain exhausted because it's been a long day and I hate this kitchen.

That's the problem with renovating one room at a time. When each room is done it makes the others look even more shabby. And the kitchen is going to be the biggest – and costliest – room to remodel. Even with the bonus we're getting from winning the Exuma account, I won't be able to afford all the supplies until next year. Not after the costs for the bathroom overran, thanks to a pipe that needed digging out and replacing.

I'm down to a few thousand dollars in my savings account and I can't take on any more debt.

I know I'm luckier than most. We have a roof over our heads and I have a job bringing in money and things are on the up. I just wish I didn't feel inadequate every time I walked into this room.

"What is it?" I ask her.

"Linc sent me this super cool t-shirt. It's French." She holds it up against her. It's black with two manga characters on it, with their names *Jeanne Et Serge*, written across the front. "Isn't it cool?"

"Linc sent you that?" They had a huge discussion about Manga the last time he was was in town. I'm touched that he remembers that.

"Yeah. A delivery man dropped it off." Her face lights up. "I'm going to wear it this weekend to Alice's party."

"You're at your dad's this weekend," I say. "Aren't you?"

"Yes." She looks at me as though I'm an idiot. "You're the one who agreed to the custody schedule."

"Maybe it's best if you don't tell him it's from Linc," I tell her.

As soon as the words escape my lips I feel like an asshole. Because I never want my kid to lie. And I'm annoyed at myself for being annoyed at Linc for sending it to her and making me ask her to lie.

Damn, it's been a hard day. I can feel a headache coming on.

"Does Dad not like Linc?"

The sauce is boiling too hard. I turn the heat down. "It's not that. It's just…" I shake my head, totally unprepared to have this conversation. "Dad is worried about him being around you, even though he shouldn't be."

"Why?" She looks almost annoyed. "Melissa is around me all the time when I'm over at their house. She spends more time with me than Dad does."

"I know." I nod. "And it's not anything you've done wrong. Or Linc for that matter. The t-shirt is fabulous. Linc is very sweet."

"He is." She nods. "And I'm wearing it. No matter what."

"Of course you are. Just ignore me." I shoot her a smile. I need to get over this. It's just that I feel extra inadequate today. I can't shake it off no matter how much I try.

And yes, some of it may be due to the Instagram photo Angela sent me of Linc at a party in Paris last night.

He wasn't with a woman. Not that I thought he would be. I'm over that kind of jealousy now. But his life is so different to mine and sometimes I find myself wondering how long he's going to stick around when he realizes just how boring it is trying to keep a roof over our heads.

"You look sad," Zoe says.

I force a smile onto my face. "I'm not sad. Just tired. Dinner will be ready in five minutes. Why don't you sit at the table and tell me about your day?"

I listen as she tells me about an experiment they did in science, and how they're studying *Macbeth* in English class but the teacher is so superstitious they're not allowed to say the name.

"We have to call it the Scottish Play," she tells me as I put our bowls on the table. She picks her spoon and fork up and twirls the noodles like an expert.

"So what do you call the character Macbeth?"

"The Scottish guy."

"Aren't all the characters Scottish?" I ask her.

"Yeah, but we're allowed to say their names. Then Jonah started calling his MacBook a ScottishBook and things deteriorated from there."

Zoe spends the evening doing her homework so she doesn't have to do it over the weekend, and I spend the time reviewing some influencer videos for the Exuma project, before sending them to Roman for his approval. And then I check the calendar and I realize with relief that I've been moody tonight for a reason.

My period is always so irregular that I don't bother tracking it, but I know the ballpark of when it's supposed to arrive. I'm smiling through my tears because at least I'm not turning into a perpetual bitch for no reason.

Linc calls at midnight my time again, while he's getting ready for work in Paris. And when I hear his voice, like the over emotional idiot I am, I burst into tears.

"What's wrong?" His voice echoes with alarm.

"I'm sorry. I'm just hormonal." If this doesn't put him off me then nothing will. "My period is due any day."

He lets out a long breath. "Thank god. I was about to book the next flight home."

"You're coming home in two days anyway," I point out, sniffling. "And you don't need to fly back because I'm an idiot." He's the one who has to cope with being away from home, and all the jet lag.

"It would be a win-win." There's a smile in his voice. "I'd get some fucking sleep at night."

"I'll give you all the sleep this weekend," I promise him. "I'll make you sleep so good, baby."

He laughs and it feels so good to hear it.

"Unfortunately, we have to go out on Saturday night."

"We do?" Well there goes my plan of not getting out of bed for two days.

"My family is in town. They want to catch up. And meet you."

My chest tightens. "Why?" I ask, because I genuinely have no idea. I'm not rich like them. Not glamorous. Linc showed me some of the photographs from his brother's wedding. The dresses there were more expensive than my bathroom cost. I know because Page Six said so.

And now I'm thinking about Jared's parents, and how they never liked me. I'm pretty sure they did some kind of happy dance when they found out about our separation.

"Because they want to meet the woman who puts a smile on my face. And I want you to meet them, too."

And now I feel worse than ever. A tear rolls down my cheek because this man knows exactly how to sweet talk.

And he is sweet. The sweetest. I miss him so much.

It's stupid to feel such a crisis of confidence, I know that. But everything inside of me feels on edge.

It's just the hormones, I tell myself. That's all it is.

If Linc wants me to meet his family then I'll do it for him.

"Okay," I say. "I'll do it."

"Of course you will. And they'll love you."

I'm not sure they will. And isn't that the bitch? Because I've fallen in love with this man. I need to tell him, but I'll do it when saying it doesn't make me cry.

"I miss you," I whisper instead. But it means the same thing.

I miss you. I love you.

God, I hope his family doesn't hate me.

CHAPTER
TWENTY-NINE

TESSA

Linc arrives at my house extremely late on Friday. I ended up getting a key made for him. Much to his annoyance, I left it under a pot at the front of the house, because I needed to get to bed and Zoe is at a friend's for a sleepover before going to her dad's tomorrow. Still, he must have found it because I wake up to him laying in my bed, his arms around my waist, spooning me from behind.

I turn to look at him and his eyes catch mine.

"When did you get back?" I ask him.

"About an hour ago." He presses his lips against mine. "Flight was delayed by an hour. Some motherfucker missed the boarding call and we missed our takeoff spot."

"Was it you?"

He smiles against my mouth. "No, but I'm guessing it was somebody important. I was the first one on there. Couldn't wait to get back to you." He pushes the hair from my face. "You look like shit, Carmichael."

"Thanks." I roll my eyes, but I can't stop the smile from pulling at my lips. I'm just so happy he's back.

I didn't know I'd find it this hard for us to be apart. And yes, some of that is my messed up hormones but the rest is him.

I can't bear to be without him.

"Seriously, did you get any sleep without me here?"

"Not much," I admit. He turns so my head is resting on his chest. He starts to stroke my hair. I always thought I'd be happy alone. I was never afraid of being the only one in the house. But when Zoe is at her dad's and Linc's in Paris I've hated the echo of silence that greets me every time I walk in.

"I told you that you should have stayed at my place," Linc says. His fingers are drawing circles on my spine.

"I'm not moving into your apartment," I murmur, closing my eyes because having him here is making me feel relaxed for the first time in days.

"You'll have to eventually," he says softly.

"Why?"

"Because this place isn't big enough for three people."

My eyes fly open again. "You want us to move in with you?" I ask him.

"I mean, not immediately." He grins at me. "We need to tell Zoe about us first. And get her used to us being together. But it's going to happen eventually. Once the Paris office is up and running and I'm back here full time I won't be hopping from one bed to another. I want you in mine."

"And Zoe?" I whisper.

"We'll get her room decorated any way she wants it. Hell, we can move into a new apartment if she prefers. We'll talk about it."

"Isn't it too soon?" I ask him.

For the first time uncertainty flits over his face. And this is a man who is never uncertain. "Is that what you think?" he asks. "Because I'm of the opinion that it can't come soon enough. I want you and Zoe living with me. If that's not what you want…"

"I didn't say that. I just…" I let out a mouthful of air. "I haven't even met your family yet. What if they hate me?"

"Why would they hate you?" he asks, a smile flitting at his lips. "They'll fucking love you. Now shut up and let me show you how much I've missed you."

"I thought you were tired."

"Never too tired for that, Carmichael. Now spread your legs and let me in."

I do as he asks, as he drags his finger along me, until he finds the part that needs him most.

"Christ, I missed this," he whispers, kissing his way down my body.

"I missed you too," I whisper and then he buries his face between my thighs and all rational thought rushes out of my brain.

———

Linc has to leave to meet up with his brothers and his father for a meeting. I should be working on the house, but instead I call Angela in a panic, because nothing in my closet looks good enough to wear to meet his family. I didn't want to spend money on a new dress, but something new is needed.

"Don't panic," she tells me. "I'm on my way."

She ends up taking me to a consignment store she knows right outside the city. She insists on sitting on a bench seat with a tie wrapped around her neck as she assesses each outfit I try on, like we're in some kind of rerun of *Pretty Woman*.

"Too flouncy," she says about the first dress. And she's right. I'm not a flouncy kind of girl, no matter how pretty the pink feathery skirt is.

"Too tight." She wrinkles her nose at the second dress. "You have a kick ass body but that one makes you look like you have a pooch."

I look down and she's right. "Ugh. I'm getting old."

"It's not you, sweetie. It's the dress."

The third one is black satin. It's as tight as the last one, but in all the right places.

"Hello boobs," Angela says, staring at the neckline. "Jesus, Linc's eyes are going to pop out."

I look down. Yeah, they really do look impressive in this.

"You look like you've had a boob job," Angela tells me, laughing. "All of you will be like this once you two are living together."

"What do you mean?"

"I mean he's rich and you'll be able to afford all the mom glow ups."

And there it is again, that little feeling of inadequacy. I don't even know where it's coming from. "Do you think I need them?" I ask, my voice quiet.

"Oh honey." She rushes over to me, hugging me so tight my boobs squash against her chest. "I was joking. Of course you don't need surgery. You don't need anything. You're perfect." She shakes her head. "I speak before I think sometimes. You know that."

"It's not you. I know you were joking. I'm just waiting for my period to start and my body feels bloated and I'm in that *I hate myself* hormonal phase."

She looks at me for a minute. "When is your period due?"

"I don't know. This week sometime."

"Are you sure you're not pregnant?"

I roll my eyes at her. "Positive." At least that's one thing I can be sure of. "I just can't understand why they're getting worse." I sigh. Because I hate feeling this way, I really do.

"Maybe you're perimenopausal."

I frown. "What?"

"You know, like about to hit the menopause. Like your body is in it's last ditch effort to keep you fertile, so it's throwing all the hormones it has at you until it finally gives up."

"You think I'm menopausal?" I ask her, a sick feeling tugging at my stomach. "I'm only thirty-five." And now I suddenly feel older. So much older than Linc's thirty-two years.

Angela's eyes widen as though she's sensed she's made things worse. "It was just a suggestion. It's probably nothing. I was just trying to help."

"But what if I am?" I ask. "Linc's in the prime of his life. He won't want to be with me."

She shakes her head. "Of course he will. I mean you won't have to worry about birth control at least."

I know she's trying to cheer me up. "What if Linc wants kids?" I ask her. And now I'm panicking again. How can a few years between us feel like a lifetime?

Any single guy worth anything isn't gonna saddle himself with a single mom. Especially not one approaching forty.

Jared's words of the other week echo in my mind. He's wrong about Linc, I know he is. But I also know Linc adores his nieces and nephews. He's going to want kids.

"Have you and Linc talked about having a family?" she asks me.

"No." And why haven't we? He's already talking about us moving in together and we haven't even spoken about the most important thing.

"Do you want more?" she asks me. And all these questions are just making me panic.

"I don't know," I say. "I'm not sure." I'm getting older, my career is finally on track. And then there's Zoe. She's getting closer to college than kindergarten. Even if she gets a scholarship, my half of her expenses are going to pretty much wipe me out.

Everything's happened too quickly. I feel like an idiot for not talking with him more. I'm in love with him, but I have no idea what he wants from me.

"You two need to talk," Angela says.

I give her the smallest of smiles. "We do," I agree. "We'll do it tomorrow. If I don't mess tonight up."

"You won't mess it up," she tells me. "You're perfect for each other. Anybody can see that."

"As long as his family does." I sigh. "Then we can get through the rest."

———

LINC

"So that's it." My father's lawyer takes the last document from Brooks and slides it into his portfolio. We've spent the last hour signing contracts and agreeing to changes in my father's real estate holdings. Nothing major, just something he likes to do every now and again. Even at his age he can't let go. He likes to move his money and properties around like a croupier at a casino. Despite the fact that Liam and Myles are perfectly capable of running his finances for him.

We also needed to add Francie – our baby sister – to the list of beneficial owners. For now her mom, Dad's current wife Julia, will represent her at board meetings. But eventually she'll take her place at this table with us.

"Well okay then. Thank you, boys." My father nods at us. I meet Myles' gaze and we both bite down a grin, because our father is the only one who thinks of us as kids still. Myles is in his forties, even Brooks and I are in our thirties.

Our dad stands and takes Julia's hand. "We'll see you at the Plaza this evening." The two of them walk out of his attorney's New York office – open on a Saturday at his request – and the six of us follow. Eli and Holden are at the front, talking about Eli's hockey team, followed by Liam and Brooks.

Myles walks beside me. "We're looking forward to meeting Tessa tonight," he says.

"She's looking forward to it, too," I reply and Brooks coughs out a laugh.

"What?" I ask him.

"Nobody looks forward to meeting our family," Brooks replies, shaking his head. "Have you seen us? It's like the wedding scene in the *Godfather*. People shake at the knees when they have to be near the Salingers."

"We're not exactly the Mafia," Myles says.

"Yeah, but we're still fucking intimidating. Do you know how many girlfriends I lost because they were scared of you guys?"

"Seriously?" Myles frowns.

Brooks shrugs. "Not everybody loves big families."

"Tessa will be fine," I say confidently. "She's not afraid of you all. She's a grown woman with a kid and a career. Five Salinger brothers aren't going to scare her."

"Of course we won't," Myles says confidently. "We're like teddy bears."

"Except for the cute and cuddly part," Brooks says.

"Bears then." Liam grins.

"Like wolves," Brooks adds. "But bigger. So you're pretty much throwing the girl you like to the wolves."

"Woman," I correct. "And I don't just like her."

All five of them stop walking. I barrage into Brooks' back.

"What?"

"I said she's a woman."

Brooks sighs. "The other part." His eyes meet mine.

"I'm in love with her." I'm not ashamed of it. "I just haven't told her yet."

"Why not?" Myles asks.

"Because I've been flying back and forth over the Atlantic for the past few weeks." I huff. "But I'm going to tell her."

"You should tell her before we meet her," Brooks says, smirking. "Because now we're going to be staring at her like she's some kind of zoological specimen."

"The woman who tamed Linc Salinger," Eli murmurs.

"Roll up and see her. Only ten dollars a look," Brooks shouts out, clearly enjoying himself.

I send them all a dirty look. "Seriously? Did I treat your women like this when you were falling in love with them?"

"Yes," they all say at once. And then they start to laugh.

"No wonder she doesn't want to meet you," I mutter. "I'm half inclined to take her out to dinner just the two of us." Not least because on Sunday night I have to catch a fucking flight back to Paris. Spending the morning at the damn lawyer's office and tonight with the family is cutting into our alone time.

"No you won't," Myles says smoothly. "Because you want us to meet her. You want us to love her the way you do. And we will. Now go home and chill out. We'll see you tonight."

As always, our big brother has the final word.

———

TESSA

"You look absolutely fuckable," Linc says, giving me the dirtiest look as we climb out of the town car he ordered. He takes my hand and we walk up the steps to the restaurant. "I keep pinching myself to make sure that you're really mine."

"I was aiming for 'meeting the parents' classy," I tell him.

He smirks. "You look like that, too."

After we went dress shopping, Angela insisted on calling her hairdresser, who somehow managed to squeeze me in.

My long hair is teased into waves that tumble around my shoulders. I put on more makeup than I usually do, though it's still pretty natural.

Linc's gaze dips to my dress again, taking in the way it clings to my body.

"You don't look too bad yourself," I say, smiling. Because this man looks like a god in a tux. I've been trying to push my conversation with Angela out of my mind. We can talk about it tomorrow. Tonight is about Linc and his family.

I'm determined to make a good impression.

"My family is going to love you," he whispers, brushing his lips against my cheek. How can he read my mind so easily. "But if you hate them, tell me and I'll disown them in a heartbeat. We'll never see them again."

I laugh. "Stop it, I know they're important to you."

"Not as important as you are," he says, suddenly serious. He squeezes my hand as we walk into the foyer. The paneled walls are painted in cream and gold, and there's a huge chandelier sparkling from the center of the ceiling. The place screams old money.

The Maitre D' recognizes Linc right away. "I spent a lot of time here with my dad when we were kids," he whispers in my ear. "Whenever Brooks and I were home from school he'd bring us here for dinner."

"Mr. Salinger," the Maitre D' murmurs. "Your party is in our private room. Angelica will take you."

"Thank you." Linc nods.

Angelica smiles at us both, her long, black slicked-back hair shining in the lamplight. "Please come with me."

When we enter the private room we're greeted by a cacophony of voices. The room is large – a small ballroom rather than a private dining room – but it's full of people. We barely make it inside before Linc gets greeted by somebody. I try to step back but he grabs my hand and pulls me to his side.

"This is Tessa," he says, sliding his arm around my waist. "Tessa, this is my kind-of-mom, Linda."

"It's a pleasure to meet you." Linda kisses my cheek as I tell her likewise. From what I can remember, Linda is Linc's older brothers' mom. "But don't tell Deandra I'm the first to meet you. She'll kill me."

From there I'm introduced to so many people my head begins to spin. I meet his brother Holden and his wife Blair, who are both glowing after their honeymoon, and then I'm introduced to Eli, his brother who is a hockey coach and make an idiot out of myself by asking what stadium they play in.

"Arena," Linc murmurs in my ear because he knows I'm clueless when it comes to sports.

And then I meet Myles and Liam, his oldest brothers. They're standing at the bar with their wives and as soon as I'm introduced their attention is firmly on me. They all shake my hand.

"I hear you have a daughter," Myles says, offering me a glass of champagne.

"Can I have an orange juice?" I ask, because champagne goes straight to my head and I'm already worried about making an idiot out of myself in front of his family.

Linc glances at me. "Everything okay?"

"I just want to pace myself." I give him a smile.

Myles passes me a glass of juice.

"How old is your daughter?" Ava, Myles' wife asks. She has such a friendly face. I begin to relax.

"She's thirteen."

"Linc has to deal with a teenager?" Liam asks, starting to laugh. "Oh boy."

"She's a good kid," Linc says and I squeeze his hand. "Much nicer than you all were when you were teenagers."

"That's because you're boys," Ava says. Then she looks at me. "I'm finding the post-toddler years hard enough. I'll have to get your advice on how to deal with teenagers."

"I'm not sure I can give any advice," I tell her honestly. "It's kind of like childbirth but years long instead of hours. You just have to get through it."

They laugh and I find myself relaxing even more. They really are lovely.

And then somebody clears their throat behind my back.

"Mom," Linc says, turning me to face her. "I was wondering where you were."

"I had to take a call." She turns to look at me, her eyes pale. "You must be Tessa," she says.

"Hi." I beam at her. She smiles softly back. "It's a pleasure to meet you."

Linc's palm is pressed against the curve of my back.

"Remind me again," his mom says. "Where did you two meet?"

"Mom, I told you. At work."

She nods. Behind her Myles and Liam are facing the bar, laughing about something. "You work for my son?" she asks. I still can't read her expression at all. I wonder if I'll be like this when I meet the partners Zoe brings home.

I hope not. I hope I'll be too busy putting them at ease to make them feel awkward.

"She works with me," Linc says. "For Roman."

"Oh yes, Roman. A good man. So are you one of the women I see him dating on Instagram?"

"I don't have an Instagram," I tell her. "That will be his French girls."

Linc starts to laugh at my reference to *Titanic*. His mom doesn't though.

"Well I should go say hello to everybody," she says. "Nice to meet you, Tessa." She leans forward to kiss Linc on the cheek. "We should catch up tomorrow. You could meet me for breakfast."

Linc shakes his head. "I can't. I'm taking Tessa to breakfast."

Her smile wavers. "Lunch then."

"I have to fly back to Paris tomorrow afternoon. Next week?" he suggests. And I immediately feel bad because I'm monopolizing his time.

"You should go to breakfast," I tell him. "I have things to do tomorrow morning anyway."

"Next week," Linc says, brooking no argument.

As soon as she leaves I let out a long breath. She barely looked at me. Is it my dress? I look down at the neckline, knowing I should have chosen something else. She so obviously doesn't like me.

My hands shake as I lift my glass of orange juice to my lips.

"Sorry," he says, brushing my jaw with his lips. "She's not great with new people."

"She was fine when she met Ava," Myles points out, turning back to us. So he must have heard the whole embarrassingly short introduction. *Great.*

Ava's eyes meet mine. She gives me the kindest of smiles. "But you're not her son, are you?" she says to Myles. "I think she's just protective of Linc, that's all."

"How many girls have you brought home to meet her anyway?" Liam asks. And then his wife – Sophie – pokes him in the ribs. "Ow."

"He didn't mean it like that," Sophie says. "Did you?"

"I don't know." Linc frowns. "I can't think of anybody I've introduced her to."

Ava looks suddenly relieved. "That'll explain it then."

"What do you mean?" Linc asks.

"You're her baby. She's not used to having to share you." Ava shrugs. "I hope I'm not like that when Charlie brings home girls, but who knows?"

"She's just slow to warm up," Myles agrees. He smiles warmly at me. "For what it's worth, we're pleased to meet you."

Liam nods in agreement. "There's just one thing I want to know?"

I force a smile onto my face. "What is it?"

"How the hell do you put up with him? Because I never could."

———

LINC

"Mom?" I say, walking after her as she makes her way across the room to Linda and Julia. "Can I have a word?"

I'm annoyed with her. And with myself. Maybe this wasn't the best time to introduce Tessa to the family, but after spending the last week fucking pining after her, I wasn't going to come here without her. There was no reason for Mom to be so cold.

Luckily Ava and Sophie have formed a protective ring around her, along with Blair and Mackenzie – my other brothers' wives – who are asking her about the Exuma project we were working on together.

I glance at my watch. In five minutes we'll sit down to dinner. And in an hour I'm going to take Tessa home and make it up to her for my mom's rudeness.

"Can't it wait?" Mom asks. "We're about to eat dinner."

"No, it can't." I take her arm and pull her over to the side. "The way you just talked to Tessa was rude."

Mom's gaze meets mine. She doesn't look sorry at all. "I'm just trying to look after you," she tells me. "I don't think she's right for you."

"You don't even know her." A wave of fury washes through me. "Do you know how hard I had to work to get her to come tonight? After this she'll probably never want to meet the family again."

"Then you have to consider if she's the right person for you." Mom lifts a brow. "You have a big family. We're not all sweetness and light. If she's going to become part of it she needs to understand that."

"You were never like this with Ava and Sophie. Or any of the others."

"They didn't have children."

I take a long breath. So here we are, at the crux of it.

"Seriously?" I ask. "You're holding that against her? You were a single mom yourself."

"And I didn't date anybody," she says, pursing her lips.

"Well maybe you should have."

For a moment the implacable mask drops. "What's that supposed to mean?" she asks. I've never seen her like this before. So fucking harsh.

"It means that instead of using me as your emotional crutch you could have found somebody your own damn age."

She flinches. "That's unfair."

"Is it? Or is it unfair to expect your kid to be the one to mop up the mess you left? Do you know how much that day I walked in on you unconscious affected me?"

Her eyes widen. "We are not going to talk about this right now."

"Of course we're not." I roll my eyes. "We never fucking talk about it. I just have nightmares about it instead. Did you know that? Because Tessa knows."

"You told her?" Mom asks, sounding appalled.

"Yes I told her. And I felt better after. I should have told somebody else a long time ago."

Mom's eyes start to glisten. "You promised…"

"I know I did. But I shouldn't have. And you should never have asked me to. So before you go being a bitch to the woman I love, maybe you should start looking at your own shortcomings."

A tear rolls down her cheek and I immediately feel bad. But before I can say anything else, she turns on her heel and walks across the room. Linda takes one look at her face and starts to follow her.

Jesus, I need a drink. As soon as coffee is served, I'm getting Tessa out of here.

CHAPTER
THIRTY

TESSA

"Your daughter is so beautiful. I hope we get to meet her soon," Ava says. She and Sophie have been so sweet to me, asking to see pictures of Zoe and showing me some of their own kids. They've already asked me to visit them in West Virginia – where they both live – this summer, and told me that everybody thinks I'm perfect for Linc.

Well nearly everybody. My stomach tightens at the memory of his mom's reaction to me.

"Thank you so much." I give her a smile. "I think I'm just going to head to the bathroom before we eat."

I need to check my make up. And catch my breath. Linc is over in the corner talking to his mom so I sneak out and head to the rest rooms.

And of course, my period has chosen this perfect moment to arrive. My stomach starts to cramp, but it feels nothing like the anxiety that's pulling at my body. I never feel like this. Like I'm constantly on edge.

I hate it.

After sorting myself out I flush and go to wash my hands. That's when I hear the murmuring.

"Just sit and calm down," a female voice says. "He didn't mean it."

"Oh, he meant it." I recognize the voice as Linc's mom. She starts to sniff. "He hates me."

The restroom has a little dressing room to the side. The kind with plump ottoman seats and mirrors, so you can touch up your makeup in comfort without having to look at toilet stalls. That's where the voices are coming from. I have to walk through it to get out of here. And if I do, they'll almost certainly see me.

I freeze, catching a glimpse of my face in the mirror. I look so pale it isn't funny.

"I'm just worried about him. I never thought he'd end up with a single mom. She's older than him, did you know that?"

"No, I didn't," the other woman says. I wonder if it's Linda. Linc says she and his mom are thick as thieves. "But does it matter?"

"What if he wants to have children of his own?" Linc's mom asks. "She already has a teenage daughter. And you and I both know her biological clock must be running out."

I almost want to laugh. She has no idea how close to the truth she is.

"Is it really any of your business?" Linda asks gently.

"That's easy for you to say. You already have grandchildren. I'm ready for mine."

Linda starts to laugh. "Are you sure about that? Imagine how angry you'd be if she got pregnant. You'd say she was a gold digger."

"I guess I would."

I swallow hard. They say eavesdroppers never hear good of themselves, and right now I feel like crap. And I'm trapped because I can't go anywhere.

"Just give her a chance. She seems lovely. Ava and the other girls seem to like her. And I trust their judgment, don't you?"

"I suppose," Linc's mom mutters.

"Come on, dry your eyes and let's go back. You and Linc can talk tomorrow."

"He wants to spend time with her instead." She just sounds sad now.

"Talk to Linc, then talk to her. Apologize," Linda urges. "Tomorrow, when heads are clearer."

She lets out a long breath. "Okay."

The sound of heels hitting tile echoes throughout, and I know they must be getting ready to leave. I tiptoe back to a stall, gently closing the door so they can't see me.

By the time I get back to the ballroom, everybody is seated at the table and the wait staff is pouring wine.

"Everything okay?" Linc murmurs as I sit next to him. He looks about as happy as I feel.

"Yeah." I nod, lying through my teeth. "Everything is great."

———

LINC

"Are you sure you're all right?" I ask Tessa as we walk to the waiting town car. What a shit show of an evening. Despite my brothers' best attempts to keep the conversation going, neither Tessa or I were particularly talkative. She barely ate. Just pushed her food around on her plate.

She nods as the driver opens the door for her and lets her in. I follow, sitting beside her, pulling her against me. When he closes the door and climbs into the driver's seat I press my lips against hers.

"I'm sorry about my family. I didn't know Mom was going to be like that."

I wait for her to agree, but instead the worst fucking thing happens.

My beautiful, strong girl starts to cry.

Not just glistening eyes or a single tear. Full blown fat teardrops with a snotty nose and huffing breaths.

Alarm rushes through me.

"Fuck, I'm sorry," I tell her, pulling her face against my chest. "I never should have made you come tonight."

I wait for her to make a joke of it, but she doesn't. I can feel the dampness of her tears wetting my shirt.

"It's not your fault," she sobs as I stroke her hair. "Your mom hates me."

"No," I whisper. "She doesn't hate you. She doesn't know you. If she did she'd love you the same way I do."

Tessa looks up at me. Mascara smudged all around her eyes. And on my shirt. Not that I give a fuck.

"You love me?" she whispers.

"Of course I do." I adore this woman.

More tears start to fall. "You shouldn't. You shouldn't love me. I'm a fucking mess."

"Baby…" I wipe the tears from her face with my thumbs, leaving more smears on her cheeks. "Of course I should love you." Then I frown. "You love me, don't you?"

She nods and relief washes through me.

"I do," she whispers. "But look at me. Your mom thinks I'm too old for you. I don't know if I can have babies. And my period just started."

My mouth drops open. I have no idea what she's talking about. "What?"

She inhales raggedly. "I'm sorry, I feel like I've let you down."

The driver starts to pull away, and I cup her face with my hands, feeling the dampness of her tears against my skin.

"You haven't let anybody down. I should have prepared you better for my family. They're a lot." I'm kicking myself. Brooks was right, my family is like the fucking mafia. "Now tell me what's happened."

We're crawling through Manhattan. I just want to get her home and make her feel better.

"My period started." She swallows hard. "And your mom was crying."

"She was? Where?" I don't even want to talk about her right now.

"In the bathroom. I overheard her. She thinks I might not be able to have kids. And she could be right."

I blink, suddenly furious. It's starting to make sense. "You heard my mom bitching about you in the bathroom?" I say, my voice low.

"She wasn't bitching. She was upset. You didn't tell me the two of you had words."

I wince. "No." And I wasn't planning to.

"She hates me. And I know you love her."

I shake my head. "She doesn't hate you. She just doesn't know you." I run the tip of my tongue along my bottom lip. "And the kid thing?"

"My periods are getting worse. Ange said maybe I'm peri-menopausal. Which could impact me having kids. And I don't even know if you want them."

"I want you," I tell her honestly. "The rest is negotiable. And there's more than one way to have children." We've barely made any progress through the streets at all. The Saturday night traffic is insane.

"Can you pull over?" I ask the driver.

"What's happening?" Tessa asks.

"Just wait here," he tells me. "I'll be right back."

————

TESSA

I take a deep breath and try to center myself as Linc climbs out of the car and disappears into a crowd on the sidewalk. Maybe he's had enough. Maybe he's going back to the restaurant without me.

Maybe he's calling his mom to tell her she's right and he's going to call it off between us.

I sit quietly in the backseat, trying not to look at the driver because I'm certain he must have heard my full meltdown.

I never meltdown. I'm so embarrassed.

Five minutes later, Linc climbs back into the car with a CVS bag in his hands. It looks full.

"Okay," he said. "I think we need to attack this one thing at a time." He pulls out a pack of painkillers. And a bottle of water. The car pulls away again. Then he pulls out two different packs of tampons – ones with applicators and ones without – and some pads.

I can't help it, I start to laugh through the tears. "You bought me tampons?"

"I'm trying to be practical."

"I think that's the most romantic thing anybody's ever bought me," I tell him. I'm not lying. Flowers are easy. But walking into a pharmacy and perusing the shelves in the period aisle?

If I wasn't already certain I was in love with him before, this would seal it.

"I love you," I tell him.

"You haven't seen the rest of what I bought yet." But there's a smile on his face. "And by the way, I'm so in love with you."

I start crying again. "I'm sorry."

"Never be sorry for showing emotion." He pulls me close, kisses my forehead.

"I want to have children with you," I blurt out. Because I'm sure of it. I want it all.

He kisses my jaw, my cheek, then my lips.

"Ditto."

———

I've never felt safer in my life. Or more loved. As soon as we walk into his apartment he makes me take the painkillers then helps me change into one of his t-shirts, while he makes me a hot water bottle and gives me a choice from the five different chocolate bars he's bought.

And then he lectures me about making a gyno appointment. I promise to do it on Monday. And he tells me again that whatever I want – kids or no kids – he's fine with that.

I believe him, too. But now I'm thinking about it, I'm more certain that I want to try for at least one baby with him. Something to talk about with my doctor I guess.

I turn to look at him. "I love you." Now that I've said it once I can't stop saying it. "So much."

"I love you too." He kisses my neck. "And I'm sorry about my mom. She isn't usually like that. I should have prepared you for them all a little better. Maybe introduced you two somewhere smaller."

"I just don't want you to feel like you have to choose between us," I tell him.

"I don't feel like that. And there's no choice anyway." He kisses me softly. "I don't want to be without you. I already told you how all in I am. I don't give a damn how she feels about that."

The painkillers are starting to work. My abdominal pains are receding. And the anxiety is, too. I make a note to talk about that with the doctor. "Thank you for being so kind to me," I tell him.

"I always want to be kind to you," he tells me. "We're a team."

My chest tightens. This man is everything. I can't believe I used to think he was arrogant. He's not. He's beautiful and he's loyal and I want to spend the rest of my life showing him how much I appreciate that.

But I also know he loves his family.

"We can try again with her," I tell him. I'm not going to let her reaction to me spoil things. We've come too far for that.

"There's no way you have to see her again if you don't want to."

"I want to," I say. Because I've realized something. I'm not scared of her. But I understand her.

I understand that his mom is the scared one. Afraid of change. Of somebody hurting her son. Or even worse, afraid of losing him. Especially after she almost lost him all those years ago when she made the worst decision she ever could.

But she's still his mom. And he loves her. So I'll give her a second chance.

"Now can we go to bed?" he asks me, tangling his fingers in my hair as our mouths softly meet. "Because I need to be horizontal with you."

"I'm on my period."

"I know. That's why I'll be keeping it PG."

I smile against his mouth. "Then take me to bed."

CHAPTER
THIRTY-ONE

LINC

Tessa is sleeping soundly in my arms when I wake up, her body warm and pliant as she curls against me. Her breaths are soft, and I take a minute to look at her.

She's so damn beautiful it makes my chest ache.

Brushing my lips against her brow, I close my eyes for a moment, remembering the shit show that was last night. A rush of fury spikes my blood as I remember the way my mom treated Tessa so casually. Like she was a piece of gum on the sidewalk.

Despite the pinkness of her skin, there are dark shadows beneath her eyes. And yeah, I'm partly responsible for that. Because I wasn't here.

Because I threw her into the dragon's den.

My phone starts to vibrate on the table beside my bed. I switched the sound off last night after receiving more than a dozen messages from my brothers – and their partners – wanting to know what happened between my mom and Tessa.

This time it's my mom's name flashing on the screen. I sigh, half-inclined to reject the call because I'm still so angry I can taste it.

But no, I need to talk to her. Because I'm not having her treat Tessa like that again. No fucking way.

Gently extricating myself from Tessa's enticingly soft body, I climb out of bed and walk over to the window, swiping the screen to accept the call.

"Hello," I murmur, keeping my voice down because I'm letting my woman sleep, dammit.

"Darling. I'm so sorry."

Even hearing her voice makes my teeth grind. "It's early," I tell her.

"It's almost eight." Her voice is soft. Apologetic even. "I didn't get any sleep. I was up thinking about last night."

"Good. Tessa overheard you and Linda talking in the bathroom. You made her feel like shit."

She inhales sharply. "She didn't?"

"Yep. And I'm so fucking pissed with you about it. You made everything a hundred times worse."

There's silence for a moment. And I know she must be horrified. I know my mom, she isn't usually like this. She's kind. Caring.

Or she used to be.

"Please tell her I'm sorry. I should never have said anything. Not to you or in the bathroom. I'm an idiot."

"Damn right you are." From my vantage point in the window, I can see the city waking up. Like the rest of us, it's a little slower on a Sunday. But soon the streets will be full of people. Heading to church. Meeting friends for breakfast.

Traveling for work. That'll be me, later.

The thought of it sends annoyance rushing through me.

"I know I don't have any right to do this," Mom says. "But can I ask you for one thing?"

"Can't it wait?" I ask her.

I just want to get back in bed with Tessa.

"Not really, no. There's something I need to do. Maybe Tessa does, too."

"What?"

"I want to meet her without you. Just the two of us. Woman to woman. So I can apologize."

I blink. Is she really asking that after everything that happened last night? "No," I respond, unable to hide the anger from my voice. "It's not going to happen."

From the corner of my eye I see Tessa starting to stir. Fuck, I was too loud. Her eyes catch mine and I feel a weird sense of serenity wash over me. I can do anything with this woman by my side.

"I need to go," I say, hanging up the call, even though my mom is trying to persuade me to let her get her way. I walk back over to where Tessa's sitting up in bed. "You're supposed to be asleep."

"Who was that?"

"My mom. Wanna hear what she wanted?"

Tessa smiles and it lights up her gorgeous face. "What?"

"To meet with you, without me. To talk woman to woman." I roll my eyes. "The gall of it."

"You're sweet when you're angry, you know that?" She rolls onto her knees and kisses the tip of my nose. I grab her and pull her closer, until she has to steady herself against my chest, her palms flat on my pectorals.

"I'm not sweet," I tell her, kissing her jaw. "I'm sexy. And strong. And masculine."

She giggles. "You are. So masculine."

My fingers slide down her side to her hip. "Say it again."

"So strong. So manly," she whispers as I kiss her throat. "Especially when you're getting chased by pigs."

I look down at her. "You just spoiled it."

"I still have the video footage," she tells me. "In case you were wondering."

"Part of our prenup will be you erasing it."

"We're getting a prenup?" she asks.

"Damn right. You'll have to sign that you'll never leave me."

She brushes her lips against mine. "Only if I get to keep the footage." Her fingers brush my neck and it sends a shiver down my spine. "By the way, I'll do it."

"Do what?" I ask, distracted by the way her other hand is tracing circles on my chest.

"Meet with your mom alone. Just the two of us."

I blink, thinking I've misheard her. But when our eyes meet there's an earnestness in them that makes me realize I didn't.

"No," I say, my stomach falling. "You don't have to do that."

"Maybe I do." She kisses me softly. "I'm not afraid of her."

"Maybe I'm afraid of you meeting with her," I mutter. "She might scare you off."

"Nothing could do that." She wraps her arms around my neck. I'm severely distracted by the way her breasts press against my chest. "I'm the one that almost scared you off."

"That could never happen." I kiss her again. I will never get enough of this woman's lips.

"Let me talk to her," Tessa whispers against my mouth. "I promise it will be okay."

I frown. "If she's a bitch again, you leave, okay?"

"I don't think she will be." She cups my face. "She's your mom. It's obvious she loves you. And it's understandable that she's worried about you. Let me talk to her."

"But…"

"And if she's a bitch, I'll be a bigger one."

Our eyes meet again. And I can see a determination there. A fierceness that slays me. The emotional Tessa of last night is gone, replaced by a warrior. I like them both so damn much.

"Okay," I say. "But I'm coming with. I'll sit at another table or something."

"You can go to another coffee shop nearby," she concedes.

I slide my arms around her and throw her back onto the mattress, then climb over her, caging her in with my arms.

"Why is it that I feel like I've just been steamrolled?" I ask her.

"You're the one who threw me on the bed," she points out, grinning.

Yeah, I was. But I still feel uneasy.

"Your mom and I are strong women," Tessa tells me, reaching up to smooth away the frown lines between my eyes. "And Zoe's going to be, too. You'd better get used to being surrounded by us."

A half smile pulls at my lips. "I wouldn't have it any other way."

———

TESSA

The restaurant Linc's mom booked for our brunchtime meeting is understated and elegant. There are families here, along with well dressed couples and a group of women in their fifties who look like they're in the city celebrating some kind of birthday, judging from the gift bags on the table.

The hostess takes me to a table in the back corner, where Deandra is waiting for me. She stands when I walk over, the most reticent of smiles on her face.

"Thank you for coming," she says simply. She doesn't offer her hand or her cheek, which I appreciate. Because I'm on guard right now. But I'm doing this for Linc. And mostly because he bought me tampons last night.

Seriously, I'm still swooning. I can't help it.

I slip into the seat opposite her, smoothing my skirt down my legs. We stopped at my place on the way here, though Linc insisted that we both shower at his place first. Which was probably the right thing to do, because even with the new shower at mine, it doesn't compare to the double shower in his place.

"Would you like a drink?" the server asks.

"Just a coffee please." I smile at her.

Deandra is drinking tea. It comes in those little teapots that hold two tea bags. She checks it for strength before pouring herself a cup.

She lifts it to her lips and takes a sip before putting the cup back down.

"I should probably start," she says, her gaze catching mine. There are little crows feet in her skin, but they only make her beautiful face more interesting. In the daylight, I can see her resemblance to Linc.

"Okay." I nod, waiting for what she has to say.

"What I said last night. All of it. Was wrong. I'm so sorry you had to overhear it. But more than that I'm sorry I even said it."

I nod, saying nothing. My eyes hold hers.

She lets out another breath. "I spent all night thinking about it. How I treated you. The awful things I said. I didn't give you a chance."

"No, you didn't," I tell her. "I was feeling vulnerable. Scared to meet Linc's family. Because he's important to me."

Her eyes soften. "I know."

"And I really wanted to impress you. To get to know you. To be your friend. He talks about you a lot and I know how much he loves you."

"I'm so sorry." Her face crumples. "I was wrong. I made assumptions I shouldn't have made about you."

I feel my back stiffen. I know what those assumptions were.

"Did you know he's never brought somebody to meet us before?" Deandra asks. "You're the first. That's why I knew how important you are to him. And as his mother, that's scary."

"He's a grown man," I tell her.

"I know he is. But he's also my son." Her eyes catch mine. "How do you think you will feel when your daughter brings somebody home?"

I let out a breath. "Happy, I hope. That she's found somebody who makes her smile." I pull my lip between my teeth. "And worried, too," I add, because I'm trying to be honest here.

"I wish I'd shown you that I was happy. Because I am. Linc deserves to be happy."

My eyes catch hers again. "He is happy," I tell her. "I care a lot about your son."

For a moment there's a crack in her mask. She blinks, the hint of a smile on her lips. She nods slowly. "I can tell that. And I'm so sorry that I doubted that. I'm sorry I hurt you both."

"Apology accepted." It's the truth. I'm not angry at her. I wouldn't have done what she did, but I understand her over-reaction. I'll give her another chance to show me that she isn't that person.

The server brings over my coffee, along with a little jug of cream and a pot of sugar. "Are you ready to order breakfast?" the server asks.

"Just an omelet for me," Deandra says.

"I'll have the same." Not that I feel like eating.

As soon as the server leaves, Deandra looks at me again. "Linc said he told you what happened when he was younger."

"The way he found you?" I ask her. "Yes, he did. He still has nightmares."

She blanches and I have to admit, I don't feel sorry for her.

"You should never have put that kind of burden on him. To keep a secret like that. He was just a child."

Deandra nods, her expression tight. "I know. I regret it. I don't want to keep it a secret anymore."

"Good." I nod. "But maybe you need to speak to Linc first. He should decide what happens next."

She blinks as she looks at me. "You're right. I will. But before I do, I feel that I need to explain to you. What I did to him. What I tried to do... I regret. So much. The things I put him through. I never want him to feel pain like that again."

I think of Zoe. The way she cried every night after Jared left. "That's understandable," I say. "But almost impossible."

"I was afraid that you would hurt him. He's always so easy going. So happy. I've never seen him like this before."

"Like what?" I ask, confused.

"In love."

That stops me in my tracks. She's not smiling but she's not frowning either. More than anything, she looks scared.

"Love is good, isn't it?"

"Until it hurts."

Oh. "Yes." I nod. "Until it hurts. But even then, it's still worth it." I truly believe that. After all my fears yesterday, falling asleep in Linc's arms made everything so much better. He makes me feel safe. Loved.

"Do you think your relationship with your ex-husband was worth the pain?" she asks, looking genuinely interested.

And I guess I could tell her it's none of her business. Because it isn't. But there's a thaw here. Something fragile that could come tumbling down at any minute.

"Yes," I say softly. "I do. Every time I look at my daughter I know for sure it was worth it." I take a sip of coffee. "But even if we didn't have children, even then, I think it was. I learned more about myself during our breakup than I had in our whole marriage. I learned what I wanted from a relationship. And that I needed to be a strong, independent woman to have one."

For the first time, her lips curl. It's the gentlest of smiles. "I wish I'd learned that."

"Maybe you did," I say. "You certainly taught your son that."

Her eyes shine as she nods. "I hope so."

"Can I give you some advice?" I ask her. "Mom to mom?" It feels weird since we're different generations. It should be the other way around. And yet she nods, looking almost excited to hear what I have to say.

"Your son loves you. He wants you to be happy. He wants everybody to be happy. But maybe you need to show him the real you. Talk to him. Stop pretending everything is okay when it isn't." I feel myself blush because I learned from my own mistake there. "Let him know it's okay not to be okay."

She gives me a watery smile and nods. "I'm going to talk to him."

"I'm glad."

"But first let me talk to you," she says. "Tell me about your daughter. Zoe, right?"

"That's right," I say, feeling relieved at the change in conversation. "She's thirteen years old but she thinks she's thirty."

Deandra gives me a soft smile. And damn if it isn't the same smile as Linc's. "Tell me about it," she says. "Even recalling the teenage years fills me with dread."

"I look forward to hearing more about that," I tell her and her smile widens. "With added photographs."

"Oh, I have them all. From baby photos to now, with all those awkward in between stages. Next time you'll have to come to my apartment and I'll show you them all."

"I'd like that." Our gazes meet and I feel myself relax. It isn't perfect, but it's a start. "Shall we call Linc and ask him to join us?" I ask her. "Put him out of his misery."

She wrinkles her nose. "I guess so." But there's a happiness in her voice that only comes from thinking about her son.

"Okay then." I take out my phone and send him a message.

"Thank you," she says softly.

"Any time." It's not like we're best friends. Or anything approaching that. But there's something here. A growing understanding.

And it's enough. Because Linc and I are adults. We don't need her approval to work.

I just want him to be happy. That's it really.

Ten minutes later, Linc walks into the restaurant. He stops at where I'm sitting and kisses my cheek. "Everything okay?" he murmurs, his expression wary.

I nod, smiling at him. He pulls out the chair next to mine and the waitress gives him a menu.

"Mom." He gives her a nod, sliding his arm behind my chair. And though he doesn't say anything, his whole body language is telling us exactly what he thinks.

If there's a side to be chosen, he'd pick mine. It makes my heart feel full.

"I'm sorry," Deandra says to him. "I've apologized to Tessa and she's graciously accepted it."

"Good," Linc says, taking the coffee the waitress brings over. "You were out of line."

"Yes, I was." Her lips part as she softly exhales. "But I'm sorry for more than that. For what I've put you through. The secret I made you keep."

Linc blinks. He shifts in his seat and his jaw stiffens. I reach out and squeeze his thigh.

"Asking a child to keep a secret like that was wrong." Her eyes fill with tears. "I'm so sorry."

He nods, taking a sip of his coffee. I go to move my hand

away from his thigh but he clamps it down with his free hand.

Like he needs the connection. Like he needs me.

"I'd like us to go to therapy," she tells him. "Talk about a way to stop it from being a secret anymore."

"Maybe." Linc nods. "I'll think about it."

"I didn't know you still have nightmares," she says. "I'd like to find a way to help them stop. If you'll let me."

He looks at me and I give him the softest of smiles. "It sounds like a good idea," I whisper.

"Okay." He looks at his mom. "We'll discuss it more when I'm back in the US full time." He glances at me again. "I don't want my nightmares waking Zoe up when we move in together."

I squeeze his thigh again. I'm so in love with this man it's almost painful. He'll put himself through the pain of reliving his past for me. For my daughter.

I'm so blessed thanks to him.

"Now let's eat some brunch," he says, calling the server over. "I have a flight to catch in eight hours, and I'd like to spend some of that with my girlfriend."

CHAPTER
THIRTY-TWO

LINC

"Are you sure you're ready for this?" Tessa asks me.

It's been two months since the disastrous Saturday night with my family. We've been juggling video calls and flights to spend time with each other while I keep the promise I made to Roman to finish the European office.

Tessa, on the other hand, has spent that time finishing the renovations in her home. She only has the kitchen left to finish, and she's graciously allowing me to help her with it. Because the woman still won't agree to move into my apartment yet.

Which I understand. Her independence is part of what I love about her. But I don't love trying to cook on a stovetop that should have been condemned during the last century, or sleep on the fucking floor because she can't decide what bed frame to buy.

On the plus side, she went to see her gynecologist the week after the family party. He ran a lot of tests and found no problems.

She also met with her ex-husband last week. To tell him that she planned to properly introduce me to Zoe as her boyfriend. She tells me it went as well as expected, which is Tessa's code word for fine.

"I don't know if I'm ready," I tell her in answer to her question. "Are you?" I've got a French comic book in my hand. According to the guy selling them in a shop down the road from the office in Paris, this one is a collector's item. And I'm not above buying my girlfriend's kid's affection.

"Well it's too late to back out now." Tessa nods at the windshield. We're sitting in my car outside the school. I arrived from Paris last night. And I spent it alone in my apartment because it's Tessa's week with Zoe. And this morning I met with Roman and told him the Paris office should be completely up and running within two weeks and I'll be staying in the US after that.

I also gave him the resumes for five European PR professionals who are looking for their next career move and have the right kind of experience to hit the ground running with the Paris office.

We've agreed that I'll go back to my old role for now, which will require a lot less travel now that we have a second office. But in reality I'm still trying to decide what I want to do in the future.

Zoe hugs her friends and smiles when she sees Tessa leaning out of the window, waving at her.

"Hey," Zoe says, pulling the back door open and throwing her backpack on the seat. "I didn't know you were coming to pick me up, Linc."

"I bought you a gift," I tell her, handing her the comic book.

Her eyes light up. "No way."

I shrug. "Way."

Her eyes meet mine and she laughs. "So are we doing this?" she asks.

"Doing what?" Tessa looks over her shoulder at her daughter as Zoe sits down and closes the door. She buckles herself in, then picks up the comic book again, thumbing through it.

"Doing the whole you and Linc are a couple thing," Zoe says, sounding almost bored. "Just promise me I'll get the biggest room in his apartment and I'm fine with it."

Tessa's eyes meet mine. She looks amused.

"I was at least going to take you out to dinner first," I tell Zoe.

She grins back at me. "Didn't you tell me not to let strange guys buy me dinner?"

"I'm not a strange guy," I point out. "I'm your new daddy."

Zoe makes a gagging noise. "Don't ever say it like that again."

"Daddy Linc?" I suggest.

She rolls her eyes at me.

"Just Linc. And that room is going to be mine, right?"

"We're here to talk to you about us dating. Not moving in together," Tessa says. "We're not doing that yet."

"I already knew you were dating." Zoe sighs loudly. "Can't I at least get something good out of this?" She's smiling though, and I know she's kidding. "I'll tell you what, if you give me the biggest room I'll call you Father Linc."

"That makes me sound like a priest," I laugh.

She shrugs. "If it fits, it fits."

"We're not moving in together," Tessa tells her, exasperation in her voice. "You need some time to get used to this first."

"No I don't." Zoe shrugs. "I need to move into a huge apartment with a huge TV."

"Zoe!" Tessa shoots me a 'help me' look.

I shrug at her, because she knows I want us to live together.

"Can I ask for one more thing?" Zoe says, as I start up the engine, because all the cars in front of us have already pulled away. And to be honest, I need something to eat.

"What is it?" Tessa asks.

"When you two get married, can I wear a tux instead of a pink dress? And if you have a kid, can I name it?"

"We're not getting married either," Tessa says uneasily.

"Yet," I add, because yeah, we are. Sooner rather than later.

Tessa's eyes meet mine. She looks genuinely surprised.

"I'm an old fashioned guy," I remind her. Tessa bites down a smile.

"He hasn't even asked me," Tessa tells her. "Calm down. We just wanted to tell you we're seeing each other, if that's okay with you."

"It's fine." Zoe shakes her head, looking down at the comic book. "Stop making a big deal out of it."

I start to laugh, pulling out into the traffic. We already decided where we were going to eat. A little Italian restaurant I love called Il Piccolo. It's been run by the same family for years. First the grandpa, then his son. Now the granddaughter runs it.

It was the place Mom used to take us when Brooks and I were kids. Dad was all about fancy restaurants, Mom was all about great food.

I'm excited to take Zoe and Tessa there.

"Can you put some music on?" Zoe asks. "The Linebackers if you could."

Tessa's still smiling. And so am I. Because this kid is completely unpredictable but she's a blast.

I get the feeling life will never be boring with her around.

———

One Month Later…

. . .

TESSA

"Oh my god, that was so good." I finish the last forkful of spaghetti and my eyes catch Linc. He's beaming because I think I love this restaurant as much as he does. We came here to celebrate his return from Paris for good. Il Piccolo has turned into our celebration location. "But I'm not sure I'm going to be able to walk after all this food."

"We can roll you home," Zoe says.

"It'll take a while," Linc replies.

"Okay, we can roll her back to your car. And then you can lift her in because you're her boyfriend and that's a boyfriend job."

Linc's eyes meet mine. Damn, I love this man. And I love the way he and Zoe get along so well. They've spent most of the meal talking about some computer game that's taking Zoe's school by storm. It involves fighting dragons and befriending elves, or something. I kind of tune it out and watch the two people I love the most bond in the sweetest of ways.

"What are you smiling about?" Linc asks, his voice soft.

"I'm happy," I tell him. And it sounds so simple, but it's not. Happiness is complicated. It can feel out of reach.

For the longest time I wondered if I'd ever feel it again.

And yet here I am, enjoying an evening in New York in a pretty little Italian restaurant, with my stomach about to explode, not because I'm having a bad period but because I'm having great food.

It doesn't get much better than this.

"Oh god, she's getting all sentimental," Zoe says. "Watch out, she'll start crying in a minute."

Linc opens his mouth to respond but then his phone starts to ring. He pulls it from his pocket and groans.

"It's Roman."

"Take it," I tell him. Because he'll be distracted if he doesn't. And we've finished eating anyway.

He nods. "Thanks." He heads outside, swiping the screen to accept the call.

The server comes over. "Can I get you anything else?" she asks.

"Can we take some cannolis to go?" I ask. Zoe's been eyeing them all night. And I'd love to try one, but later. "Six assorted ones. And the check please."

"Of course."

"Linc's gonna be mad at you if you pick up the check," Zoe says. The girl can read my mind. But I'm not going to let him pay for everything. I still like my newfound independence.

I shrug. "He'll learn to live with it." He'd better.

"I like him," she says. And it makes my heart clench.

"You do?"

"Yeah. He's good for you. He's funny and he has great taste in comic books." Her face suddenly turns serious. "I think he'll be a good addition to the family."

And now my chest feels as full as my stomach. "You know you're my number one, right?" I say softly. "You'll always come first."

"That's fine until I go to college." She nods. "But after that you're gonna have to let me go. I'll be an adult. Doing adult things. Probably things that I don't want my mom to know about."

"Zoe!" My mouth falls open.

"It's true. I'm glad you and Linc have each other. It takes the pressure off me." She shrugs. "By the way, I'm staying at Maisie's tomorrow night. She's having a sleepover. So you and Linc can do all the embarrassing things you want without me there to supervise."

I start laughing. I can't help it. "Sometimes I can't decide if you're my daughter or my mother."

"Tonight I'm your daughter. Because I can't afford to pay for dinner."

Linc walks back in right as I'm signing the check. He frowns. "This was supposed to be my treat."

"It's okay," I tell him. "I'm just trying to buy your affection."

"By affection she means sex," Zoe says.

I shoot her a look. There are some things kids can't say out loud. This is definitely one of them.

"Sorry." But she doesn't look it.

Linc grins. "Come on. Let's get you both home."

The family comes out of the kitchen and Linc hugs them all, before they swamp Zoe and I with hugs, too. The granddaughter gives Zoe the bag with the box of cannolis, and then the three of us walk outside into the early evening air.

Linc puts one arm around my shoulders, and the other around Zoe's as we walk to his car that's parked up the street.

To a casual bystander we must look like any other normal family. Eating early, then heading home for the evening.

"What did Roman have to say?" I ask him. In the excitement of leaving, I'd forgotten to ask about his phone call.

"He just wanted to update me on how the European office is going."

I look up at him. "And?"

He smiles softly. "And he's happy with the new guy. He's already bringing in new business."

"That's fantastic."

"So do we get to move in with you now?" Zoe asks. "Because I seriously need to start packing if we do. I have a lot of stuff."

"That depends on your mom. Whether she's ready." His

voice is even. He's not making this a big thing, which I appreciate so much.

In another month I should have the remodel finished. The kitchen is already underway. Whatever happens, I'm going to keep it. Linc wants me to as well. I'll either rent it out, or he can move in with us.

It's my choice. That's what he says.

But the idea of this big man having to share my small bed and the three of us all trying to use the bathroom or get breakfast together in the morning just doesn't make sense. Not when his apartment is so much bigger.

My one reservation is Zoe. But she's right. I have five more years of her, and then she'll be grown. I can't be leaning on her to be my support. Not the way Linc's mom did with him.

"Mom?" Zoe says. And I realize we've reached Linc's car. She's standing in front of us. Linc's arm is still around my shoulders.

"Sorry." I smile at her. "I was just thinking."

"I know." She rolls her eyes. "Have you stopped now?"

"Yeah," I say. "I have."

"Good. So are we moving in with Linc or not?"

I look at the man who's changed my life. The one who I know will be there for me and Zoe, no matter what. His gaze is easy, but I can tell he wants to know, too.

So for once I put my heart before my head.

"Yes," I say firmly. "We are."

Before I can say anything else, Linc swings me into his arms, his mouth pressing against mine as Zoe lets out a whoop. His kiss is soft, and I can feel his lips curling into a smile beneath mine.

"Thank God," he says. "Now let's go home."

"To whose home?" Zoe asks. "Yours or ours."

He reaches out to ruffle her hair. "Same thing, kid. Same thing."

EPILOGUE

TESSA

Later that year...

Mariah Carey's voice echoes through the apartment, promising that she doesn't want a lot for Christmas, as I slowly blink my eyes awake. The bed is empty apart from me, and I roll over to look at the time.

Damn, it's nine o'clock. And there's so much I need to do. I sit bolt upright. How the hell did I sleep through my alarm?

When I get downstairs I see two familiar heads facing the television. There's some kind of air fight going on between dragons, and Zoe groans as one of them dies and falls down to the ground.

"That's not fair, I taught you that move," she says.

"You snooze you lose," Linc tells her, putting down the controller. "Alright, it's time to wake up your mom."

"One more game," Zoe says. "Please?"

"You can keep playing," I tell them. "I'll make the coffee."

On hearing my voice, Linc turns around to look at me. His hair is mussed up, and he's wearing the t-shirt that Zoe bought him with 'Bonus Dad' written across the front. We opened our gifts yesterday on Christmas Eve – European style, as Linc called it – because Jared will be picking Zoe up any minute and taking her to his folks' house for a few days.

It's been four months since Zoe and I moved in. We reached a good rhythm fairly quickly. Linc and I share most of the chores, though he insists on keeping his cleaner which I insisted on paying half for.

We all take turns cooking. Even Zoe's learned how to make a few mean pasta dishes.

And he's even gotten used to dealing with Zoe's hormones. And mine, too, when it comes to that. Our periods are pretty much in sync these days, so when one of us begins I tend to send him an SOS.

And he comes home with bags of candy and comic books for Zoe. Plus cannolis for me.

I make sure he knows how much we appreciate him.

Since Zoe's going to be gone for a week, Linc and I decided to take time off work and enjoy a short vacation. Just the two of us. Our bags are packed and we're due to leave at lunchtime. I'm so excited for some alone time with him it's not funny.

I start up the coffee machine, putting in an espresso pod for Linc, followed by a decaf one for me. Then I froth up the milk while I watch Linc let himself get beaten by Zoe.

I love the way he only does it occasionally. He never lets her win all the time, but he always seems to know when it's the right moment to step back.

Watching the man I love be the sweetest step dad to my daughter makes everything inside me ache in the sweetest of ways.

We eat breakfast and then I send Zoe to grab her bags. The buzzer rings right as she's leaving her bedroom. Through the crack in her door I can see it's a typical teenage mess. When she's back from her trip I'll make her tidy it up, but for now I'm choosing my battles.

"Come here," I say to Zoe, as Linc goes to open the door to Jared. They're not exactly friends but they tolerate each other for Zoe's sake. I hug her tightly, pulling her against me. "Be good," I tell her. "And have fun."

"I'd rather be coming with you," she grumbles.

"No you wouldn't. There's going to be a lot of PDA going on."

Public Displays of Affection. The teenager's worst nightmare.

"Ugh." She looks up at me. "Thank you for a great Christmas."

"Thank you for celebrating it early with me." I kiss her cheek and hug her again, then I pick up one bag while she picks up the other.

Jared is standing in the doorway. Linc is standing in the hallway, his arms crossed.

"Hey Dad," Zoe says, handing him her bag.

"Hey Zo."

She turns to Linc. "I guess I'll see you after New Years."

"Yeah, you will." He hugs her and she hugs him back hard. "Have a good time. And if you need us, call."

"I won't." She winks at him. "I don't want to disturb your PDAs."

"Tessa." Jared nods at me.

"Hi. Merry Christmas," I say to him.

"And to you." He takes Zoe's other bag from me. "You ready?" he asks Zoe. "We gotta get a head start on the traffic."

"Yeah. I'm good."

She blows me a kiss and the two of them head down the hallway to the elevators. I stand and watch until they step inside and then I gently close the door.

"You okay?" Linc asks, his eyes wary.

I take a deep breath. No parent likes spending Christmas Day without their kid. But it happens all over the world. "Yeah," I say. "Do we need to go, too?"

"Another half an hour," Linc tells me. "Come here." He reaches for me, his fingers sliding between mine, then pulls me against his body. Cupping my face with his warm palms, his eyes catch mine.

"Next year you get her for the whole holiday," he reminds me.

"She'll be fifteen. And a bigger pain in the ass."

He laughs. "I know you don't mean it."

No, I don't. I ache for her.

But then I've been aching a lot this month. In all kinds of ways. "We should enjoy this," I tell him. "This is our last Christmas just the two of us."

"Until Zoe decides she has better things to do than spend time with us." He grins.

"No." I shake my head slowly. "We won't be alone then, either."

"Why not..." He slowly trails off as realization replaces the frown lines on his face. "What?" he asks, his eyes searching mine. "Are you?"

"Pregnant?" I whisper. "Yes."

A huge grin pulls at his lips. "You're kidding me."

"No, I'm not." We made the decision a few months ago to stop using birth control. Because yes, my doctor couldn't find any fertility problems, but I'm still heading toward my late thirties. If we want a baby, we needed to do it soon.

"How long?" Linc asks, staring at my stomach like he can't believe his baby is in there.

"Six weeks," I tell him. "So we have a while to go."

"When did you find out?"

"Yesterday." I'd suspected for a few days, but with the holiday season and getting ready for us all to leave the city I'd finally gotten around to taking a test on Christmas Eve morning while I was cooking the ham. "I wanted to tell you when we were alone. I hope that's okay."

"It's more than okay," he says, looking at me tenderly. "It's everything." He looks down again. "Can I touch your stomach?"

"There's nothing to feel, but go for it."

So he does. And as his palm splays out against my stomach there's a look of wonder on his face. "Eight months," he says. "And then we get to meet her or him."

"Yes." I nod.

When his lips touch mine I feel the emotion in his kiss. His arms wrap around me, pulling me closer until our bodies are pressed together.

"Are you happy?" I ask him when our kiss finally ends.

"So damn happy you wouldn't believe," he tells me. "Even though you spoiled my surprise."

"You have a surprise?" I ask him, blinking. "Don't tell me you're pregnant too."

He starts to laugh and it's a beautiful sound. Putting his hand in his pocket, he pulls out a little box. It's dark red and velvet and I have to swallow hard because I think I know what's inside it.

"I was going to ask you in Exuma," he tells me. "In our cottage."

"Ask me what?" I say softly, even though I think I know. Because I want to hear him say it. Because I know what my answer will be.

He slowly opens the box and the most beautiful sapphire ring is inside. It glistens beneath the lights of our apartment.

"Tessa Carmichael," he says, his voice clear as he suddenly drops to one knee in front of me. "You and Zoe are the loves of my life. You've made me feel complete. And now this little one is added to the mix and I'm so fucking happy I think I might combust." He leans forward to kiss my stomach. "Will you do the honor of becoming my wife?"

My eyes are shining as I reach for him, because I feel complete, too. He makes everything better by just existing. I can't imagine my life without him.

I thought that love was scary, but it's the lack of it that I hate. He's taught me to live again, to love again.

To have hope where I thought it didn't exist for me anymore.

"Yes," I tell him, feeling like I'm about to explode with happiness as he stands and kisses me softly, sliding the ring onto my finger. "Yes, please. I can't think of anything I'd rather be."

THE END

DEAR READER

Thank you so much for reading STRICTLY THE WORST. If you enjoyed it and you get a chance, I'd be so grateful if you can leave a review. And don't forget to check out my free bonus epilogue which you can download by typing the following URL into your web browser: https://dl.bookfunnel.com/nw9scaz3qg

The next book in the series is BROOKS' story - join him and all the Salinger brothers in STRICTLY PRETEND.

I can't wait to share more stories with you.

Yours,

Carrie xx

ALSO BY CARRIE ELKS

THE SALINGER BROTHERS SERIES

A swoony romantic comedy series featuring six brothers and the
strong and smart women who tame them.

Strictly Business

Strictly Pleasure

Strictly For Now

Strictly Not Yours

Strictly The Worst

Strictly Pretend

THE HEARTBREAK BROTHERS NEXT GENERATION SERIES

A steamy and emotional small town / big family romance series, set
in West Virginia.

That One Regret

That One Touch

That One Heartbreak

THE WINTERVILLE SERIES

A gorgeously wintery small town romance series, featuring six
cousins who fight to save the town their grandmother built.

Welcome to Winterville

Hearts In Winter

Leave Me Breathless

Memories Of Mistletoe

Every Shade Of Winter

Mine For The Winter

ANGEL SANDS SERIES

A heartwarming small town beach series, full of best friends, hot guys and happily-ever-afters.

Let Me Burn

She's Like the Wind

Sweet Little Lies

Just A Kiss

Baby I'm Yours

Pieces Of Us

Chasing The Sun

Heart And Soul

Lost In Him

THE HEARTBREAK BROTHERS SERIES

A gorgeous small town series about four brothers and the women who capture their hearts.

Take Me Home

Still The One

A Better Man

Somebody Like You

When We Touch

THE SHAKESPEARE SISTERS SERIES

An epic series about four strong yet vulnerable sisters, and the alpha men who steal their hearts.

Summer's Lease

A Winter's Tale

Absent in the Spring

By Virtue Fall

THE LOVE IN LONDON SERIES

Three books about strong and sassy women finding love in the big city.

Coming Down

Broken Chords

Canada Square

STANDALONE

Fix You

An epic romance that spans the decades. Breathtaking and angsty and all the things in between.

If you'd like to get an email when I release a new book, please sign up here:

CARRIE ELKS' NEWSLETTER

ABOUT THE AUTHOR

Carrie Elks writes contemporary romance with a sizzling edge. Her first book, *Fix You*, has been translated into eight languages and made a surprise appearance on *Big Brother* in Brazil. Luckily for her, it wasn't voted out.

Carrie lives with her husband, two lovely children and a larger-than-life black pug called Plato. When she isn't writing or reading, she can be found baking, drinking an occasional (!) glass of wine, or chatting on social media.

You can find Carrie in all these places
www.carrieelks.com
carrie.elks@mail.com

Printed in Great Britain
by Amazon

45531650R00189